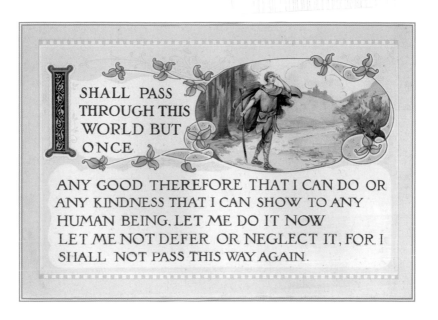

I SHALL PASS THROUGH THIS WORLD BUT ONCE

ANY GOOD THEREFORE THAT I CAN DO OR
ANY KINDNESS THAT I CAN SHOW TO ANY
HUMAN BEING, LET ME DO IT NOW
LET ME NOT DEFER OR NEGLECT IT, FOR I
SHALL NOT PASS THIS WAY AGAIN.

Doi Chaang Coffee is proud to be associated
with this book. It reflects a personal
philosophy, and one that Doi Chaang chooses
to follow as its corporate philosophy.

Doi
CHAANG
COFFEE CO.

www.doichaangcoffee.com

Praise for *Beyond Fair Trade*

Beyond Fair Trade tells the extraordinary story of how the traditionally illiterate hill tribes in a small mountain village in Thailand overcame warlords, opium production, deforestation and poverty—all through coffee and help from Canadian entrepreneur John Darch and Thai visionary Wicha Promyong.

Julie Angus, author of *Olive Odyssey*

A rich and resonantly detailed account of an unlikely partnership that enabled the hard-working tribespeople of a remote coffee-growing village in Thailand to emerge from poverty and obscurity to success in the refined new world of fine coffee.

Kenneth Davids, *Coffee Review*

Doi Chaang is where the bar is presently set—the absolute gold standard for good.

Todd Carmichael, founder of La Colombe and Adventurer-Host of the Travel Channel's *Dangerous Grounds*

With scholarly and sensitive detail, Mark Pendergrast tells the story of the once despised Akha hill tribes of northern Thailand, tracing the culturally traumatic but ultimately successful transformation from raising opium poppies to harvesting a more stimulating crop: organic arabica coffee beans.

William E. Mitchell, author of *The Bamboo Fire: Fieldwork with the New Guinea Wape*

Mark Pendergrast relates the story of coffee in Thailand against a backdrop of the confluence of economics, anthropology, agriculture and the extraordinary capacity of humans to influence their own worlds.

Ric Rhinehart, Executive Director, Specialty Coffee Association of America

Beyond Fair Trade completely surpassed my expectations. This is an uplifting account of how coffee and the dedication of a few outsiders is helping the Akha escape the poverty that has haunted them for so long.

Linda Aylesworth, Global TV News Reporter

Mark Pendergrast has written an extraordinary book about how a poverty-stricken hill tribe in a remote village in Thailand became internationally famous for its coffee, and how a Canadian businessman and Thai entrepreneur helped make that happen.

Pisan Manawapat, Ambassador of Thailand to Canada (2013-2015)

Beyond Fair Trade does an admirable job of tracing the evolution of the Doi Chaang Coffee Company and showing how corporate social responsibility can be part of a successful business strategy.

Philip Calvert, Canadian Ambassador to Thailand

I celebrate the story of Doi Chaang in Thailand as a force for change. I believe that through trade justice, communities like Doi Chaang and world markets can meet and thrive together.

Tom Smith, Executive Director of Fairtrade Canada (2012-2015)

Mark Pendergrast

BEYOND
FAIR
TRADE

How One Small Coffee Company Helped Transform a Hillside Village in Thailand

GREYSTONE BOOKS

Vancouver/Berkeley

Greystone Books Ltd.
www.greystonebooks.com

Doi Chaang Coffee
110-807 Powell Street, Vancouver, BC, V6A 1H7
www.doichaangcoffee.com
Phone: 1-866-924-2264

Cataloguing data available from Library and Archives Canada
ISBN 978-1-77164-047-3 (pbk.)
ISBN 978-1-77164-105-0 (epub)

Editing by Lesley Cameron
Cover design by Peter Cocking, text design by Jennifer Griffiths
Cover photograph by iStockphoto.com
Photographs by Mark Pendergrast
Map on page x by Carol MacDonald
Printed and bound in Canada by Friesens
Distributed in the U.S. by Publishers Group West

The author gratefully acknowledges the permission of Paul Lewis and the Payap
University Archives to include their texts in this publication.

We gratefully acknowledge the financial support of the Canada Council for
the Arts, the British Columbia Arts Council, the Province of British Columbia
through the Book Publishing Tax Credit, and the Government of Canada
through the Canada Book Fund for our publishing activities.

Greystone Books is committed to reducing the consumption of old-growth
forests in the books it publishes. This book is one step toward that goal.

Dedicated to
Wicha Promyong,
*visionary humanitarian and
lover of life in all its forms*

"I shall pass through this world but once. Any good therefore that I can do or any kindness that I can show to any human being, let me do it now. Let me not defer or neglect it. For I shall not pass this way again."

FAVORITE SAYING OF ELIZABETH DARCH (1909–2013),
MOTHER OF JOHN M. DARCH

CONTENTS

ON THE MOST basic level, *Beyond Fair Trade* tells the extraordinary story of Doi Chaang Coffee, a coffee cooperative on a remote mountainside in Thailand, and the Vancouver coffee company, half-owned by that cooperative, that imports and roasts its beans, then sends half its profits back to the co-op farmers, most of whom belong to the Akha hill tribe. Wicha Promyong, a charismatic, shrewd Thai, provided essential leadership to the Akha in growing their coffee, roasting it, and creating a coffeehouse chain in Thailand to sell it. In Vancouver, Doi Chaang Coffee chairman John M. Darch emphasizes that he founded the company not as a charitable venture but as a sustainable, alternative form of capitalism that provides a new business model, a win-win approach that provides equitable profit for all.

If that were all there were to the story, it would indeed make a fascinating case study in global partnerships. But *Beyond Fair Trade* is far more than that. It is part travelogue, part anthropology, part business/marketing, part drama, part social equity tale. And, as with any venture involving human beings, there are complications, misunderstandings, friction, challenges, and con-tinual evolution. The partnership between the Canadians and their Thai suppliers has already been tested as coffee prices fluctu-ated during the perennial boom-bust coffee price cycle. Although the Canadian firm shares profits equally with the Akha, there are as yet few profits to share, and John M. Darch has invested a signif-icant amount of his personal fortune in the venture.

I was first attracted to the Doi Chaang story because it was so unusual. For one thing, I had never heard of excellent coffee com-ing from Thailand, and having written *Uncommon Grounds*, the history of coffee, I would have been an obvious person to know about it. But my ignorance wasn't unusual. A few years ago, virtu-ally no one in the specialty coffee industry was interested in beans from Thailand, where, as in Vietnam, most of the coffee that *was* grown was robusta, an inferior bean with a higher caffeine con-tent and a more bitter taste than arabica, which generally brews a superior cup. So when I heard that Doi Chaang beans were arabica, organically grown and harvested, then meticulously processed and sorted, I tried brewing some. I quickly became a convert.

In August 2012, I called John M. Darch for a phone interview, then wrote an article for my semi-regular coffee column in *The Wine Spectator*, focusing on the quality and characteristics of the coffee, which is what the magazine's readers, people on the look-out for superior wines and other beverages, are interested in. But I found myself fascinated by the story of the Akha hill tribe, one of several tribes that migrated into the northern Thai moun-tains. The Akha had no written language and, until a few decades ago, they had little contact with the outside world. They lived in thatched-roof bamboo homes, practiced swidden (rotating) agriculture, and hunted for wild game in the jungle. They had an elaborate set of spiritual beliefs and phenomenal memories. They were a peaceful, egalitarian people who usually preferred to flee rather than fight.

In Thailand, however, they ran out of room. They were running out of land as more hill tribes immigrated, more children were born, and Thai loggers destroyed the forests; they had nowhere left to go. They resorted to growing poppies as a cash crop— scraping opium from the scored seedpods—an activity that brought them into increased contact with Thai authorities. Eventually, in the mid-1980s, the Thai military, under pressure from the United States, destroyed the poppy crop and terrorized the hill tribes. Although there were many well-meaning efforts to promote substitute cash crops, none were very successful, and some were even disastrous, leading to further deforestation, the use of dangerous pesticides, and crushing debt.

Their fortunes began to turn only in 2001, when Adel, the young former headman of the village of Doi Chang, approached Wicha Promyong, an old friend of Adel's father, Piko. With Wicha's help, they began to grow, harvest, and roast their own coffee, establishing the Doi Chaang brand. In 2006, John Darch met Wicha and was impressed with his and the others' efforts to take control of their lives. He founded his coffee company in Vancouver, British Columbia, the following year, precipitating a new approach to business and a new way of life for the Akha.

Some of this might sound too good to be true. A bona fide Canadian business that seeks profit but shares it with those who provide the raw material, halfway around the world? I can attest to the accuracy of this claim. I traveled to Vancouver, Canada, and Doi Chang, Thailand, to meet the people behind the "Beyond Fair Trade" logo, and I saw for myself what the company is doing and how it is doing it. My personal perspective, recounted in chapters 8 and 9, offers an unbiased, outsider's view of Doi Chaang Coffee's operations.

The Doi Chaang partnership between a Western company and its non-Western suppliers is unique, as far as I know, but I don't want to give the impression that the Vancouver company is alone in its concern for the welfare of those who grow the beans they roast. That is the entire basis for the Fair Trade certification, and the organic stamp also makes sure that coffee laborers do not breathe pesticides during their workday. In addition, some coffee companies are directly involved in communities at origin, helping to build schools and health clinics and encouraging more sustainable agricultural methods.

Starbucks has an admirable certification system of its own, called Coffee and Farmer Equity (C.A.F.E.) Practices. Community Agroecology Network (CAN) promotes sustainable coffee growth, research, and trade innovations in Latin America. CoffeeCSA. org is a consortium of organic coffee cooperatives from Ethiopia, Guatemala, Peru, Nicaragua, and Mexico. Its beans are roasted in Sacramento, California, but most of the profits go directly to the farmers. Food 4 Farmers is a Vermont-based organization that is working with communities in Latin America to build long-term solutions to chronic hunger in coffee-growing regions. Grounds for Health, which is supported by various coffee companies, is a charity that helps test for, prevent, and treat cervical cancer in coffee-growing regions, which have unusually high levels of that form of cancer. There are many other organizations and coffee importers and roasters that work directly with coffee farmers.

The Doi Chaang story illustrates the importance of all such efforts and offers a different model for a kind of compassionate capitalism that directly links growers and roasters. The two main protagonists in this story, Wicha Promyong and John M. Darch, are in some ways mirror images of one another from different continents: daring entrepreneurs, visionary workaholics who inspire and lead, but who can drive their colleagues crazy. These unusual men became positive change agents across two continents. The story of Doi Chaang Coffee is also their story.

The narrative also features a multi-layered saga involving the history and culture of the hill tribes of Thailand, of Thailand itself, and of the opium trade, from ancient Sumeria to its apotheosis in the Golden Triangle of Southeast Asia (aided and abetted by the British, the French, and the CIA), as well as the history and cultivation of coffee, from its origin in Ethiopia to tropical mountainsides around the world. Readers will also learn about stevia, the plant from which natural low-calorie sweeteners are made; potash, one of the three principle ingredients in fertilizer; and cordyceps, a fungal alternative medicine. In addition, the saga introduces a cast of fascinating characters, without whom coffee would not be transforming lives. It also explores the impacts, both positive and negative, of sudden wealth on a previously marginalized tribal village. These are issues many people will face as the global village becomes ever smaller.

This is a story of inspiration and hope. When cultures meet, they sometimes collide, but they can also reinforce, teach, and help one another.

CHAPTER 1

The Akha

AZY, STUPID, IGNORANT, dirty, illiterate, immoral, criminal, opium-addled. That's the way many Thai citizens once regarded the hill tribes who lived precarious lives in the remote mountains of northern Thailand, eking out a living through subsistence agriculture, selling a few crafts such as weaving, producing illegal opium in recent times, and, in the remote village of Doi Chang, cultivating coffee.

Most of the farming families in Doi Chang are Akha, a culture that may have originated in Mongolia and that can be traced through at least seventy generations, back 1,500 years, according to the Akha Heritage Foundation. "Civil unrest has led them to migrate practically throughout their existence, although they eventually settled in Yunnan province of southwestern China for a significant period of time," foundation literature states. "Tibetan and Chinese influence helped shape their culture. Wars of recent centuries once again led them to travel south."

Despite their marginalized status and uncertain existence, they proudly maintained their traditions and way of life; they regarded themselves as a kind of chosen people. They did not try to protect themselves through military prowess. Rather, they sought peaceful accommodation. Mostly, they just wanted to be left alone. The center of their universe was the village, wherever it might be. The resourceful Akha would cultivate a small area on a mountainside that no one else wanted. In general, they rotated fields around an established village for years, practicing what anthropologists call *swidden agriculture*, which has commonly been termed "slash-and-burn," a more pejorative term that implies environmental destruction, whereas the Akha had a profound respect for the mountainsides where they lived.

The Akha would cut trees to make a clearing, then burn the fallen trees and underbrush, clearing only sufficient space to grow their mountain rice, corn, squash, and other crops. They also foraged, hunted, fished, and kept domestic animals. They rotated their crops, often leaving fields fallow for ten years or more as part of the rotation, allowing nutrients to be replenished before the field was burned again in preparation for replanting. They were not nomads, since they were not constantly on the move. They would, however, move their village periodically. Their homes, made of bamboo, wood, and thatch, were sturdy but relatively easy to construct.

Some tribes wandered into Burma, Laos, Vietnam, and Cambodia; after World War II, many moved to the Golden Triangle area of Thailand, the notorious source of much of the world's opium and its derivatives, morphine and heroin. (The Golden Triangle area includes parts of Burma, Laos, and Thailand, with Burma comprising the largest portion and Thailand the smallest.)

For reasons long forgotten, the Akha were considered the lowest of the low, even among the other hill tribes such as the Lisu, Lahu, Karen, Hmong, Mien, Dara-ang, Kachin, and Lua, as well as the Shan and Chinese Haw. By the mid-1990s the Akha constituted a majority of the people who lived in the remote, inaccessible village of Doi Chang in Chiang Rai Province, yet they lived below—literally and figuratively—the Lisu who lived in the village before the Akha arrived.

Despite how they were viewed, the Akha have a rich culture and heritage, though with increased contact with the more "civilized" world of mainstream Thailand and television representation of other lifestyles, their cultural heritage is being eroded and diluted. "The Akha have always been a peaceful people," according to the Akha Heritage Foundation, "interested only in living quietly in the forest as their ancestors taught them. Until recently, they have succeeded, but migration is no longer an option and their survival now rests on the benevolence of strangers." The story of the Akha in Doi Chang, however, challenges the accuracy of that statement. The saga does indeed involve benevolent strangers, but the tribal community proved itself capable and resourceful on its own.

In the Beginning

THE AKHA WERE largely egalitarian, without a formal class structure, though they did have a hierarchy in place. The village council of elders, composed of the head of every household, made most decisions. The village priest (dzoema), also called "the father of the village," was the most important figure. Well versed in the Akha Way, he ensured that rituals were conducted properly, and he was treated with great respect and deference. The village headman (buseh) took care of dealing with lowlanders, regulations, and disputes. In addition, there were two spirit specialists. The spirit priest (pima), who was always male, repeated incantations to call back wandering souls or recited ritual texts during important occasions such as funerals. The shaman (nyipa), either male or female, could go into a trance, riding a horse into the underworld where spirits and ancestors dwelled. Finally, the blacksmith (baji), another extremely prestigious villager, forged the sacred knife used by the spirit priest. The men of Doi Chang were expected to memorize their patrilineal descent back over fifty generations to an Akha named Sm Mi O, reputedly the first human (à la Adam in the Judaic tradition), who came from Jadae in Yunnan Province in China, a kind of Mecca for the Akha.

This egalitarian society was also a patriarchal society. When a woman married, she left her family to become part of her husband's clan. Women took on a disproportionate share of the work both in the fields and at home. Yet as she aged, she could become a "white-skirted woman" who was especially honored and who could conduct many important rituals on her own. Despite their lack of official power, Akha women were clearly strong-willed individuals, as illustrated by the story of the fate of the first Akha man to take a wife (described by anthropologist Cornelia Kammerer in her dissertation):

> Long ago, when the sky and earth first appeared and human beings were first born, Apoe Miyeh [the supreme Akha deity] asked an Akha man if he wished to marry... A spirit woman, sometimes described as half-tiger, half-spirit, emerged from the woods. She wore no clothes; her body was covered with thick matted fur. Her fangs long, her fingernails like sickles, and her toenails like hoes, the promised bride walked noisily onto the path... Together they returned to the village, where after their marriage the spirit wife killed and ate the first Akha husband.

Then the spirit woman asked another man to marry her. "You eat people," he observed. "I would not *dare* marry you!" But she promised not to eat him, allowing him to knock off her fangs and claws, and she suggested that he build an interior wall separating her living area from his. And that is why, the story explains, women and men live on separate sides of an Akha home, though they can visit one another when others are asleep.

The Akha language, part of the Tibeto-Burman linguistic family, appears to the uninitiated to be simple, since it consists primarily of one-syllable words with an initial consonant followed by a vowel sound, but there are twenty-six possible consonants, including a kind of glottal stop, and thirteen vowels. Perhaps most important, there are five different tones: high, middle, low, and two varieties of "creaky" tones made by constricting the larynx. The tone of a vowel is extremely important, because the same consonant-vowel combination can have five different meanings, depending on the tone used; for instance, the word "Akha" can mean "the tribe," "a crab," "in between," or "later."

There is no native written form of the language. The Akha have a rich oral tradition and a wealth of myths to explain their world. One Akha creation myth—and there are many—asserts that, in the beginning, an all-powerful God called Apoe Miyeh created the sky, where "owner-spirits" lived. God had nine sons, known as "children of the sky." One of these sons, M G'ah, created the Earth—three pieces of clay and three white rocks, from which water flowed—then rain, moon, stars, clouds, grass, wild raspberries, and vines, followed by birds, termites, squirrels, fish, crabs, and other animals, and finally people. The Earth was at first very small, but it kept shaking and gradually grew larger. Initially, the sky was quite close to the ground, with twelve suns and twelve moons, but as people shot down eleven of each, the sky rose higher and the hot rocks cooled.

At first there was no distinction between humans and spirits, who were born of the same parents and lived together. In heaven and on Earth, there was no serious sickness, and people grew over 10 feet tall. They lived a long time, perhaps for hundreds of years, and everything in the world could speak, including birds, trees, animals, grass, wind, water, and earth. After the first eleven generations, however, a father chopping a tree accidentally felled it on his son, whose shoulder was impaled by a branch. Although the father pulled out the branch and the wound healed, people never grew so tall again.

In another story, a dragon caused a huge flood that lasted seven days and seven nights, and everyone drowned except a small boy and girl, who floated in a giant gourd, the Akha version of Noah's Ark. Afterwards, God gave them a magic wand to bring the dead alive. "From that day to this," the Akha told an ethnographer in the 1960s, "the people followed what they could of the religion God had taught them, but since they had died and risen from the dead, they forgot many of the old customs."

The Akha Way

BUT THEY REMEMBERED enough of the old ways to be guided by them. The people followed the Akha Zah, the "Akha Way," which emphasized everyday rituals and stressed strong family ties. They believed in a form of animism, in which all beings and many locations or objects possessed a spirit. Thus, both people and rice were considered to have souls. Rice was the most important food item and was a crucial part of Akha rituals, in which ancestor spirits were asked to help provide a good harvest. Every house had an ancestor shrine. All their rites were designed to maintain harmony, fertility, and continuity. As anthropologist Deborah Tooker observed, "The drawing of Akha village boundaries served to protect village inhabitants from negative external forces." Each village traditionally had at least two "spirit gates" to ward off threatening spirits and entice favorable ones.

Much of what we know of traditional Akha beliefs and daily life comes from an extensive ethnography written by Paul W. Lewis— an American Baptist missionary and anthropologist who with his wife, Elaine, worked among the Akha in Burma from 1947 through

1966, and subsequently worked with the hill tribes in northern Thailand from 1968 through 1989. The Human Relations Area Files at Yale published his *Ethnographic Notes on the Akhas of Burma* in 1969. Anthropologists Leo Alting von Geusau, Cornelia Kammerer, and Deborah Tooker also did field work in Akha villages in the late 1970s and early 1980s, adding new insights into their way of life.

In late 1980 and early 1981, writer Frederic V. Grunfeld and photographer Michael Freeman spent three months in an Akha village down the mountain from Doi Chang; they published a book, *Wayfarers of the Thai Forest: The Akha*, the following year. Grunfeld concluded:

> It gradually became clear to me that underlying the apparently random and spontaneous nature of Akha village life was a complex tissue of the unwritten rules of *Akha Zah*. These govern the villagers' relations with each other, with animals, with the natural world and its powers; they specify the correct way of doing everything, from building a house to laying out a village, from planting the rice to serving a meal, from welcoming the new year to dealing with outside communities. For the Akha, therefore, there is no real distinction between the level of ritual or prescribed behavior and the level of secular daily life.

Paul and Elaine Lewis made a similar observation in their lavishly illustrated 1984 book, *Peoples of the Golden Triangle*: "The Akha Way determines how they cultivate their fields and hunt animals, how they view and treat sickness, and the manner in which they relate to one another and outsiders. It is all embracing."

An Akha folktale explains that long ago, the different tribes took baskets to receive their customs from God. All the other tribes carried loosely woven or torn baskets, but the Akha brought finely woven baskets suitable for carrying rice. That is why they have more detailed customs than the Lisu or other hill tribes.

If all humans lived as the Akha did and embraced the same belief system and way of life, there would probably have been no wars to displace them, since they seldom fought with one another. Murder was virtually unknown, although they did practice infanticide, smothering twins at birth, since they were considered "human rejects," along with babies born with the wrong number of fingers or toes. The house in which such children were born was burned, and the parents were treated as though they were guilty in some way.

Paul Lewis heard of one instance in which the Akha purportedly resorted to violence against adults. Around 1955, Chinese Kuomintang (KMT) soldiers (nationalists who fought against the Chinese Communists) camped in an Akha village in Burma, seven of them lodging with the village priest. "Some of the village children came running and told him that the soldiers were taking wooden decorations off the village spirit gate and using them in their fire for cooking rice and curry." When the priest objected, the soldiers beat him and "told him he was crazy." Back at his house, the priest recited his entire genealogy, then asked God and his ancestors for help. "He then took up his machete, and he and his son killed all seven men in his home, and then went up and killed the four men at the gate." Though the soldiers had guns, they couldn't shoot, presumably because the ancestor spirits prevented them. But in general the Akha preferred to use their wits rather than force against their enemies.

The Justice System

THE AKHA HAD a relatively informal, common-sense justice system and no jails. The elders and the headman would hear both sides of a case and pass judgment, usually within a day. If the trial lasted several days, waiting for witnesses to return from a trip, for example, the headman might be bribed. If the people uncovered evidence of bribery, however, the headman would often be ousted.

There were three levels of crime. A minor offense would involve stealing small things from a person's house, such as firewood, or killing someone's chick if it strayed into the wrong garden. Such cases were often dropped, or the fine assessed as free drinks for the elders. A more serious offense was actually entering someone's house to steal something. For that, the offender had to give a pig, return the stolen goods, and sometimes pay a fine. If they stole something from the bamboo section containing the ancestor altar goods, they also had to pay for a ceremony that involved a spirit priest and various sacrifices. The third and most serious offense was "wronging another's wife"—that is, adultery. Paul Lewis asked if murder would also fit into this third category, and the answer was affirmative, but "perhaps there are not enough murders in Akha society that they categorize it along with the more 'common' crimes." For these more serious offenses, a water buffalo or two pigs would be assessed.

In the vast majority of the world, suicides outnumber homicides. Human beings seem to be unique among animals in their tendency to kill themselves. Yet it was almost unheard of for an Akha to commit suicide. "As to the Akha's attitude toward suicides from other tribes," wrote Lewis, "they always seem dumbfounded that anyone would do such a horrible thing."

As their justice system implied, the Akha believed in personal property. People could sell their houses if they moved to another village, but they had to give some of the money to the village, half of which went to a community fund and half to the elders. They could also sell their fields or gardens. If someone was fined for a crime but had no money to pay, the elders could force him to sell a field or animals.

If a villager asked to borrow something, then a neighbor was obliged to lend it, though that didn't apply to someone from another village. If the borrowed item was lost or broken, it was supposed to be replaced. Since the person who did the borrowing was often very poor, that sometimes didn't happen. If a poor person was repeatedly fined and couldn't pay, he could be kicked out of the village.

In the past, there was one disturbing form of property. The impoverished Akha would sometimes sell their children into slavery to another Akha, though such servants were treated as part of the new family and were freed when they later married.

Superstition

THE AKHA BELIEVED that their world was filled with spirits, some of whom could be helpful, but many of whom were potentially dangerous. They were divided into "inside" spirits, who existed within the village gates, or the "outside" spirits of the jungle. Although the Akha could no longer see them, they could tell when the spirits were active at night, because the dogs would bark and howl. The Akha developed elaborate rituals to placate or frighten away malevolent spirits. Because the spirits feared saliva, for instance, the Akha would spit when anxious. Spirits were also afraid of fire, gunshots, and the sharp edge of a machete.

Nonetheless, one had to be on guard against offending the spirits and incurring bad fortune. Similar to the Chinese practice of feng shui, the Akha believed that the placement of people and objects was crucial. The cemetery had to be located far from the village in the forest, for example. Villages were built on a slope, with the lower section associated with impurity.

Although the Akha collected a variety of healing herbs and practiced folk medicine, they relied heavily on spirit priests, as well as a shaman who could go into a trance and visit the spirit world, a kind of hell below the earth. The shaman could discover which spirit was eating someone's stolen soul and what meat the spirit might prefer as a substitute. Then an appropriate chicken, pig, or goat would be sacrificed. They had many other superstitions as well. If a cow or dog climbed up on the roof of a house, for instance, it was considered a bad omen, since a household spirit was luring them there. Once a year, each family would make an offering to this spirit. If the shadow of a flying crane fell on someone, that person would be partially paralyzed. Seeing two snakes entwined or two crabs skittering in opposite directions were bad omens.

Smallpox and other contagious diseases were of grave concern. If an Akha had visited a village where an epidemic was raging, he would perform a "follow-me not" ceremony as he neared his own village, to keep the illness from following him home. The entire village might perform an epidemic protection ceremony. If the plague were some distance away, they might just sacrifice a chicken, but if it were nearby, they would kill a large black dog, mounting its snarling head atop the village gate. Lewis recounted that in 1950, he witnessed such a ceremony—but the villagers also asked him to send a vaccinator to protect them.

When a contagious disease did break out in their village, each Akha family would make little clay models of all their animals, including a person riding a horse, to represent the plague riding out of the village. Then they put the clay figures in a dish, where everyone would spit on them. All the dishes were brought to the village priest, who would sacrifice a white rooster, giving some of the meat to the figurines. Then he would say, "There is no place for you here. Go to a place where there is plenty of room. There is no means of getting food here. Go to a place where food is plentiful." The villagers would then throw the clay figurines into the jungle.

The Akha would sometimes wear an amulet or take finely ground herbs to treat or prevent illness. But when they did get sick, they remained stoical. They had no concept of resting to get over a disease. They would keep on working until they simply couldn't go on.

Village Life

THE AKHA WOULD choose a village site near a good water source and fertile land where they could establish their fields. A wide avenue led down the center of the village, convenient for driving animals out to pasture, and a bypass path always led around the village, to be used during special religious ceremonies that weren't to be interrupted, to carry sick people, or to be taken by someone just passing through. If visitors chose to go through the village, they were obliged to stop and have tea in someone's house, where they would often also have their legs and arms massaged after walking a long way.

The men assembled the bamboo and wood for a new home, while the women cut grass stalks to make the thatch, carrying big bundles on their backs. When all was ready, the head of the household would call villagers together to build the house, which usually took several days. During the construction, a dog had to be sacrificed and eaten, which disgusted some other tribes, who called the Akha "dog-eaters."

The head householder dug the first hole for the main post. Digging holes was a perilous enterprise, since a human shadow should never fall into a hole, which would bring bad luck. The householder sprinkled water, three pinches of rice, salt, ginger root, and egg into the main posthole. A partition divided the men's side, in the front, from the women's. The ancestor shrine would be hung on the women's side of the house near this post. Houses were sturdy and easy to repair. The thatched roof had to be replaced every seven or eight years. Up to thirty people could live in an extended family home, though usually ten or fewer lived there.

Great care was taken in preparing a field for one of the fifteen varieties of rice the Akha grew. First they marked the field, hoping for an auspicious dream that night. The men then cleared the underbrush with their machetes on an appropriate household day. The night before and night after the householder cut the first tree in the field, tradition dictated that he and his wife had to refrain from intercourse.

After all the trees and brush were cut, they were left to dry for several months; then the men decided, in consultation with nearby villages, on the day for burning the new fields. The Akha week had twelve days, named for different animals—sheep, monkey, chicken, dog, pig, rat, buffalo, tiger, donkey, rabbit, fox, horse—each with its own characteristics and rules. For instance, no one could put a post into the ground on Tong La, the day of the donkey. The best days to start a fire were: Kheu (dog), so that the fire would jump like a dog; Yah (pig), so that the fire would root around; or Home Yah (monkey), so that it would spread quickly. Kha La (tiger) was a bad day, since the fire might burn incompletely, in stripes. Boys would set the fire with beeswax, then blow buffalo horns to summon the wind. When the fires had burned out, the village priest or an elder would call out, "Tomorrow don't go anywhere. We are going to have ceremonial abstinence for the fire." This was to assure that the fire would not burn anywhere it should not.

Because rice was the staple crop, great care was taken to make sure that the soul of the rice field was not frightened off. Hand hoes were used for weeding—never machetes. Chicken sacrifices were made in the small "spirit hut" near the field, though the poultry could be taken back home to eat that night. Every aspect of the agricultural cycle had its own carefully prescribed rituals.

In addition to rice, the Akha also planted cotton, peanuts, soy beans, chili peppers, squash, cucumber, cantaloupe, pumpkin, tomatoes, greens, beans, onions, ginger, barley, gourds, sunflowers, tobacco, indigo, poppies, and banana trees. They made alcoholic beverages from corn and rice, though most public drinking occurred during the New Year's celebration or at weddings. One or two men in a village were often known as heavy drinkers. Many Akha smoked tobacco in pipes, and a few chewed it. Others chewed betel nuts, though they had to purchase or trade for them. Opium, made from poppies, was mostly used as a medicine or painkiller, but some men became addicted to it. Young men usually did not smoke opium, because then no girl would want to marry them. Once a man was addicted, he usually became useless as a provider and needed money to feed his habit.

In addition to growing their food, the Akha kept domesticated animals such as water buffalo, pigs, goats, and chickens. Dogs and monkeys were both pets and potential food if the need arose or if a ritual sacrifice was necessary. They kept cats to control rodents, while caged parakeets or other jungle birds were apparently just for pleasure. The Akha men were great hunters and trappers. "Even when the men are not actually hunting," noted Paul Lewis, "they talk about it constantly." Their favorite game animal was the barking deer. Young boys usually drove the deer toward the older men, who were waiting with their crossbows or homemade guns. Boys shot birds with slingshots, while men put up a large net to capture flocks as they funneled through a narrow passage. A spring-pole snare caught larger fowl. They also built traps for bamboo rats and other small game. A sharp stick was set to impale wild boar, tiger, or deer, though these traps were also dangerous for unwary people. Hunters were respectful of mountain spirits and left some of the kill for them, saying, "You all eat. Don't let us be afflicted by spirits. May that which is good never cease, and that which is bad never be encountered."

The Akha also fished, though without hooks. They would attach a liana vine to a stick and weave an earthworm into the end of the vine to attract a fish, then swoop under it with a net or basket. Others made dams in streams and diverted the fish into nets. Yet others specialized in catching fish with their bare hands by reaching into holes on the bank, though they risked catching a poisonous animal as well.

They also sought out other wild edibles, including herbs, wild apple, mango, cherry, raspberry, and chestnut, along with various leaves and flowers. They ate bamboo shoots and tendrils from particular vines. They dug up wild yams if short of rice. Birds' eggs, spiders, cicadas, grasshoppers, praying mantises, and grubs were all collected and consumed. Mushrooms that grew on logs, rocks, and trees were mostly edible, but they avoided ground mushrooms, many of which were poisonous.

Akha boys would catch a wasp, tie a string to it, and then race after it to find its nest, where they would dig up the larvae to eat. In a similar way, villagers could follow bees and smoke them out for their honey.

Women performed most of the domestic chores, rising at dawn to pound (husk) the rice, fetch water, cook, gather firewood, cut and carry 10-foot-high bundles of imperata grass for thatch, and forage for wild edibles. They spun cotton and made cloth that they dyed, embroidered, and appliquéd. Girls began to learn such tasks by the time they were seven years old.

The meals, during which the oldest male always ate first, and the women and children last, were tasty and varied, prepared in a wok or stew pots, with spices (hot or mild), mushrooms, roots, flowers, game birds, pork, chicken, or crunchy fried termites. Every meal featured nourishing mountain rice. Other dishes might include pickled beets, wild honey, omelets, or curries.

Through the Seasons

THE AKHA CALENDAR had twelve months that corresponded roughly with their Western equivalents. Thus, the first month of the year, Pare Lar Bar Lar, paralleled January. Since most readers will find it easier to refer to their own calendar months, those are used here. In January, they prepared agricultural land by weeding and felling trees. February was the month for rest from much labor, as well as a month for courting. Women spun cotton thread, weaving and embroidering blouses and skirts. In March, the onset of the three-month dry season, it was very hot and time for the burning of the fields.

April was the beginning of the new growing season, with various ceremonies, such as the dedication of the spirit house near the fields. In May, the fields were planted in anticipation of the rains. Four ceremonies occurred this month, including one to bless the first rice planting, to repair a holy well, a ground-beetle catching ceremony for a rice pest, and finally, a ceremony to apologize to all the insects that were killed during the cultivation.

In June, as the four-month rainy season commenced, there was a ceremony with a sacrifice to the source of the river, the ever-flowing supplier of water. During this month, everything was supposed to be growing strong—trees, animals, even the cricket in its hole developing strong wings. In July, as the rice grew ankle-high, the Akha weeded for the first time, often during heavy rains. They conducted a ceremony for "making a merit in the rice field."

Near the end of August, the three-day Swing Ceremony commenced, which was a fun-filled way to further ensure a good rice harvest. Women went to the holy well for water to bless the rite and prepared special rice cakes with salt and sesame seeds. A large swing was constructed with four long wooden poles tied together at the top, holding a woven vine strong enough for two Akha to ride on a horizontal stick held at the bottom. Sometimes it would swing out over the edge of a cliff. They also made a smaller swing for children. The Akha sang special songs and recited poems during this time.

In September, there were rituals such as the Plucking Chicken Ceremony and the Evil Driving Out Ceremony. This latter event was a favorite with the boys, who got to run repeatedly through the houses and the village with wooden clubs to chase the evil spirits away.

October, the last month of the rainy season, featured the harvest. Nature was bursting with ripe fruits and the rice was ready, with an appropriate New Rice Eating Ceremony. The harvest continued into November, when the rice was beaten and threshed, then stored in a barn, for which appropriate rituals were performed. This was the time to choose rice seed for the next year's planting as well. Finally, in December the rice barn was officially opened for use with a Top Hitting Ceremony, and near the month's end, New Year's was celebrated.

Thus, the Akha lived in a traditional, well-regulated culture, in tune with the seasons. While they feared and placated the spirits, they also had plenty of human spirit themselves. During the New Year's ceremony, boys made and spun tops, trying to knock opponents' toys out of the circle. Girls played a pitch-and-toss game with beans. Children sometimes strode tall on stilts; other times they rode a kind of three-wheeled wooden go-cart, greased with the rind from a fruit, that could go dangerously fast down hills. During some festivals, children climbed up a greased bamboo pole to reach a prize.

In another game, children would set two long bamboo sticks on the ground, slapping them together rhythmically while a boy jumped in and out. They increased the speed until his ankle was caught, and then the boy had to manipulate the bamboo himself. They played variations of tag, tug-of-war, and hide-and-seek.

Those too old to play active games would sometimes have a smoking competition, seeing who could turn their burning tobacco as red as possible, followed by a kind of quiz game, and then more smoking. The one whose pipe lasted longest was declared the winner.

As they worked in the fields or spun cotton in their homes, the Akha sang joyful or plaintive songs to stave off loneliness or just to pass the time. During ceremonies, they would dance in their finely embroidered clothes and headdresses, loaded with silver coins and feathers, accompanied by wood drums, gongs, cymbals, and wooden flutes.

And at night, mothers would sing lullabies to their children, such as this one:

Oh little girl, little girl,
Come to sleep, come to sleep right here.
Oh little girl, Mama is here,
So don't cry, don't you cry.
Nobody is scolding you little one,
No one at all.
If you continue to cry,
All the other mothers will call you fussy.

The Akha were appalled when they learned that some ethnic Chinese not only scolded their children but would hit them—not just with their knuckles, but with sticks. The Akha would never tolerate such behavior.

Opium

NO HISTORY of the Akha would be complete without a history of opium, whose story stretches back thousands of years, and which became an important, illegal cash crop for the Akha. Humans probably discovered the magical properties of the poppy plant before they learned to brew alcohol. Neolithic villagers in Switzerland left behind poppy seeds and pods around 4000 BCE, and the Sumerians were cultivating the lovely paper-thin flowers in the Fertile Crescent of the Tigris-Euphrates rivers by 3400 BCE. Some authorities have opined that Arab traders introduced poppy cultivation and opium to China as late as the sixth century, but it probably arrived much earlier in the Far East. In *Opium: A History*, Martin Booth wrote:

> Opium was either brought home by Chinese seafarers who were sailing as far as Africa in the first century BCE, or introduced by Buddhist priests from Tibet around the first century CE... or, just as likely, it arrived from India via Burma, where Chinese merchants were trading in jade and gemstones as early as the third century BCE, or from Bactria (central Asia) whence the famous Chinese explorer, Chang Chien, traveled in 139 BCE, meeting the remnants of the Greek civilization of Alexander the Great there.

There is no question, however, that the Arabs did spread opium through extensive trade, and the ninth-century physician known as Avicenna advocated opium for the treatment of diarrhea, dysentery, and eye diseases. Avicenna was also an addict, writing poetry in praise of the poppy. He died at fifty-eight, probably from an overdose of opium mixed with wine.

Around 1520, the German-Swiss Philippus Aureolus Theophrastus Bombastus von Hohenheim, known as Paracelsus, combined medicine and alchemy, dispensing pills he called laudanum (from the Latin word for "praise"), with opium its main ingredient. In 1546, a Frenchman visiting Turkey observed: "There is not a Turk who would not purchase opium with his last coin; he carries the drug on him in war and peace."

Opium's popularity quickly spread. In 1603, Shakespeare acknowledged it in Othello, referring to "poppy [and] all the drowsy syrups of the world." In the 1660s, British physician Thomas Sydenham dispensed opium dissolved in strong red wine or port. Following the lead of Paracelsus, he called it laudanum and wrote: "Here I cannot but break out in praise of the great God, the giver of all good things, who hath granted to the human race, as a comfort in their afflictions, no medicine of the value of opium."

Throughout most of history, opium was consumed orally, either eaten as a solid (along with spices to make its bitter taste more palatable) or dissolved in a drink. But after smoking tobacco was introduced from the New World in the sixteenth century, people began to smoke opium in pipes for a quicker impact.

In 1700, British physician John Jones published *Mysteries of Opium Reveal'd*, asserting that the drug promoted "Ovations of the Spirits, Courage, Contempt of Danger, Magnanimity… Euphory… Satisfaction, Acquiescence, Contentation, Equanimity." Yet Jones also described the horrors of withdrawal, which brought on "intolerable Distresses, Anxieties and Depressions of Spirits, which in a few days commonly end in a most miserable Death, attended by strange Agonies."

Cultivating Poppies

POPPIES ARE ANNUALS rather than perennials, though they self-seed quite nicely. In Asia, they grow best at higher elevations, at 3,000 feet or more above sea level. The seeds sprout in warm, moist conditions and grow about 3 feet tall, producing a single blossom some ninety days after germination. The four delicate overlapping petals offer various shades of white through red and purple. Inside the flower is a ring of pollen-bearing anthers.

Insects must quickly fertilize the plants, since the flowers last only a few days. After the petals drop, the globular seedpod grows to the size of a small egg, bluish green with a waxy surface. The pod's outer skin protects the wall of the ovary, which produces over a thousand tiny black seeds. Once the pod dries, the seeds loosen and are dispersed through holes in the crown when the wind blows the swaying stem.

Opium is harvested before the pod dries, however, by making shallow parallel vertical incisions on the seedpods, beginning about a week after the petals have dropped. It is a delicate, labor-intensive process that must be done by hand, using a specialized metal tool. The cuts should be neither too shallow nor too deep. The sticky white latex sap oozes out and coagulates on the pod surface, where it turns brown and is scraped off the following day, using a blunt blade. The pods can be harvested repeatedly over the brief twelve days during which the pod is ripening. When the pod has dried, the sap flow ceases, and seeds can be collected for the next year's planting.

The raw opium is sun-dried for several days. As it loses water, it becomes pliable, like putty, and can be beaten and molded into bricks, then wrapped in leaves or plastic. If properly prepared, it does not ferment or rot. To purify the opium further, it must be cooked in boiling water, sieved, and reduced to a clay-like consistency. Opium is an ideal product for trade and distribution because it is compact, non-perishable, and always in demand. Where there is trade, there is money. And where there is money, there is frequently conflict.

Seeds of Conflict

IN 1685, by imperial decree, China tentatively opened the port of Canton to trade with Europeans, though the western "Barbarians" were kept at a distance. The Chinese exported tea, silk, spices, and other products, in return for which European traders sent silver, iron, tin, pepper, cotton, and opium. The East India Company, that venerable British institution, conducted most of the trade. The Company virtually ruled much of India from 1700 until 1833, when its monopolistic charter lapsed.

Although the Chinese grew some poppies, the Indian opium supplied by the British was superior and better for smoking. It was so popular that the emperor prohibited the smoking of opium in 1729 out of concern for the growing addiction of his subjects, though opium imports weren't restricted until 1799. That didn't stop smuggling, and the British exploited their opium monopoly in India to push sales for all they were worth.

Warren Hastings, the Governor-General of the East India Company, was disturbed that many Indian laborers were becoming opium addicts, so he discouraged such Indian consumption. Meanwhile, back in his native Britain, opium remained legal and widely consumed. Samuel Taylor Coleridge and Thomas De Quincey were famous opium addicts of the early nineteenth century, while in 1850 novelist Charles Kingsley wrote that the British housewife needed "her pennord o'elevation, to last her out the week"—that is, a penny's worth of opium. Victorian opium sedatives were commonly used to quiet crying babies.

After the East India Company charter lapsed in 1833, other British enterprises took over the opium trade with China, notably Jardine Matheson & Company, owned by William Jardine and James Matheson. Jardine called the sale of opium "the safest and most gentleman-like speculation I am aware of." The founders became enormously wealthy, and their firm still thrives, though its website makes no mention of opium: "Founded as a trading company in China in 1832, Jardine Matheson is today a diversified business group focused principally on Asia."

American entrepreneurs also jumped into the opium trade. In 1830 the first fast clipper ship, the Red Rover, was able to make three round-trip passages a year to carry opium from India to China. Despite the official Chinese ban on the drug, addiction levels grew dramatically. When the Chinese made a serious effort to stop the opium trade, a British ship fired on a Chinese junk in 1839, starting what came to be known as the Opium War. That war ended three years later with the victorious British forcing China to open more ports to trade. As part of the treaty, Britain got Hong Kong as a colony. The Second Opium War (1856–1860) ended with another British triumph and the legalization of opium importation, albeit with a tariff.

Helpless to stop the continued importation of the drug, the Chinese decided to grow their own rather than continue to enrich the British, but that meant subjugating highland ethnic rebels of Yunnan Province, including the Chinese traders called Haw in Thailand (many of whom were Muslims) and the Hmong tribe. The imperial Chinese forces broke the rebellions with repeated massacres of men, women, and children in the late nineteenth century. In response, some tribes migrated into Burma and further south. These migrations would span a century.

Meanwhile, the Chinese were cultivating opium. By 1885, China was growing twice as much as it was importing. An 1888 article in the London Times reported, "A third of cultivation [in Yunnan Province] is devoted to poppy fields [and] this huge stock of Chinese opium is raised for the supply of scores of millions who never smoked before." Two years later, the Chinese emperor revoked the official opium prohibition, sanctioning the domestic crop.

Despite various attempts to reverse the policy, and the successful revolution of 1912 led by Sun Yat-sen, poppy cultivation remained a driving force in Yunnan, the mountainous area of southern China where the Akha and other hill tribes lived before migrating south. After 1916, political chaos ensued, with warlords battling for control. "In some areas, opium cultivation became virtually mandatory," wrote Martin Booth in his history of opium. "Local warlords used it as a source of income to fund guerrilla warfare. Farmers were forced to abandon food production and cultivate poppies." This pattern would be repeated throughout Southeast Asia for decades to come.

A 1921 visitor to Yunnan wrote, "We heard much about the poverty of the district and the increasing cultivation of opium poppy. It is tragic to see this when a few years ago the land was filled with crops needed for the daily food of the people. In some parts half the crops are opium, and it demands a great deal of labor!"

Meanwhile, the hill tribe migration continued. "Their movement south was primarily to flee fighting between warlords and bandits and rampant disorder in late nineteenth century [and] early twentieth century southern China," wrote Ronald Renard in *Opium Reduction*, his book about opium in Thailand. "As the minorities moved south, the cash-cropping of opium moved with them."

The Chinese Haw became the primary opium traders, carrying the product in long mule-trains through the mountains. They supplied opium to the black market in Thailand, where a royal monopoly had been in place since the British pressured Siam (as Thailand was then known) to legalize the drug in 1855. The Thai government set an artificially high price on legal opium for the Bangkok opium dens, so the Haw smuggled cheaper produce through the mountains, where, along the way, they also bought a small amount of the drug from hill tribe farmers.

Opium and the Akha

THE AKHA and other hill tribes may have grown poppies for medicinal purposes for centuries, but opium only became a cash crop in the 1800s, thanks to the Opium Wars and British traders. Before that, the drug was probably only a minor part of their lives. According to anthropologist Leo Alting von Geusau, opium is not mentioned in any Akha ritual texts or songs. In the book *Plants and People of the Golden Triangle*, however, Edward Anderson recounts this Akha legend about the origin of opium:

> There was once a girl so beautiful that men came from all over the world to court her. Of these many men, only seven gained her affection and became her lovers. One day, all seven arrived at her house at the same time. She decided to make love with all of them, even though she knew it would make her die, because it was better than choosing only one man, thus making the others bitter and causing conflict. The girl asked her people to care for her grave, promising to send up a beautiful flower (opium) that would grow from her heart. She also said that anyone who tasted the fruits of this flower would want to taste them again and again. Finally, she warned them to be very careful, for the fruits bore both good and evil.

It would appear, then, that the Akha had been aware of the seductive, dangerous qualities of the drug for a long time. Still, it was only through the influence of the British in the nineteenth century and the Chinese, Burmese, and Americans during the twentieth century that opium became a major problem. As Ronald Renard observed, "Where there is opium cultivation, there will be opium use and then opium addiction. Because opium is such good medicine and also because of the lack of alternatives in the hills, opium was widely used for various ailments. This got a lot of the users addicted." Even walking through a field of poppies with harvested seedpods could produce a mild narcotic effect.

In 1934, a British advisor to Thailand's Ministry of Finance proposed that the hill tribes in northern Thailand should be encouraged to grow more opium in order to discourage smuggling from Burma. That way, he said, tribal people could become integrated into Thai life and become "more civilized." In 1938, the government decided to promote poppy cultivation in Chiang Rai, but World War II intervened and the plan was apparently dropped.

Some Akha men proved to be particularly vulnerable to the drug. Paul Lewis was studying at Eastern Baptist Theological Seminary in 1946. As Lewis was preparing to depart for Burma, his instructor, Dr. James Telford, who had worked as a missionary in Burma in the 1930s, warned him that a disproportionate number of Akha were addicts. In his work during the 1950s and 1960s, Lewis found that to be true. More Akha than Lahu were habituated to opium. "As many as 25 percent of some Akha villagers took opium, and about 5 percent were seriously addicted," Lewis recalled. In the next few decades, the problem grew worse, so that one writer in 1983 estimated that 30 percent of Akha adult males in Thailand were opium addicts.

Cold War Opium and the CIA

IT WAS ONLY after the Communists took over China in 1949 that opium cultivation in Southeast Asia exploded. Through harsh measures, the new Communist dictatorship of Mao Zedong successfully wiped out Chinese poppies, leaving a huge gap in the world market that was filled by hill tribe cultivation in Burma, Thailand, and Laos.

The Kuomintang (KMT) forces of Chiang Kai-shek's losing Chinese Nationalist Party regrouped in Burma. Partially funded and armed by the US Central Intelligence Agency (CIA), the KMT invaded southern China in 1951. After the invasion failed miserably, the KMT forces set up camp in northern Burma in the Shan

States. To support themselves, they turned to opium, levying an annual tax on every poppy farmer and becoming an opium militia.

The Thai military rulers, who took power in a 1947 coup, lined their own pockets and personal fiefdoms through opium sales and graft. "General Phao, head of the CIA-equipped and -trained national police force, took personal control of the opium trade and, in exchange for CIA support, furthered KMT political aims, protecting their supply lines and opium business interests and establishing the Burma to Bangkok opium corridor," observed Martin Booth in *Opium*. "By 1955, Phao's police force was the largest, best organized trafficking syndicate in Thailand." Although Phao was ousted in 1957, the corruption and flow of opium continued, even after opium use and cultivation in Thailand were officially outlawed in 1958.

In 1961, the Burmese government drove the KMT into Thailand and Laos. In Thailand, the KMT soldiers were called civilian refugees, and they were soon escorting caravans of hundreds of opium laden mules, guarded by armed troops, through the mountains, including villages such as Doi Chang. General Li Wen huan ran the KMT smuggling operation from his private mansion near the city of Chiang Mai, in the district just to the south of Chiang Rai.

For the next thirty years, many in the Thai military and Border Patrol Police worked with the KMT and other opium dealers to keep the border with Burma relatively safe, while extracting profitable kickbacks. In his book *The Politics of Heroin in Southeast Asia*, Alfred McCoy documented the confusing, kaleidoscopic, shifting alliances and politics of poppy production in Southeast Asia. "Thailand," wrote McCoy, "defended its frontiers with warlord allies who transformed the borderlands into zones of controlled chaos." Even while the US government officially launched a war on drugs, the CIA quietly supported the opium trade as part of its anti-Communist efforts. "The Cold War was also fought with covert operations that encouraged alliances with warlords and criminal syndicates at the flash points of global confrontation," wrote McCoy. "As the CIA mobilized tribal armies in these rugged highlands, their warlords used the agency's arms and protection to become major drug lords... The opium trade relieved the agency from the prohibitive cost of welfare for tribes... Control over this critical cash crop allowed the CIA's chosen warlord to command tribes, clans, and villages in bloody wars that ground on for years."

In 1965, a US Agency for International Development (USAID) document stated, "Thailand is currently of enormous strategic importance in terms of U.S. national interests [because] Thailand is located in the midst of the all-out struggle between the Free World and Communist Forces of Southeast Asia." That same year, the CIA helped to fund the new Tribal Research Center in Chiang Mai, intended to study the "hill tribe problem," as it was regarded by the American and Thai governments. At the opening ceremony of the new center, the General Secretary of the Southeast Asia Treaty Organization (SEATO) said, "I need not remind you...that it is among minority people that Communist propaganda and agitators find a fertile field for their subversive activities."

Although the Tribal Research Center was ostensibly founded to help the hill tribes, and did indeed do some important research, the attitude toward the hill tribes was generally negative and patronizing. In a 1967 report, UN-funded German social anthropologist Hans Manndorff wrote about the "problems" that hill tribes allegedly caused—forest destruction, opium growing, border insecurity—and, although ostensibly sympathetic to the hill tribes, he assumed that they had to be forced into Thai society: "Of course, it is no longer possible for the government to leave these ethnic minorities entirely alone today. It is the inevitable logic of events in our times that administration and modernization are extended even into those remote parts of the country which were traditionally self-sufficient." He suggested "the government should consider ways and means of creating loyalty to the Thai nation, so as to facilitate the integration of [the hill tribes] into the social, economic, and political life of the country." Manndorff recommended setting up experimental demonstration areas to promote cash crops to replace opium, as well as centers for health, education, and welfare.

Thus, while opium was illegal, and the hill tribes were blamed for producing it, the CIA and some corrupt Thai officials continued to wink at the charade of anti-drug enforcement. In a staged media event in March 1972, General Li Wen-huan appeared on US television to denounce the opium trade. As the cameras rolled, one hundred mules loaded with 26 tons of opium deposited their load on a huge bonfire, for which the Thai military, with covert funding from the CIA, paid US$1.85 million. Li vowed that this was the end of the opium trade, but most of the material burned was just poppy straw, and General Li continued to profit from opium for years to come.

By now it was not just opium but also its refined product, heroin, which was being smuggled. Heroin was a relative youngster compared to opium. In 1874, a pharmacist in London, Britain, was looking for a non-addictive alternative to opium and morphine. He experimented by boiling morphine with acetic anhydride, creating what came to be known as heroin. By 1898 heroin was being mass-manufactured in Germany by Bayer Laboratories, which touted it as a powerful, safe painkiller and gave it the trade name of Heroin, from the German word *heroisch*, meaning heroic. Within a few years, it became clear that heroin was indeed addictive, but by then its use and manufacture had spread widely.

Although pure heroin wasn't simple to manufacture, it was more concentrated and easier to smuggle than opium, and it didn't have the characteristic odor that gave away the presence of opium.

It was also easier to smoke, snort, or inject, and quicker to take effect. And it could be cut with chalk or other white powders to maximize profits.

Heroin use gradually increased in the first half of the twentieth century but its use exploded during the 1960s in the United States, where the number of addicts rose from 50,000 to 500,000 from 1960 to 1970. During the Vietnam War (1965–1975), heroin was the drug of choice for many miserable, frightened, disillusioned American soldiers. The swelling number of US addicts led to President Nixon's announcement of a "war on drugs" in June 1971, the beginning of a hopeless, counterproductive effort that only made drugs more unsafe and expensive, lining the pockets of criminals, dealers, warlords, and authorities who looked the other way.

In 1974, a rival appeared to contest General Li and his KMT opium squad. He was Khun Sa, an old nemesis, whom Li had defeated in a 1967 opium war. Half-Chinese and half-Shan, Khun Sa had been imprisoned by the Burmese military in 1969. Upon his release in 1974, he quickly rebuilt his opium empire, based in the remote hilltop village of Ban Hin Taek in Thailand's Golden Triangle region, near the Burmese border. There he built a major heroin refinery. In the crop year of 1976–1977, his army of 3,500 combatants accompanied twelve caravans, each with over one hundred mules, carrying 70 tons of raw opium.

In 1977, the Thai military, trying to protect itself against the perceived threat from Burmese Communist Party troops (who also made money from opium) across the border, tried to forge an alliance between Khun Sa and General Li, hosting a meeting between the two. They proposed a cozy marketing agreement with Khun Sa and Li in return for arming both to fight the Communists. But the two warlords refused to work with one another. Around the same time, the American government was giving military aid to the repressive Burmese government, which claimed that it was fighting against opium cultivation among the rebellious hill tribes of Burma.

On January 21, 1982, under Thailand's Prime Minister Prem Tinsulanonda (uncorrupted by opium money), the Thai military turned on Khun Sa, attacking his stronghold in Ban Hin Taek with 1,500 troops, jet fighters, and helicopter gunships. A survey of the captured village revealed luxurious villas, a hospital, a brothel, and seven heroin refineries. Khun Sa quickly rebuilt a major heroin outpost just across the border in Burma at Homong, declaring it the capital of his "Free Shan State," where he remained for the next fourteen years. From there, he launched an attack on March 11, 1984, against General Li's mansion in Chiang Mai, detonating a truck loaded with 7,000 sticks of dynamite that destroyed the building and left a huge crater in its place. General Li survived, since he was in Bangkok at the time, but his opium empire crumbled as the Thai government finally cracked down on the KMT forces with whom they had cooperated for so many years. Khun Sa remained the undisputed, self-described "King of the Golden Triangle" until 1996.

CHAPTER 2

Culture Clashes

ACCORDING TO an Akha proverb, "One does not have the ability to throw away our customs, any more than a buffalo has the ability to have its footprints one place and its body someplace else." Unfortunately, the modern Akha of northern Thailand, including those in the village of Doi Chang, have found it increasingly difficult to maintain their traditional way of life. Especially since the 1960s, their culture has faced threats from other tribes, the police, the army, Communists, anti-Communists, fundamentalist missionaries, so-called environmentalists, warlords, and drug dealers, as well as the encroachment of "civilization" in the form of cheap mass-produced clothing, television, and a cash economy where becoming a prostitute was a way to survive in the city.

The first Akha tribe moved into Thailand in the late nineteenth or early twentieth century, followed by a few others in subsequent years, but the major migration took place after Burmese dictator Ne Win staged a 1962 military coup. The Loimi Akha, named for a mountain in the Shan State of Kengtung in

Burma, began to migrate out of Burma into Thailand in the late 1960s to avoid violent conflict. "Groups such as the Akha [were] caught in the cross-fire between forces of the central Burmese government and the forces of various independence, communist, and opium armies," wrote one observer. Or, as anthropologist Leo Alting von Geusau put it, the Akha sought to escape "increased incidence of violence, robbery, murder, and the destruction of property in the mountain areas of east Kent Tung state [in Burma.] Like many other highlanders, [they] came over the border after being robbed of surplus silver and cattle, some even in a state of near starvation."

In 1980, the first three Akha families settled in the village of Locha in northern Thailand, southwest of the town of Chiang Rai, though the village was more commonly known by its Thai name, Doi Chang, which meant "Elephant Mountain," since the mountain on which the village sat could be taken to resemble an elephant's head and trunk. Brothers Akur and Luko and their cousin Asar, together with their families, were the pioneers, escaping villages to the north on Doi Tung mountain, where the violence between drug warlords and the government was becoming a daily threat, and where the soil was depleted, the forests disappearing. They had all been born in Burma, where the chaotic violence and forced labor had driven them across the border. Now, in typical Akha fashion, a few families tested out the new village, sending back reports the following year to encourage others to relocate as well.

Doi Chang, up a remote mountainside about 30 miles southwest of the city of Chiang Rai, was a Lisu village. Since the Akha traditionally established their own separate communities, this was an unusual relocation. But there were advantages. There was still some unoccupied forest here and no warlords. The small valley, tucked just below the mountaintop, offered springs and streams with fresh water. Because it took many hours to walk up or down the mountain, the location was sufficiently isolated from lowland Thai interference. The entrepreneurial Lisu were glad to sell nearly level land for housing, and there was enough surrounding sloping land to clear for fields so that there was initially no charge for claiming them.

Over the next few years, as news of the fertile soil and relative isolation and peace spread, more Loimi Akha arrived, through word of mouth and family ties. Three of these newcomers were men named Aha, Piko, and Agui, plus a spirit priest and shaman. And in January 1982, as the bombs were exploding in Khun Sa's compound at nearby Ban Hin Taek, a wealthier Akha named Aso fled the Doi Tung area, heading for Doi Chang with his family and relatives, including his two younger brothers and their families; his father, who was in his sixties; and his uncle, who brought along his two sons and their families. In Hue San, his previous village on Doi Tung, Aso had bought goods such as battery-operated transistor radios for resale and had accumulated one hundred cows. He sold them and bought land in Doi Chang, adding to the nucleus of the new Akha village, now home to some one hundred Loimi Akha, downhill from about 700 Lisu. The first Lisu had moved there in 1921, replacing Hmong villagers who had sought fresh land. The Lisu were the predominant tribe and generally looked down on the Akha as inferior, despite the two tribes having much in common.

The Lisu

LIKE THE AKHA, the Lisu had traditionally practiced rotational swidden agriculture, growing mountain rice as their primary food crop and opium poppies as an important supplemental cash crop. They, too, believed in ancestral and forest spirits. The sun, moon, trees, hills, guns, and crossbows all had their own Lisu spirits. A guardian spirit shrine was located above every Lisu village to ward off evil spirits and disease, serving a similar function to the Akha village gate, and the Lisu, too, kept ancestral altars in their homes. While the Akha had their werewolves, the Lisu believed in weretigers that could possess people.

Both tribes had village priests and shamans, though in his trance, the Lisu shaman was ridden by the spirits like a horse, whereas the Akha shaman rode atop a spirit horse. A Lisu shaman could make a spectacular show of chasing illness from a house by spraying hot lard from his mouth over a torch, producing fireballs worthy of the Wizard of Oz. Both tribes told stories of a great flood, and the Lisu, too, believed in one superior God they called Wu Sa. They also practiced various rituals and animal sacrifices to ensure good outcomes and harvests, reading the lines in a pig's liver to determine which spirit might have been wronged.

Although there were many similarities between the Akha and the Lisu, however, they were different in other crucial ways. Unlike the Akha, the Lisu were intensely individualistic and competitive. "A Lisu always wants to be first," wrote Paul and Elaine Lewis in their 1984 chapter on the tribe. A Lisu household appeared to be continually trying to "keep up with the Joneses," so to speak. While the Akha held fiercely to their traditions, the Lisu's cultural basket was quite loosely woven and easily modified to take advantage of new circumstances.

In 1982, the same year that many of the Akha arrived in Doi Chang, a Dutch anthropologist named Otome Klein Hutheesing moved to the Lisu village of Doi Lan, 4 miles down the mountain from Doi Chang, to conduct field work. She lived there for four years. A third of the Lisu wives she interviewed had grown up in Doi Chang.

At first, the Lisu completely baffled her. "For many, many months, their world of living appeared to me like a huge surrealistic painting," wrote Hutheesing in her book about her experience, bearing the rather arcane academic title of *Emerging Sexual Inequality Among the Lisu of Northern Thailand: The Waning of Dog and Elephant Repute.* "I groped for objects in their dimly-lit habitat, I stumbled across roughly-hewn doorsteps, fell through shakily-constructed platforms, bumped into unexpected protrusions of a never-finished wall." Eventually, however, she became a seemingly accepted member of the village. "I became one of them as I shared the meals, the quarrels, as I sowed rice and maize, scraped the poppypods, sang and danced with them."

The subtitle of her book refers to traditional Lisu expectations. Men were like dogs—brave, adventurous, and sometimes rather irresponsible. Women were supposed to be like elephants—not in terms of size, but shy, reserved, and well-behaved, as female elephants were perceived to be. While men and women had different roles, Hutheesing argued that they seemed to be equally valued. It was only as their traditional life unraveled that the relationship between the sexes became unbalanced.

Given what she observed, however, most readers would conclude that Lisu men always had the upper hand. While women could visit nearby villages, it was only men who ventured down the mountain into town to sell maize or opium and buy bullets. Men were stronger and had nine souls versus seven for women. Men hunted and cut down trees, while women cooked and pounded rice. During sexual intercourse, men made "hae-hae" sounds when they climaxed, but women were expected to remain quiet. Lisu men had formal given names but were often called by descriptive nicknames such as Bad Leg, Big Head, Wide Eyes, Big Shit Body, Ear Not Good, Kinky Hair, or Opium Smoker. Women, too, had nicknames, such as Little Bird or Big Mouth Lady.

The women complained to Hutheesing about the men's gambling, gallivanting, and opium smoking. "Her husband drinks every day, every day he is drunk," one Lisu woman told the anthropologist about a woman married to a man named Bad Leg. "He is not ashamed. Why is this? Because of what woman is... Woman is like elephant. Man is like dog. She has to be shy. A man does not. If he divorces, he can get another wife. A woman waits. A man is never shy when he makes a child in the forest (without marrying her). He is a dog."

Hutheesing summarized the limitations imposed on village females: "To have to adhere to the dictates of elephantlike timidity restricts the world of movement of a Lisu female and restrains the expressions of her psyche. She, for example, seldom trades or sells a pig in a nearby village. She is not supposed to laugh too loud, she should not be short-tempered, not drink tea nor alcohol. Her only pleasurable outlet is the chewing of betel [nuts]."

The concepts of "repute" and "shame" were deeply embedded in Lisu culture. The Lisu talked about feeling shame in many circumstances, such as providing inadequate food to guests or a woman waking up later than her husband. "Children are soon told that they ought to know about shame," Hutheesing observed. "If a father cannot pay money for the acquisition of a bride for his son, there is shame." This feeling of shame, so foreign to the Akha, could have mortal consequences for the Lisu. Hutheesing told the story of a Lisu wife who told her husband, "Give the rifle to the son. You are too old to go to the forest and shoot." When her husband accused her of wanting her son for a mate instead of him, the woman felt such deep shame that she swallowed poison and died. Unlike the traditional Akha, the Lisu sometimes resorted to suicide (or murder) when matters of honor were involved.

Looking Down on the Akha

IT MUST HAVE been difficult for the pioneering Akha who established themselves downhill from the Lisu in Doi Chang, since most Lisu held the Akha in low esteem. Akha girls were said to have fat legs because they ate dog meat. "In general being married to an Akha," Hutheesing observed, "is interpreted as a loss of repute." Nonetheless, she noted, "five Lisu boys of the village have recently married Akha girls, who are looked down upon, but for whom no bride-wealth needs to be paid." While Lisu women may have lamented their status, they told the anthropologist that Akha women had it even worse. As Leo Alting von Geusau wrote, "The Akha are much more frequently subject to adverse comments than other groups."

The Thai lowlanders spread rumors that the Akha washed only once a year. It was widely claimed that Akha girls practiced "free love" and that Akha men were all opium addicts. And as far back as 1929, a missionary in Burma wrote about the "low standard of morality" of the Akha, complaining of "licentious orgies among the unmarried." Another missionary wrote in 1962 that the Akha were a "malodorous and filthy people" and conveyed the misinformation that during annual rites, an Akha man was assigned to deflower village virgins. An anthropologist observed that "Akha women in particular are considered by Thai to be sexually uninhibited, wild like the forests they inhabit." In 1982, a Taiwanese journalist claimed that "the Akha can't even count up to ten, [so] they have been unable to undertake work of a higher cultural level." He described "a family squatting in a small circle and helping themselves with revoltingly filthy black hands to a pot of rice that was covered with flies."

It is little wonder, then, that Aje, the son of Aso, Doi Chang's unofficial Akha headman, should have felt inferior. "I didn't want to be an Akha," he recalled. "Akha were the lowest, the poorest, the outcast, with no citizenship." Because he was relatively well-off, Aje's father sent him to Chiang Rai to attend a private Christian missionary school in 1975, when Aje was nine years old. There he wore a school uniform—white shirt, blue shorts, black shoes—and learned to speak fluent Thai. "I had a pretty good Thai accent. I didn't wear Akha clothes. I could pass for non-Akha," he said.

Yet he was torn. "If I *had* to be an Akha, I wanted to be the *pima*, the spirit priest, the big man with power and privilege. I had concluded that Buddhism was for the Thai and that Jesus was the white man's God." Sure, he heard Christian stories in school, but they were similar to many Akha tales, and the Akha had more dramatic, interesting myths. But one night in 1981, when Aje was fifteen, he attended a movie about a missionary among New Guinea headhunters. During the intermission, a preacher asked a question that resonated deeply: "Do you want to have a friend who will be with you at all places and all times?" Aje accepted the altar call. Ironically, once he accepted Jesus as his personal lord and savior, he became proud to be an Akha, now that he had a special calling to proselytize. "I was not shy to be Akha or Christian."

The following year, when Aje returned home to the village of Hue San on Doi Tung for his school break, he found to his shock that his family was no longer there. "They were all gone. It was quite a traumatic experience." He learned that they had moved south to Doi Chang, a Lisu village. "It was unthinkable. You just didn't see Akha move to a non-Akha village." But that is where he found his family.

Changing Life in Doi Chang

IN JULY 1982, an American anthropologist named Deborah Tooker moved to Doi Chang, first staying with Aso's younger brother, Alae, and his family. They subsequently built her a nearby hut of her own, where she lived for three years, conducting field work that eventually resulted in a book, *Space and the Production of*

Cultural Difference Among the Akha Prior to Globalization: Channeling the Flow of Life. In the book, she named the village "Bear Mountain" rather than Doi Chang (Elephant Mountain). The villagers called her Michu, an Akha name, or Palama, which meant "foreign white woman."

Tooker documented the traditional way of life that the Akha reestablished in their new home. They built three village gates to define the upper, lower, and side boundaries. The gates separated the domestic life of the Akha village from the external world, which included antagonistic forest spirits, the Lisu, and lowland Thai. Outside each gate they placed a carving of a man and woman, with the male figure sporting an oversized, potent penis. Adopting powerful symbols of the modern warfare they had fled, they gave the man a carved rifle and placed a wooden airplane model atop the upper gate. Near that main gate, they built a swing for the annual harvest festival and a clearing for the courting yard where young people danced, sang, and flirted in the evenings. They built their homes from bamboo, wooden poles, and thatched grass and hung up the ancestor shrines they had brought with them.

With appropriate rituals and on auspicious days, they cleared fields and planted dry mountain rice and corn. In the fall, after the corn was harvested, they sowed poppy seeds to produce opium, their primary cash crop, to be harvested in January and February. There was not enough land to grow sufficient rice for each family, so the cash from the opium crop was used to purchase extra rice.

They also needed cash to pay Beno, the bald-headed Lisu headman. As a show of honor and respect, it was customary for Lisu villagers to pay a small amount during their ceremonies or to donate pigs or chickens for sacrifices. The Akha found that they, too, were expected to pay for the predominant Lisu rituals.

Only two Akha spoke Thai, so they generally relied on the more sophisticated Lisu to conduct business. Beno himself had realized at a young age that he had to learn from lowlanders. In 1959, when he was twenty, he volunteered to work for free for three years on a farm in Chiang Rai, so that he could learn to read and write in the Thai language. (He knew the family because they were opium dealers.) Back in Doi Chang, he worked with the Thai army's anti-Communist efforts. The military trained him to be a paramedic, so he became a kind of public health clinician until he was elected the village headman in 1970—an office he held for twenty-eight years. To make extra money, Beno grew opium poppies and boarded tourist trekkers in his home for 20 baht a night (30 baht = $1.00 approximately, a fair amount of money at that time).

Thus life in Doi Chang village was not an ideal situation for the Akha, but it was better than many others, and more Akha moved to Doi Chang during the 1980s.

Crop Substitution Programs

IN 1983 the Thai-German Highland Development Program arrived in Doi Chang to help the Akha and Lisu convert from illegal opium production to other sustainable cash crops. This was one of several such efforts in Thailand to entice hill tribes away from poppy cultivation.

The first crop substitution program grew out of the king's interest in the hill tribes. The widely revered Thai monarch King Bhumibol Adulyadej (Rama IX) was a polymath who played jazz and composed music, painted portraits, never went anywhere without his camera, built and raced sailboats, wrote books, and invented scientific instruments. He first began to visit Hmong villages in 1967.

Two years later, the king decided that the hill tribes should stop growing poppies for opium. Not only was it illegal, but it also left the tribal people in a state of perpetual debt bondage. Each year, they took out goods on credit from village shopkeepers, paying for them with opium, and at year's end, they were no richer. Hill tribes made little money from opium. Traders might buy raw opium for US$20 that would be sold for US$90 in Chiang Rai, $110 in Bangkok, and $2,000 in the USA. They were in no position to bargain because, without connections or influence, they would be arrested if they complained.

During the annual royal winter sojourn at the Bhubing Palace in Chiang Mai, the king and queen would travel to remote regions in helicopters or by jeep, then hike up mountains to visit various hill tribes, bringing gifts such as blankets, mosquito nets, clothing, medical supplies, rice, iodized salt, vegetable seeds, notebooks, pencils, and candy. In 1969, King Bhumibol established the Royal Project to test various crops for the hill tribes.

The king's first idea was to encourage fruit trees, after he found that peaches fetched higher prices than raw opium. The humanitarian king emphasized that opium poppies should not be destroyed until viable alternatives were in place. Unfortunately, the price of peaches plummeted when his program resulted in overproduction.

But the real push for crop replacement programs came in 1971, when one of US president Richard Nixon's top advisors, Egil "Bud" Krogh, Jr., flew to Thailand and let it be known that the United States would help pay for programs to find alternatives to opium poppies. Over the next two decades, a variety of initiatives came and went, including projects cosponsored by the United Nations, Germany, Norway, the Netherlands, Sweden, the United States, Japan, Australia, and New Zealand (with the member countries offering support independently of their UN membership). Most lasted only a few years and, while well intended, were ineffective top-down affairs.

The missionary anthropologist Paul Lewis wrote scathingly in 1985: "The tribal people themselves were not brought in at the planning stage. The program was brought to them, with the general attitude, 'Aren't you lucky! Look at the wonderful goodies we are bringing to you!' If they found that any villagers did not like what they proposed, they sometimes talked them into accepting it one way or another."

Administrators of such programs referred to the "hill tribe problem," implicitly blaming the mountain people. At best paternalistic, their attitude was sometimes overtly hostile. "They [hill tribes] only know how to hold out their hand to get what they want," wrote one public welfare administrator in 1982. "Their conscience (a sense of their full responsibility as Thai citizens) is still not developed to a satisfactory level." Another Thai development official summarized the prevalent attitude:

> They [the hill tribes] are thought to have a unique way of life, which poses a threat to the majority Thais. The problems perceived as generated by the tribal peoples are: their traditional practice of shifting cultivation, destruction of the forests and deterioration of soil and water resources, frequent migration, opium cultivation and addiction, and their propensity for illegal behavior or other misconduct.

Responsibility for the hill tribes was scattered across eleven Thai government ministries, under which were thirty different departments and 168 agencies. A former Thai administrator of the ironically named Center for the Coordination of Hill Tribe Affairs and Eradication of Narcotic Crops (COHAN) recalled his frustration. "Our attempts to solve the hill tribe problem received little interest... Whether it was government policy, plans or projects, each were scattered about the various agencies with no unity or purpose or action. There was no real coordination or close contact exercised... The whole business evolved into one of extended and complex conflict among the Thai government agencies." He concluded, "The hill tribe problem can be compared to a balloon. If you squeeze it here, it bulges elsewhere. If you squeeze it in too many places, it bursts with a bang."

Given this background, it is hardly surprising that the Thai-German Highland Development Program did not involve the Akha or Lisu of Doi Chang in planning sessions. Instead, the Thai-Germans concluded that tomatoes were the most appropriate crop for the mountain villagers, along with cabbages, kidney beans, and some experimental coffee, peach, and apricot trees.

The Akha were willing to give it a try. As anthropologist Leo Alting von Geusau wrote in 1983, "They [the Akha] are interested and willing to accept beneficial changes, but only if they believe that drudgery will be reduced, that some profit will accrue, that they will be treated like equals by those who advise a change, and that they can trust their benefactors not to exploit them." Though they were not treated as equals by the Thai-Germans, the villagers were eager to explore profitable alternatives, so both the Lisu and Akha farmers planted tomato seeds and accepted the chemical fertilizer and pesticide that came with them. "The good faith shown by highlanders is often amazing," wrote one observer later that decade. "They will go along with extension worker plans even though they are well aware that they face serious transport problems."

The Thai-Germans also paid for the construction of a new dirt road to the south, connecting Doi Chang with the main road between Chiang Rai and Chiang Mai, near the city of Mae Suai. Although the new road was almost impassable at the height of the rainy season, when it turned into a muddy quagmire, it allowed the farmers to get their tomatoes down the mountain. The Chinese Haw families in the village, who helped trade opium, owned pickup trucks and charged for transportation down the mountain. Still, the new crop yielded a profit during the 1983 and 1984 seasons, since tomatoes grew in the mountains when it was too hot for the plants in the lowlands. Encouraged by the success, the Thai-Germans stopped subsidizing the seeds, fertilizer, and pesticide, since the villagers could now pay for them.

The Opium Raids

THE VILLAGERS SOON had no alternative but to rely on tomatoes as their main cash crop. In December 1984, without notice, the local police searched village homes for guns and drugs. The next month, the dreaded Thahan Pran—many of them criminals recruited into the military in lieu of prison—rampaged through the village and decapitated field after field of poppies, lopping off the ripe seedpods with their machetes just before the harvest. They stayed in the village for several days, heavily armed and drunk from the homemade rice liquor they stole.

The raids ended poppy cultivation in Doi Chang, though a few Lisu continued to grow them in more distant, hidden locations for a few years. There was much discussion of where else the Akha might move, but there were few options. They had reached the end of their long migration.

In 1984 and the following year, attracted by the Thai-German project, three other governmental units moved to Doi Chang. The anchor program was the Wawi Highland Agricultural Research Station, which commandeered 3,000 rai (about 1,200 acres) of sloping land just up the mountain from the village. The villagers could do nothing about the confiscation of their fields, since they held no legal title to them. The Lisu, who had farmed it the longest, were particularly angry. "They wanted to slit my throat," recalled Bandid Jangnam, the agriculture station's founding director. So, like most other people in Doi Chang, he carried a gun. When one of the road construction crew was shot, rumors circulated that a Lisu had done it.

The only Lisu who welcomed the agricultural station, and who urged others to give up their land for it, was Beno, the village headman. He thought that the researchers would eventually help the villagers make a living. Soon after Bandid arrived at the agricultural research station, someone shot Beno in the leg, though it wasn't clear why.

A few Buddhist monks also moved up the mountain, living in a bamboo grove where statues of Buddha had been placed the century before. They walked down into the village every morning to beg, and despite the hill tribes' poverty, the villagers gave them food.

At the same time, a "mobile unit" of the Department of Public Welfare (DPW) moved from Doi Lan to Doi Chang, lodging with the new agricultural station, and more Thai teachers (who spoke neither Akha nor Lisu) arrived to teach at the primary school in the village. All of the Thai socialized primarily with one another (one referred to individual villagers as "it"), and the incompetent head of the DPW unit spent most of his time elsewhere. Administrators at the agricultural station told Deborah Tooker that the Akha, whom they hired for 35 baht per day (a bit over a dollar), were diligent workers, unlike the Lisu.

Impinging Modernity

ALSO AROUND THIS time, a lay "doctor" was hired to dispense medicine (if he was around), but for any serious medical problem, villagers had to travel down the mountain to hospitals in Mae Suai or Chiang Rai. This they did as often as they could, since they were losing their faith in traditional Akha healers.

There were plenty of health problems among the hill tribe population. According to one survey, infant mortality among hill tribe children under five years old was 21 percent, due to infectious diseases and malnutrition. Women and children were second-class citizens who ate after the men, even though the women did the bulk of the work. A 1986 nutritional survey of a different Akha village revealed that only nine of fifty-three children were of normal weight, with nineteen exhibiting severe malnutrition. Those who were breastfed were better off, but once they were weaned, they lost weight steadily. Two of the five-year-olds died a month after the study ended. A survey of ten Doi Chang households revealed that 90 percent of the families had inadequate rice supplies, and 19 percent of the children were chronically malnourished.

Yet the modern world was crashing into Doi Chang, even as the children went hungry. The Chinese Haw, some intermarried with Lisu, ran restaurants and shops selling lowland goods in the middle of the village and operated rice mills. They now opened two video theaters, powered by their pickup truck motors or generators. These theaters showed Chinese and Thai movies, bringing loud violence, sex, and consumer culture to the villagers who were willing to pay 5 baht apiece. On men-only nights, they sometimes showed pornography.

Doi Chang took on the character of a town in the Wild West. As tomato sales continued to bring a modicum of wealth to farmers, highway robberies became common on the mountain roads. When five Akha resisted, two were shot and seriously wounded. All gave up their money and wristwatches. A government official tried to extort money from a wealthy Lisu by falsely claiming to have found a bag of heroin in his house. When farmers carried guns for self-protection, they were stopped by soldiers and fined for the illegal possession of firearms. Nonetheless, Beno, the Lisu headman, openly carried a pistol on his hip. He also made money by turning his large home into a guesthouse for the occasional tourist.

Many of the Lisu and Haw spoke Thai, whereas few Akha knew the national language. Aso, the Akha headman, had to serve as their interpreter. When a Thai visitor offered an expensive course

(100 baht) to teach the Thai language, only Akha women signed up, donning their headdresses for class in a vain effort to master the language. Instead, they only learned the names of a few common objects. The illiterate Akha, who signed documents with their thumbprints, valued any papers they received, touching them reverentially as if they were sacred objects.

Among those papers were thirty-year leases for the use of 15 rai (6 acres), for which the Akha had to pay a tax. Akha who had no Thai ID or insufficient funds could not participate, and many Lisu refused to sign up, since they regarded it as their land already.

That land was becoming denuded of trees. Despite the popular perception that slash-and-burn agriculture was at fault, most of the trees were cut down by legal or illegal Thai loggers. In 1985, a logging company with a concession from the Royal Forestry Department cut down a large swatch of forest along the road between Doi Chang and Doi Lan. "There is an elongated 'graveyard' of logs (over 1500 of them) that stretches itself over more than seven kilometres on the path leading to [Doi Lan]," wrote Otome Hutheesing. "Who are the culprits? Certainly not the hill minorities like the Akha and Lisu who live nearby."

Long gone were the days that a missionary recalled in 1974, writing about the hill tribes:

> It is difficult now, back in civilization, to evoke the sense of freedom that comes upon a man when he stands on a mountaintop and looks out over tens of thousands of acres of fertile and unexplored land in the valleys below. It is only then that a man knows that, given the wit and will to survive, he need not bow his head to any government, any ideology.

Most of the remaining agricultural land in Doi Chang was stripped of trees and terraced to grow relentless rows of tomatoes, which often required irrigation. Profits remained high in 1986 and 1987, allowing farmers to buy increasing amounts of chemical fertilizers and pesticides, which they needed as the monoculture attracted more pests. As Duangta Sriwuthiwong, a keen-eyed, skeptical researcher in Doi Chang, observed sarcastically in 1988, the farmers' "favorite shop" in Chiang Rai sold fertilizer and pesticide, "many kinds of amazing products for saving their crops," manufactured in Germany, Sri Lanka, or Bangkok. "Where has all the money gone?" she asked rhetorically. After a heavy rain, farmers rushed into their fields to spray pesticides before it was too late. Few protected themselves from the noxious fumes, which made them ill.

Forced Relocation and the Miracle Crop

THE THAI GOVERNMENT viewed Doi Chang as a success story in the fight to replace opium with other crops. In March 1986, the head of the DPW unit oversaw a ritual public burning of 3,000 kilograms of poppy seeds and opium smoking pipes and tools, as headmen Beno and Aso looked on, along with many villagers in their traditional dress. In February 1987, there was a repeat performance for Thai prime minister Prem, who brought the Malaysian prime minister to Doi Chang by helicopter for more opium-burning in front of TV cameras.

A few months later, in September 1987, the Thai police and civilian "Village Defense Volunteers" carried out a series of dawn raids on thirteen hill tribe villages in Chiang Rai Province in order to "repatriate" supposedly illegal immigrants to Burma. American anthropologist Cornelia Kammerer, who had worked among the Akha, wrote in outrage: "Houses and granaries were torched; livestock were stolen or purchased at farm-sale prices; rice nearly ready for harvest was left in the fields; and villagers were forced, sometimes at knifepoint, to hand over their silver ornaments... They were herded onto trucks and dumped at the Burmese border."

Some villages were burned. The commander of the Third Army dismissed concerns about the torched homes, saying that they were "only huts." One devastated Akha man asked in bewilderment:

> Is it really true that we are no longer allowed to establish fields? We are so sad. Now we have been living for years in this country which we have come to love as our home. We have never before had quarrels with the Thai and now we have to leave our villages and emigrate in order not to starve.

Doi Chang was spared, but most villagers knew friends whose homes had been destroyed. Recalling the opium raid of 1985, they were terrified, posting lookouts on the road to give advanced warning.

But there was no advanced warning for the collapse of tomato prices in 1988. Other hill tribes, encouraged by the success in Doi Chang, had begun to grow the lucrative crop as well. "The cultivation of tomatoes," observed Otome Hutheesing in nearby Doi Lan, "had gripped populations from all corners of the area like a disease." As a result of oversupply, the price collapsed. John McKinnon, a rural development consultant hired to study Doi Chang, documented that in 1988 the "miracle crop" had failed. "Through to the beginning of the 1988 rainy season," he wrote, "farmers persisted, unaware of the fragility of the market and the fact that they were the captives of a few road-head traders." The price of tomatoes dropped to 1 baht per kilogram, half of which went to pay for transportation. "The 1988 season has been a disaster," McKinnon concluded.

The consultant submitted a scathing report that year. The crop substitute program had been a dismal failure. "Serious indebtedness, declining productivity of the land, and a profound erosion of community morale appear to be the results," he wrote. The few who continued to grow small fields of rice did so to "reassert their belief that they can grow food for themselves, that they know that rice is the food of their ancestors [and] for certain ritual offerings." McKinnon wrote that there were "few reasons for optimism. The [former] cropping assembly of opium/rice/maize allowed a more leisurely approach to farming activities, a wider range of domestic food plants were grown, [and] the impact on the environment was much less destructive."

The situation at the end of 1988 looked bleak, he concluded. "No farmers have legal rights to the land they work, yet they are caught up in a profound political, economic, and social process which threatens to completely change their way of life. This is no game. It is a fight for survival."

That same year, the Thai-German Highland Development Program, claiming victory, moved on to another province.

Even though the price for tomatoes had dropped precipitously during the 1988 season, the hill tribe farmers of Doi Chang hoped that the next year would be different. They had little choice, since growing opium poppies was no longer an option, and they needed a cash crop. So they grew tomatoes again, along with more cabbages than the previous year. By now, however, the soil was becoming badly depleted and plant pests such as nematodes (worms) were becoming more of a problem, so the farmers had to go further into debt to buy more chemical fertilizer and pesticide. John McKinnon wrote about the appalling outcome:

The 1989 season was particularly bad. When the crops were ready to harvest, the road became virtually impassable, the price of tomatoes dropped to next to nothing, and the cabbages were so heavily treated with lethal sprays and smelled so bad that truckers from Bangkok refused to load them. Tomatoes and cabbages rotted in the fields. By this time the Thai-German Project had moved on to other activities and new areas, so it did not have to face up to the price the community was paying for going along with adopting the introduced crops. In that season three men died of respiratory arrest, most probably caused by spraying insecticides.

Two young Lisu women committed suicide because the men they planned to marry could not come up with sufficient bride wealth.

Coffee: A Better Option?

AS THE VILLAGERS of Doi Chang faced the last decade of the twentieth century, they were desperate for a way to make a living. Many of the Lisu opted to move. Over the course of the 1990s, they sold out to their Akha neighbors and tried to integrate into Thai society in Chiang Rai, Chiang Mai, or even Bangkok. Doi Chang gradually became a predominantly Akha village. The farmers who remained, whether Lisu or Akha, hoped that coffee might be the crop that would at least prevent starvation.

Lisu headman Beno, noted for his shiny bald pate, was one of those who chose to remain in Doi Chang. Out of curiosity, he had brought the first coffee plants—about a thousand seedlings from the Lahu village of Hue Mat San—to Doi Chang back in 1977, but after the initial encouraging harvest a few years later, they had not done well. The price declined and many trees succumbed to disease. In 1984, the Thai-German project gave 7,000 coffee seedlings to sixteen Doi Chang farmers—eight Akha and eight Lisu—who planted them on a total of seven experimental acres. They were of the arabica species, superior to the robusta that grew at lower elevations, but the Caturra and Catuai seedlings they planted were subject to coffee leaf rust, a fungus with the fierce Latin name, Hemileia vastatrix, and only 4,958 of the trees survived.

In 1986, the Thai-Germans gave nineteen farmers another 7,400 seedlings, still arabica, but this time they were of the Catimor variety, which was more resistant to coffee leaf rust. Most of these trees survived (6,530 of them), offering more hope for coffee's success in the village, so in 1987 another thirty farmers were given seedlings. The farmers weren't particularly interested in coffee, but they received an ID card identifying them as a member of the coffee growers' group, and for those who had no Thai citizenship cards or rights, the symbolic weight of any kind of official identification was great.

It takes three or four years for seedlings to grow into mature, bearing coffee trees. The first small harvest, then, would have arrived in 1987. Two years later, in July 1989, the International Coffee Agreement (ICA) expired, due to discord between Brazil and the United States and widespread discontent with the global quota system. Despite an avowed belief in free trade, the Americans had supported price-support quotas because of Cold War fears that poverty-stricken coffee farmers would turn Communist. With the collapse of the Berlin Wall in 1989, the United States no longer cared. When the ICA fell apart, coffee-growing countries dumped their stockpiled beans onto the world market, driving prices on the C-market down from $1.15 to 65 cents a pound or lower.

The Akha and Lisu of Doi Chang had no idea why coffee prices suddenly bottomed out, but they knew they could only sell their beans in Chiang Mai for 40 or 50 baht for years to come.

Nonetheless, by the time their Catimor trees were producing ripe red coffee cherries in 1990, coffee had become the last best hope for some kind of reliable, semi-profitable crop.

Unfortunately, bringing coffee to market wasn't as simple as it was for tomatoes or cabbages. You couldn't just pick it, wash it, bag it, and throw it on a truck. Coffee is ripe when the green berry turns a rich wine red (or in some varieties, yellow). It looks a bit like a cranberry or cherry, though it is more oval-shaped. Growers can test a coffee cherry by squeezing it between thumb and forefinger. If the seed squirts out easily, it is ripe. What is left in the hand—the red skin, along with a bit of flesh—is called the pulp. What squishes out is a gummy mucilage sticking to the parchment, a thick protective layer somewhat similar to the skin on peanuts. And like peanuts, coffee seeds usually grow in facing pairs. Inside the parchment are the seeds (somewhat inaccurately called coffee beans), which are covered by a diaphanous silver skin.

One problem with coffee is that the cherries do not ripen all at once. If you strip them all off simultaneously, as many Doi Chang farmers did in the 1990s, you get a combination of ripe and green beans, which is just one of many ways to ruin the eventual taste in the cup.

As agronomist Jacques Op de Laak, who worked at a coffee research station in Chiang Mai, observed in 1992: "Being a complicated crop in terms of technology, management, investment and delayed returns, coffee put farmers' interest, patience, reliance, and adaptability to the test." He added, "Adequate knowledge and experience must be built up at all stages of the production cycle, i.e., planting, fertilization, field management, disease and pest control, weeding, harvesting, and processing."

Years later, Op de Laak wrote more candidly:

I was not really optimistic about highland coffee cultivation in the northern Thai hills when I finished my assignment at the

Highland Coffee Research and Development Centre at Chiang Mai University in 1992. Arabica coffee after all was virtually exclusively grown by hill tribe farmers who were at that time sort of spoon-fed (with seed, loans and training and extension services) by numerous Highland Development Programmes financed by various overseas donors. At that time these HDP's were gradually winding up their involvement and left the farmers at the mercy of often unscrupulous traders and buyers from the lowlands.

The Thai-German managers probably gave the farmers some instructions about how to harvest and process the coffee, but by the time of the first serious harvests, the project advisors had departed. The Wawi Highland Agricultural Station was still there, but it was further up the mountain, and though the Thai agronomists experimented with coffee, little of what they discovered or advised filtered down to the growers below.

Farmers consequently did what made the most sense to them, which was to use the oldest traditional method of removing the bean, known as the dry or natural method. Both the ripe and unripe cherries, along with buds, twigs, and leaves, were stripped from the branches, then spread to dry, either on a dirt patio or up on the thatched or corrugated metal roof of a house. Unless they were turned several times a day, the beans were likely to ferment, and if it rained and they were not covered, that likelihood became a certainty. Fermentation resulted in unpleasant or "off" tastes. The beans might also lie on the ground for so long that they would develop mold or absorb other unpleasant earthy tastes—iodine-like and malodorous.

When the skins were shriveled, hard, and nearly black, the Akha farmers' wives threw them in their rice-pounders, which could be heard every morning thudding throughout the village to remove husk from stored rice. These pounders were made from long levered poles that could be lifted by a foot treadle and then let fall so that a wooden mortar slammed heavily into a hollow log. The process removed the dried skin and mucilage from the coffee beans, which, bruised, fermented, and still covered in parchment, were ready to sell to a trader down in the lowlands. It never occurred to the Akha to roast and brew their coffee—they drank tea.

The truck ride down the rutted dirt road to get to Chiang Rai took four hours during the dry season, and more when it rained, and then it was at least another three hours to drive south to Chiang Mai, where the coffee traders were preparing to go home in the late afternoon. They took one look at the dusty, bedraggled Akha farmers and knew that these hill tribe rubes were riper for the picking than their coffee. They offered miserable prices, hardly paying the cost of the gas to get there and back.

But what choice did the farmers have? They weren't going to drive back up the mountain with their load. So they sold for whatever they could get and went home, arriving exhausted and hungry long after dark. It is little wonder that most coffee farmers eventually cut their coffee trees down in frustrated rage.

End of an Era

BY THE LATE 1990s, the traditional life of the Akha was noticeably eroding, as Deborah Tooker noted when she made a return visit to Doi Chang in December 1997. Although there was still no electricity (that would arrive soon afterwards), VCRs (run by batteries or generators) had introduced the villagers to Thai culture and modern mass-produced goods. The village, including the agriculture station up the hill, had grown to hold about 135 households, with well over a thousand people. "More and more land was purchased for a cash price or even rented for cash on a monthly basis," Tooker observed, "creating a division between the 'haves' and 'have-nots'.... A new wealth-based ranking system, part of a more global capitalist system, was developing."

Many Akha now worked as wage laborers for the agricultural station, punching a time clock and maintaining a seven-day week rather than the traditional twelve-day cycle and more natural flow of activity. Mass-produced goods, including surplus Western-style clothing, were replacing homespun cotton and elegant appliqué and embroidery. Many homes were built with lumber, cement block, and tin roofs rather than bamboo and thatch. Women now donned their silver-laden headdresses only for special occasions. People maintained a small token rice field only so that they could perform old rituals, and some homes were built with separate kitchens, keeping a symbolic cooking area near the sleeping mats, although no meals were prepared there anymore.

Tooker also found evidence of more addiction, crime, and violence. She met an Akha heroin addict, the younger brother of the *pima*, who looked terrible, emaciated, and desperate. Two days later, he was dead, shot by Lisu from whom he had stolen in order to pay for his drugs. She heard about Akha suicides, inconceivable in the traditional past. Both men and women had intentionally consumed insecticide to end their lives. The one positive change of this modernity movement was the 1998 Akha decision to stop killing twins and children with missing or extra fingers or toes at birth.

Increasingly, tourists found their way up the mountain to visit Doi Chang, and to appeal to them, some Akha traditions were modified to be performed outside their usual time. The Swing Ceremony and children's top-spinning games, for instance, were put on display for paying tourists. "A stage was constructed for the performance of Akha dances and songs and an Akha rock band," Tooker noted.

Yet the traditional lifestyle was becoming less appealing in general. "As Akha are increasingly incorporated into the Thai nation-state," wrote anthropologist Cornelia Kammerer, "Akha men who in bygone days would have jovially competed with one another to gain knowledge of their *zah* instead eagerly attempt to attain as much education in the Thai school system as possible." More children were receiving a formal education, which meant learning to be literate in Thai, not Akha, and many of those children were educated in lowland schools, often run by Christian missionaries.

Missionaries were also having an impact up in Doi Chang. In 1992, Akha headman Aso's younger brother Alae had converted to Catholicism. Aso consequently forced his own brother to move outside the village gates. Yet in 1995, Aje, who had graduated from Mahidol University in Bangkok with a degree in public health and had become a missionary, convinced his father, Aso, to become a Baptist and burn his ancestor shrine. Aso refused to move, creating resentment and friction. Three years later, when he fell to his death from his balcony, the villagers concluded that the angry ancestors had toppled him.

Tooker discovered that there were now five distinct Akha factions in Doi Chang, in addition to the remaining Lisu, Chinese Haw, and Thai government employees.

One traditionalist group, including Piko's family, would no longer permit addiction or drug dealing. One of the paradoxical results of the end of poppy cultivation was an increase in heroin addiction, since homegrown opium was no longer available. Smuggled from Burma, heroin was relatively cheap, convenient, and highly addictive. Methamphetamines were also being made in Burmese labs and were becoming popular, called *Ya Ba*, or "crazy medicine."

A collection of essays critical of the impact of development projects on the hill tribes—*Development or Domestication?*—was published in 1997 and included a chapter on drug abuse. "The age group of highland drug addicts is shifting to younger people," the authors wrote, "especially among the heroin users."

Young people were more likely to sniff glue or solvents and to use amphetamines. More women were also becoming addicts. Why? "People's difficulties in coping with the extremely rapid changes in their socio-economic environment, including pressures on them [to] alter their lifestyles, have led to psychological and spiritual stresses, which in turn are a major cause for addiction."

Missionary Positions

INDEED, ACCORDING TO anthropologist Cornelia Kammerer, the economic hardship of those animal sacrifices was one motivation for Akha conversion to Christianity. In 1968, a frustrated missionary had described the Akha as "deeply steeped in their own animistic religion and apparently well satisfied with their own complicated culture, language, and society." But by the 1990s, Kammerer estimated that "roughly one-fifth to one-third of the approximately 200 Akha villages are fully or partially Christian." The main reason, she concluded, was poverty. "I had no chickens, I had no pigs [for sacrifices]," an elderly Akha woman explained as her motivation for conversion.

Christianity offered an alternative that the canny missionaries called the Jesus Zah. A typical Protestant missionary skit showed an Akha throwing down the heavy burden of the Akha Zah in order to accept Jesus. "Most Akha converts to Christianity are simply seeking a replacement zah that is cheaper and easier than their own," Kammerer concluded. Yet many converts in Doi Chang denied that economics had anything to do with it. Their children who attended mission schools influenced them. Kammerer also noted that Catholics allowed the continuation of many Akha rituals, whereas most Protestants spurned them and banned rice liquor.

Still, the transition to either form of Christianity could be relatively painless. Like the traditional Akha, Christians buried their dead in coffins, while Buddhists practiced cremation, and new Christian converts could continue to wear their Akha clothing, speak the Akha language, and maintain their patrilineal affiliation.

While the missionaries meant well and did help in many ways—encouraging education, bringing medicines and vaccines, discouraging drug addiction, helping to sell tribal handicrafts, providing help in acquiring Thai ID cards—they also clearly disrupted traditional beliefs and lifestyles, especially by encouraging parents to send their children to Christian boarding schools. In her memoir, Without a Gate, published in 1990, Overseas Missionary Fellowship (OMF) missionary Jean Nightingale wrote that she and her husband, Peter, "both loved the Akha," but they thought that the Akha belief in spirits meant that they practiced "demon worship." They demanded that converts burn their ancestor shrines, which they called "demon shelves."

This attitude appalled Matthew McDaniel, an American who in 1991 had moved to the remote northern Thai town of Mae Sai, just across the border from Burma. He bought glass trade beads to sell back in the States. In his first week there, McDaniel heard two old women speaking in a strange, poetic-sounding tongue. He asked a young woman what it was. "Akha," she said. "We are Akha." He learned that their villages were up in the mountains. Another day he noticed a little malnourished Akha boy with an ugly open sore on his shin, so McDaniel bought some antibiotic powder, gauze, and tape.

With no medical training, he found himself regularly tending to such minor wounds. "When I had the money," he later wrote, "I bought vitamins, lots of Band-Aids, salve ointment for scabies, and anti-fungal cream for cradle cap." He would also escort women and children to the hospital on the south end of town. If he hadn't gone with them, "the police would shake them down."

Disturbed and intrigued, the American began to seek out the Akha. "I made my way into every Akha village I could find, high in the mountains," visiting over 200 of them. He brought food and medicine and sometimes paid for a well or pipe from a spring to the village. In the hills, he found that Thai soldiers or Royal Forestry Department officials were forcing some villages to relocate. Border Patrol Police and "Black Shirts" (criminals conscripted into military service) could do anything they wanted. "As a common practice the police arrested Akhas on trivial charges," McDaniel recalled. "Some Black Shirt commandos raped Akha women in remote regions." Sometimes when McDaniel took the bus from Mae Sai to Chiang Rai, the police would stop the bus at checkpoints and make Akha without ID papers get off.

"I then discovered there were missionaries working with the Akha. At first this came to me as quite normal, a good thing," McDaniel wrote. "But as time went by, I found that not all was well. The missionaries were clearly critical of Akha culture and were removing the children from their families." The missionaries claimed that they were helping orphans, but often parents had given their children to the missionaries, hoping to give them a better life.

McDaniel, who later married an Akha woman and founded the Akha Heritage Foundation, became a fierce critic of all missionaries, somewhat unfairly lumping them all together. For instance, he claimed that Paul Lewis, the Baptist missionary and anthropologist, was committing "genocide" against the Akha by offering birth control services, including tubal ligation, which McDaniel called forced sterilization. Yet Lewis helped only women who already had four or five children and were eager for the operation.

Among other places, McDaniel visited Doi Chang, where he put up some of his "Missionaries Suck" posters. He was particularly harsh on Aje and his Akha Outreach ministry, claiming that Aje required new converts "to dramatically turn their backs on anything Akha ... Aje wanted anything that endeared him to Western missions." On the contrary, Aje insisted that he valued and sought to save Akha culture, which is featured on the Akha Outreach Foundation website.

In 2004, Matthew McDaniel was expelled from Thailand after numerous run-ins with authorities, including a class action suit against a project initiated by the Thai royal family. In Thailand, it is strictly forbidden to criticize the royal family, although it is acceptable to protest against the government. After a sojourn in Laos, he moved with his family to the United States, where he continued to highlight the plight of the Akha.

Prostitution and AIDS

ONE UNEQUIVOCALLY GOOD THING that a missionary accomplished was the establishment of the New Life Center in Chiang Mai in 1987. Paul and Elaine Lewis were increasingly concerned about hill tribe women who had come to the lowlands, desperate for work, and who had become prostitutes, euphemistically called "service women." Two years before the Lewises retired and returned to the United States, Elaine founded the New Life Center to provide an alternative lifestyle, including education, vocational training (mostly making tribal handicrafts for sale), health care, and "a wholesome Christian atmosphere with emphasis on worth and dignity" for young women who had either been prostitutes or were at risk.

A 1993 survey of 225 hill tribe villages in northern Thailand showed that of 1,683 women employed outside the village, 610 of them—well over a third—were prostitutes. "Tribal girls and young women, with little education and a near total lack of knowledge of the world outside, became prime targets in the sex industry," wrote two Lahu women who worked with the New Life Center in 1997. "Some of the girls are knowingly sold into prostitution by their families, which are extremely poor, often addicted to opium or heroin, and feel they have no other alternatives for survival." But those were a minority. "Most are either lured into prostitution with the promise of paid employment in urban areas, or seek out such employment on their own... All too often they are tricked into what appear to be good-paying jobs in restaurants, private homes, or businesses. Knowing little Thai language and having little education, villagers are relatively easily fooled in this way."

In one case, a man posing as a teacher visited a tribal village, offering urban educational opportunities for girls. Some families jumped at the chance, paying 700 baht apiece for seventeen girls to go with him. All were then sold into sexual slavery. Once in a brothel, it was difficult to escape, since the local police, subject to bribes, would frequently track them down and return them. "Some Akha and other prostitutes, better labeled sex slaves than sex workers, are shackled and imprisoned," observed one anthropologist in 1993. As the Lahu New Life employees wrote:

> The prostitutes themselves face considerable danger if they fail to service enough customers or try to run away. Physical beatings, including on the head, are standard. Another method is to dunk the girl's head under water until she complies. We have met girls who have been beaten on the legs with rods, beaten on the face with high heel shoes, who have lost all of their teeth from beatings, and some who have gone deaf as a result.

By this time, many "service girls" were contracting AIDS, which reached epidemic proportions among prostitutes in Thailand during the 1990s. The HIV infection rate in brothels in northern Thailand ranged from 30 percent to 90 percent. Until they began to show clear signs of AIDS the girls were forced to continue to service customers (and transmit the disease), but then they were thrown out to die alone. Some returned to their home villages, pretending to suffer from another disease, since they were ostracized if their AIDS infection was discovered.

Doi Chang Approaches the Millennium

BY THE END of the 1990s, the village of Doi Chang was in the midst of a chaotic, troubled transition. While Thailand had been experiencing robust economic growth during most of the 1980s and 1990s—part of the so-called "Asian Miracle"—the boom had only marginally impacted remote hill tribes, and even then it often had a negative impact. Because of the expanding economy, the government was able to pay for agricultural extension efforts and eventually brought electricity to the village, but it also contributed to lowland Thai expansion up the mountainsides and higher prices for the consumer goods that more and more Akha were forced to buy as part of their new lifestyles. Then in 1997, the Thai economy collapsed after the baht was cut loose from its fixed exchange rate with the US dollar, which rippled outward to cause a global recession.

No one in Doi Chang followed or understood any of these developments, although villagers were impacted when various services were curtailed and employment opportunities in lowland towns dwindled. What the Akha did understand was that their lives were changing. The traditional Akha way of life, with rotational farming based on rice cultivation, was gone. The rituals that they still clung to seemed more and more anachronistic. Most villagers were poor in the midst of a land of plenty and could not figure out how to do any better. Extended families were fragmenting as young people sought jobs in Chiang Rai and elsewhere. Village elders no longer commanded as much respect and power. The future held little hope.

Yet despite all of this, the Akha remained philosophical and essentially upbeat. They had survived worse. They would find a way to survive this. In December 1997, near the end of a visit to Doi Chang, Deborah Tooker had a three-hour conversation one night with a few Akha. She asked them to reflect on their past and present situation:

> With the backdrop of beatings, torture and misery in Burma, the Akha were willing to accept that changes, even the loss of Akha identity, were inevitable and even positive. After dwelling long on the sad past of the Akha in Burma, one man turned the conversation by saying, "*Ma mui-eu je neh jaw mui je do la-eu*" ("Good has come out of all our hardships"). After this he elaborated by saying that despite the mixed turn of events in the last 30 years, he appreciated the region and land of [Doi Chang], and he was happy in his present circumstances... Despite the dramatic social changes the Akha had gone through, we (this small group of 7-8 people, including Akha, westerners and Thais) would not [otherwise] be sitting here, enjoying each other's company.

But leaders of the younger Akha generation were not so willing to accept their poverty and powerlessness. Surely, there must be a way to maintain their autonomy even if they had to find a way to make money and fit into the Thai economy. Adel, the young Akha who had replaced Beno as the headman in Doi Chang in 1998, when he was only twenty-eight years old, pondered what could be done.

CHAPTER 3

Wicha Finds the Way

ADEL WAS THE son of Piko, an Akha village leader and one of the few Doi Chang farmers who kept trying to grow and sell coffee. Piko had noticed that coffee trees are hard to kill. New growth sprouted from the stumps of the trees that had been cut down, and in a few years, they began to bear fruit. Though untended and unpruned, they produced enough for Piko and a few others to sell, albeit for a pittance. Those frustrating coffee trips to Chiang Mai made a lasting impression on young Adel.

Like all Akha, Adel has a confusion of names. His real Akha name was Kopeo Saedoo. The first syllable of an Akha person's name is taken from the last syllable of the father's name. Thus Adel's real name, Kopeo, derived from his father Piko's name. His first nickname as a baby was Modeh, because he was born without hair, like a bald neighbor named Modeh. But as a child he couldn't pronounce that, and it came out as Adel, which stuck. Since Akha names are either too unfamiliar or otherwise foreign-sounding for Thai officialdom, Akha tribal members also adopted Thai names. Adel's was Panachai Pisailert. He wasn't sure of his real birthdate.

On his Thai ID, his date of birth was given as January 1, 1972—but all Akha birthdates were listed as January 1. Adel thought he was in fact born some time in 1970, the seventh of nine children of father Piko and mother Bu Chu.

As a child, Adel recalled picking the beautiful poppy flowers and making garlands of them in December and January, then helping to score the seedpods and collect the opium sap during the harvest in February and March. He watched his father and other men roll the rubbery raw opium into big balls and wrap them in banana leaves, to be sold to Chinese Haw traders. Adel's family ate the empty poppy pods and used the seeds as seasoning.

When he was around nineteen years old, in 1989, Adel, who had quit Doi Chang's inadequate school after the second grade and could speak only a few words of Thai, first accompanied his father to the lowlands to sell coffee. The road was nearly impassable on that first trip. They took the beans down with a horse and cart, then rented a pickup truck to go to Chiang Mai. It took more than eight hours to get there. "Up in the village, a messenger from a trader had promised us 22 baht per kilo," Adel remembered, "but when we got to the city, they only paid us 12 baht."

They returned to Doi Chang that same day, arriving late at night. It never occurred to them to overnight in the lowlands. "We had no idea where to stay. We had no identification. Sometimes we were stopped by the police. We just wanted to get back home."

Like the other villagers, Piko eventually cut down his coffee trees, but he was one of the few who resumed harvesting and processing them when the trees grew back. By that time, the price for green coffee beans had gone up somewhat, though Adel had no idea why. In the late 1990s, major cities on the Pacific Rim were beginning to imitate the Western world, discovering the joys of high-grown arabica coffee through coffeehouses that at first catered primarily to foreign tourists.

By 1998, Adel had left Doi Chang and was living in Chiang Mai, where he had opened a shop selling Akha handicrafts and "antiques," old tribal items that now fetched cash from tourists. Like many other Akha, he had been forced to the lowlands to make a living. Adel may have been illiterate and missed out on a formal education, but he was shrewd and enterprising, and his Thai speaking skills had improved dramatically.

He was also recognized by his fellow villagers. In 1998, they elected him the first Akha headman of Doi Chang, to replace Beno, who was retiring. The villagers (the majority of whom were now Akha) chose Adel in hopes that he might be able to bring some of his business acumen and lowland connections back to the mountains. His father, Piko, was well respected, and Adel's youthful energy could help.

Adel closed his shop and moved back to Doi Chang, where, as he knew, people were barely eking out a living, in part because most of them had no Thai identification papers. Over the next year and a half, he was able to secure the all-important Thai ID for many of the villagers. Proving to the district officers in Mae Suai, the small city at the base of the mountain, that an Akha had been born in Thailand was challenging, especially when the written records said they had been born in Burma, which was often the case. "I couldn't read or write," Adel recalled, "so I could only talk on their behalf."

His other major focus was on calling for a ceasefire in the Lisu-Akha conflict in Doi Chang. "I tried to be a mediator, asking people to come and talk reasonably together," Adel said. His efforts to promote reconciliation were only partially successful, since the tension had been simmering for two decades. It was hard to build trust, but he had made a start.

One challenge proved to be too much, though. Adel could not see a way to raise the standard of living for the Akha or Lisu, and he disliked feeling that he was expected to achieve the impossible. He resigned in 1999, after seventeen months as headman. A moderate, conciliatory Lisu named Suchat replaced him for three years, but all the subsequent headmen in Doi Chang were Akha.

The situation in Doi Chang remained dire. The mountainside around the village was nearly barren of trees, with the exception of some 200 acres of coffee shrubs, most of which had regrown after being cut down and abandoned. Otherwise, only scraggly patches of second-growth trees, along with a few peach, apricot, and macadamia nut trees, grew here and there between the tomato and cabbage fields. Village farmers continued to spend money on chemical fertilizers and pesticides that sickened them when they inhaled the fumes. And prices continued to fluctuate unpredictably. Many Akha worked for just over a dollar a day at the agricultural research station up the mountain, but they brought back little useful information to the farmers in the village.

Most of the Lisu families had fled down the mountain, looking for better-paying jobs and trying to assimilate with the lowland Thai. Beno, now retired, remained in Doi Chang, but his daughter, Chome, worked for IMPECT, a hill tribe development agency in Chiang Rai. Beno commented with apparent pragmatism that in thirty years, the Lisu would all be Thai.

As anthropologist Deborah Tooker concluded, "A hill swidden subsistence rice economy and a semi-autonomous local political system, on which a comprehensive form of Akha identity is based, … is no longer viable … Incorporation into the larger national and global scene brings with it both losses, reflected in Akha nostalgia for older forms of collective identity … and gains, reflected in Akha acceptance of, and even strategizing within, the new regime." Adel was more than interested in strategizing within the new parameters, but he could not figure out how to carve out a better life for his people.

With help from Akha relatives in the Yunnan Province of China, Adel began an import-export business, selling hill tribe chicken parts (livers, lungs, and guts) and eels to the Chinese and bringing back potatoes to sell in Thailand. While engaged in this enterprise, he discovered that Chinese coffee beans were being imported into Thailand. *That's strange*, he thought. *We grow coffee in Doi Chang. Why can't we sell our own coffee?*

Around that time, in the fall of 2001, Adel's fifteen-year-old niece Apa asked her father, Leehu, for advice on a school project. She was attending a Christian high school in Chiang Rai, and her assignment was to bring something from her hometown to sell at a school event. Leehu, who was helping his father, Piko, with his frustrating coffee sales, said that he could have some of their coffee roasted in Chiang Mai and Apa could take that. Apa bought an automatic brewer from the Big C store in Chiang Rai and brewed coffee at the school fair, selling it for 20 baht (about 65 cents) per cup. The coffee was a hit. She sold 45 cups and gave the 900 baht (about $30) to her father.

Leehu was astonished. His teenage daughter had made more profit from the roasted, brewed coffee than he made selling 20 kilos of green beans in Chiang Mai, and she still had a few bags left over. When he told his younger brother Adel about it, Adel decided that coffee might be the solution to the chronic village poverty after all. If city people were crazy enough to pay that much money for a cup of coffee, why not take advantage of it? But he didn't know how to go about it.

Enter Wicha

ADEL THOUGHT OF Uncle Wicha. *If anyone would know what to do, it would be Wicha.* Wicha Promyong was not really Adel's uncle, but the peripatetic Thai man had roamed throughout the mountains for decades, since Adel was a little boy. Wicha had slept in Piko's house sometimes, sharing meals, laughing, singing, and telling stories of other villages he had visited. Wicha had traveled widely, even to Europe. He spoke Akha, Lisu, and Thai, as well as English and a smattering of French, German, and Mandarin. Such a man of the world might be able to give good advice, might be able to find a way for the Akha of Doi Chang to break out of their poverty with coffee. So late in 2001, Adel ventured down the mountain to see Wicha. His timing was fortuitous. Wicha, then around fifty, was pondering his next big project. He was doing well enough with what he called his antiques store, selling traditional hill tribe goods, secondhand clothing, and army surplus uniforms from both the US Army and the Viet Cong. But he was growing bored.

Through his wanderings, Wicha had come to love the hill tribes and their way of life. He was particularly fond of the Akha, with their deep sense of their culture and place in the cosmos. He knew that unwanted change had been thrust on them. He had seen it for himself, had despaired over the forced relocations, the violence, the drug addiction and prostitution. He listened with sympathy and attention as Adel described his quandary and asked for advice.

"Tomorrow I will come up the mountain," Wicha told Adel. "I will visit with your father, my old friend Piko, and I'll have a look around. Maybe we can figure something out. I can't be sure of anything, but I will try." Adel rose to leave, expressing his gratitude even as he towered over the smaller man. Wicha stood barely over 5 feet and looked so skinny that the wind might blow him away. His hair was close-shaven, but he sported a scraggly beard and mustache and wore long braids down his back and an earring in one ear. Yet he walked and talked with the self-assurance of a much larger man.

The next day Wicha, true to his word, drove for several hours up the rutted dirt road to the village, with its scruffy children, chickens, and pigs dodging out of the way. He took tea at Piko's home, greeting his old friend and his wife, Bu Chu, and Piko's mother. Then, accompanied by Adel, Wicha walked around the village. It was essentially as he remembered it—small family compounds with vegetable gardens between them—but there were fewer pole, bamboo, and thatch-covered huts and more structures that looked like the poorest homes down in the city. Here, however, the corrugated metal roofs atop ramshackle boards were signs of relative wealth.

They got in Wicha's truck and drove up toward the ridge to the northeast along the rutted dirt road, passing fields of tomatoes and cabbage. Wicha shook his head as he saw a farmer spraying. "I hate this kind of crop," he said, gesturing at the man in the field as they bounced and swayed past. "They cut down all the trees, and they use all those chemicals." They crested the hill, coming down into a higher valley, going toward the satellite village of Ban Mai (which means "new village"), where many of the Chinese Haw and Akha had settled. Here in the high valley Wicha saw spindly coffee trees, with their glossy green leaves and berries.

"This is where my father still tends his coffee trees," Adel said. "But I don't know why he bothers. There isn't much money in it. Still, as I told you, Apa sold her brewed coffee for a lot of money. Maybe we can figure out how to do that." Wicha stopped the truck. He loved all kinds of shrubs and trees, and he wasn't familiar with coffee. As Adel explained how the Thai-German project had given them the trees and how they had been frustrated by the subsequent low coffee prices, they walked through the fields. Wicha touched the leaves, picked a few of the ripe red berries, and kicked at the earth with his shoe.

"You know," he said, "coffee has become very popular in Bangkok. They have coffeehouses where people pay a lot for just one cup, and they sit and talk over it, as we do with tea. Even in Chiang Rai some tourists ask where they can find good coffee. Maybe Apa's experience at the school fair wasn't so unusual. Perhaps there is something we could do to get a better price. Let me look into it."

Leehu gave Wicha the rest of the roasted coffee that Apa had not brewed. Wicha didn't like coffee—he preferred tea—but the next day, back in the lowlands, he took the coffee to a dealer in Chiang Mai, who brewed it and declared that it was quite good, despite containing some over-fermented, bug-eaten, and broken beans. Wicha had his new project. He set out to find out how to grow, process, and brew the best coffee.

He went to Chiang Mai University, which was noted for its strong agricultural program. When he walked into offices unannounced and explained that he wanted to talk to a coffee expert about how to help the Akha, the secretaries politely told him to take a seat. Then they disappeared and came back, shaking their heads. *Sorry, the professor is too busy. Sorry, the professor is in class. Sorry, you have to make an appointment.*

"Excuse me," Wicha said, when a distinguished-looking man in a tweed jacket and wearing a tie strode by in yet another office. "Excuse me, sir, but I am trying to help the Akha..." The man recoiled from Wicha, who was dressed in his customary informal clothing—baggy pants, an unbuttoned shirt over a black t-shirt, a gold chain around his neck—and backed quickly out of the room. "I'm sorry. You will have to make an appointment. I have no time to talk to any Akha today."

So that's it, Wicha thought. *They think I am Akha. No one wants to waste time on the Akha.* He turned to go, when a woman who had just walked into the office and overheard the conversation asked, "Can I help you? I have to go soon, but I could spare a few minutes."

The woman was Patchanee Suwanwisolkit, an agronomist who would go on to write two books about coffee cultivation. She invited Wicha into her office and listened patiently as he explained the situation. "Yes," the agronomist said, "I've actually been up to Doi Chang before, years ago, when I was a graduate student. I remember how muddy the road was and how difficult it was to get up there, and how frightened I was by the stories about violence and bandits." Wicha assured her that he would pick her up in Chiang Rai to drive her up the mountain and that she would be perfectly safe with him.

There was another problem. "Doi Chang is out of my jurisdiction. I am only supposed to be giving agricultural extension advice in Chiang Mai Province. But if I were to go there on my own time, on a weekend, I suppose no one could object. And if you have 50 baht, I could sell you this basic book about coffee cultivation to start your education," she said, grabbing a book off her shelf.

A Lifetime's Preparation

ALTHOUGH WICHA PROMYONG'S adventurous life may have seemed somewhat random up to that point, it might be seen, in retrospect, as perfect preparation for the role he was to play in helping the Akha of Doi Chang become world-renowned for their coffee. It is unclear exactly when he was born. His birth certificate said 1955, but he later said that it was late by as much as five years. He was probably born in the early 1950s, the seventh of ten children of Cham and Sudnit Promyong. He enjoyed keeping his age a bit of a mystery, always joking that he was twenty-nine when he was obviously well beyond that milestone.

His father, Cham, was born in southern Thailand in 1901, the son of a relatively wealthy Muslim landowner, though Wicha said that his grandfather wasn't rich but smart, claiming land when it cost a pittance, and that the family was land-rich but not so flush with cash. The family's original surname was Mustafa, an Arabic name, but his grandfather had changed it to Promyong, a Thai name, in order to assimilate better.

Wicha's father had studied Islam in Egypt, then science and law in Europe. He was still in Europe on June 24, 1932, when a revolution ended the absolute monarchy that had ruled Siam, as it was still called, for 700 years. The current lineage, the House of Chakri, had begun in 1782 with Rama I, a military leader who declared himself the monarch, established Bangkok as the capital, and fathered forty-two children. Rama VII was ruling at the time of the 1932 revolt.

The revolution was led by rising young middle-class leaders, both civilians and military men, who had, like Cham Promyong, been educated in Europe. Cham rushed back to Siam to support the revolution, becoming a leader of young Muslims who believed in modernity and democratic change.

Rama VII, a moderate who had tried in vain to institute a constitution, only to be blocked by the powerful traditional princes, defused the potentially violent situation by agreeing to the new constitution that stripped him of most power other than his title. The monarchy subsequently had some of its power restored, but Rama VII abdicated in 1935. His successor was his nephew Rama VIII, a nine-year-old boy attending school in Switzerland. He remained there, with Thai-based regents ruling in his stead, until after World War II.

The handsome young king, who held a law degree, was an instant hit among his subjects, and as the chief representative of the minority Muslims in Siam, Cham Promyong was one of his advisors. Tragically, Rama VIII died in 1946. His brother, Rama IX—more commonly referred to as King Bhumibol—succeeded him to the throne, where he would remain for an unprecedented length of time. It was King Bhumibol who championed the cause of the hill tribes and began the Royal Project to help them.

Wicha was born in the Phra Pradaeng district just south of Bangkok, when his father was in his fifties. His mother, Sudjit, was considerably younger. Wicha wasn't sure of his own birth date, but he knew that he entered the world on a moonlit night and that his brother ran to call the old midwife in the village. "My father owned 5 or 6 acres there. He had land here and there around Thailand, which he inherited from his father. Promyong is a big name in Thailand, and people think we are very rich, but that isn't true. My father was a very good man—everyone loved him." Cham Promyong spoke multiple languages and was clever at anything he set his mind to learn, according to his son. He was a generous man, who "gave away all" to anyone who was in need.

Wicha grew up worshiping his father, but mostly from afar, because as the head of the Thai Muslims, Cham was rarely home. Wicha's mother was the steady rock on which he built his young life. "My mother raised ten children, virtually alone. She was a tough woman," he said. "She wasn't scared of anything."

Wicha, who did not enjoy school, quit when he was fifteen and sold ice cream with a friend to make some money. Despite this, he won a scholarship from the University of Pakistan, but only briefly attended classes. "I couldn't sit still like that for very long," he recalled. After a few months, he ran away. He stayed for a while in the Peshawar district of northern Pakistan, now infamous as a Taliban stronghold, but at that time, it was simply a wild area where nomads and other itinerants lived. Peshawar was a fascinating, ancient multiethnic city. Then he hitchhiked across the border to Afghanistan and ended up in Kabul for several months. "I lived cheap cheap," Wicha recalled. "I would stay in a place that charged five rupees a night, but I would offer to help to sweep or wash dishes, and I usually could stay for free, or they even paid me." He would befriend older men who worked at the inns, and they gave him better food. Meeting other travelers—Japanese, Australians, Germans, American hippies—Wicha learned to play the guitar and harmonica from street musicians, and he began to smoke hashish with them to get high while he played. He learned rudimentary English and sang Bob Dylan, Joan Baez, and other folk or protest tunes.

Then it was on to Iran, but only for a short time. In Tehran, he was walking one morning with a group of Americans and Europeans when some Iranian boys ran up and began harassing some of the women, grabbing at their breasts. "It happened just right in front of me," Wicha recalled, "so I fought with them to stop them." After six days in an Iranian prison, he was released and hopped a mini-bus going to Turkey. He still had about $60 he had saved from his days in Kabul. He continued to wander, passing through Turkey, Bulgaria, and Yugoslavia.

In Austria he met Terry O'Sullivan, a Brit who said he knew a way to sneak into West Germany, where border guards were strict about keeping vagrants out. O'Sullivan planned to cross over by walking through the Black Forest. They got lost in freezing temperatures. "I didn't know what to eat. It wasn't like the jungle in Thailand. There were just tall pine trees. We were starving. The bread in my rucksack saved our lives." Maddeningly, he couldn't open the can of sardines he had brought. They kept walking west, following the sun, and finally they saw smoke rising into the sky from a fire. A rural farmer gave them hot soup and let them rest a while, then showed them the highway, where they walked and hitchhiked to Chiemsee, the island where mad King Ludwig had erected a huge unfinished castle.

For a month, he and Terry O'Sullivan toured Germany together. "Terry had worked in South Africa and had money. I only had sixteen dollars left, so he paid for everything." Then O'Sullivan left for England. Wicha stayed in Germany, sleeping in parks and washing in underground bathrooms for a while. He eventually found work in Chinese restaurants, where he could eat and sleep in a corner in return for washing dishes and cleaning bathrooms. In Hanover, he met some musician friends, joined a band, and found steady work in a restaurant.

Then, in October 1973, a student revolution broke out in Thailand, protesting against the military junta and demanding a new constitution guaranteeing democracy. A crowd of 400,000 protestors gathered, and the regime agreed to free political prisoners and promised to adopt a new constitution the following year. Nonetheless, police subsequently attacked students, who retaliated with vandalism. Tanks, helicopters, and soldiers were brought in, and over one hundred students were killed. Finally, King Bhumibol intervened and announced that the military government had resigned.

With the student rebellion making international news, Wicha flew back to Bangkok. He stayed for four months, joining protest songwriter Surachai Jantimatorn and his rock band. It was a time of incredible energy, excitement, chaos, and optimism. Students continued to call for strikes and sit-ins to protest everything from Thailand's trade imbalance with Japan to the CIA's role in funding the Thai military. But nothing had really changed, even under the supposedly "democratic" regime. Corruption and violence continued. The right wing and military surged back to power in 1976, with increased assassinations of student leaders and other protestors. Surachai Jantimatorn and his fellow musicians, known as Caravan, fled Bangkok, hiding out in rural areas. They were able to return from exile only after amnesty was declared in 1979.

After Wicha's brief but intense four months in Thailand, he left again, this time flying to England, where he spent the next four years doing whatever was needed to survive. One day a young Scottish woman named Brenda Douglas came to a Chinese restaurant to buy chicken. She was intrigued by the young Thai man who served her. They began to see one another and fell in love. By this time, Wicha was tired of the British weather and was homesick. He and Brenda flew back to Thailand in 1977, where they were married. The following year, their daughter, Chada, was born.

Wicha was distraught when he went back to see his father's old home. What used to be a "garden plantation" was now covered with smoke-belching factories. The water was filthy. "All my plants had died from the pollution." And his mother had sold his beloved Harley-Davidson motorcycle.

He bought a small farm on the outskirts of Bangkok, but he wasn't happy. "I didn't know what I was doing. My way of life was to struggle. I couldn't settle down." He left Brenda and his daughter in Bangkok and began to travel restlessly again. He preferred the city of Chiang Mai, farther north, which was far less crowded and polluted, so the family moved to a rental house there with two-year-old Chada.

Wicha began to roam through the hills, getting to know the hill tribes, buying "antiques"—old opium scales, jewelry, animal traps, weapons, homespun embroidered clothing—from them to resell in a store he opened in Chiang Mai. He opened a factory to make rustic furniture from twisted tree limbs and other "found" wood. "It seemed like I started a new business every day," Wicha remembered.

Although he was a good businessman and enjoyed the money he made, Wicha was always generous and tried to help the downtrodden. When he happened to meet an ex-convict who was down on his luck, for instance, he hired him to work in his furniture factory, and that led to many other former prisoners seeking work there.

After seven years in Thailand, Brenda had had enough. Wicha was rarely home, she worried that Chada would not receive an adequate education in Thailand, and she missed her family. In 1984 she left Wicha, without rancor, to return to Scotland.

Free to roam at will in northern Thailand, Wicha continued to create new enterprises, including a pig farm, despite the Muslim prohibition against pork. "At that time," he said, "I knew a lot about the northern mountains, the jungle here and there. No one else knew the jungle the way I did. So I worked for many people as an advisor."

Another project involved research on stevia, a plant that showed promise as a natural low-calorie alternative to sugar. Wicha explained, "They tried to grow stevia in Thailand, starting in 1982," which is when he was hired. This was one of the crop replacement schemes supported by the Thai military in villages that supposedly held communist sympathizers. Wicha, who loved growing things, became an expert on the plant. "Once I study something, I go deep into it," he said. He worked nearly full-time on the stevia project for seven years and part-time for another four years.

Stevia, which is native to subtropical and tropical regions in the western hemisphere, is part of the sunflower family. The leaves of the stevia plant are intensely sweet, but most stevia products produce a bitter, licorice-like aftertaste. Wicha claimed that Thailand produced a superior strain, but it could not compete with cheaper stevia products from China, Brazil, the Philippines, and elsewhere.

During his stevia research, Wicha met Nuch, a Thai secretary at the stevia factory. They were married in 1984, though he warned her from the outset that he was a traveling man, unlikely to stick around for any length of time. He stayed home long enough, however, to father four children—Chanoot, a boy, born in 1986, two daughters, Nootcha (1988) and Picha (1990), and another son, Pichai (1995). They all had nicknames starting with K—in descending order, Khem, Kwan, Kern, and Koon.

Chiang Mai was turning into too much of a big city for Wicha's taste, so in the late 1980s, he moved his growing family farther north to the smaller, more intimate city of Chiang Rai, where he reopened his antiques store. Here he was closer to many of the hill tribes. He continued to make forays up into villages in the mountains, including Doi Chang, and he hired a crew of buyers to work for him throughout the mountains of Thailand, Laos, and Burma. His store was named one of the top five antique shops in the world.

Not all of his ventures succeeded. In Chiang Rai, he opened a large restaurant with an adjacent retail market where members of hill tribes—mostly Akha, Lisu, and Hmong—demonstrated how to make traditional handicrafts and silversmithing. The business provided important income for the impoverished tribes. "He would throw himself into everything he did," his daughter Kwan remembered, "whether it was antiques, plants, food, or building design." Her father sometimes frustrated her with his generosity. "I was a selfish kid, and I would try to stop him from giving everything away."

Her parents would help anyone with a problem. "When I was very young," Kwan recalled, "the antiques store was in the middle of town, and a poor boy from the south of Thailand came by. Mom fried him an egg and some chicken, so he came by every day, and he told them he was an orphan. Years later, when we opened our first coffeeshop, this scruffy hippy guy, with lots of beads, said hello and asked if my parents remembered him. He was that boy. And it wasn't just him—there were many others like him. My parents helped so many."

But the restaurant and hill tribe market went bankrupt in 1992, after demonstrations in Bangkok against the military regime led to massacres and riots. Tourism, on which Wicha's businesses relied, dried up, and business for his antiques shop slowed down as well. Fortunately, King Bhumibol intervened, which led to new elections, and a civil war was averted. But for much of the next ten years, Wicha struggled financially.

Kwan, who was a young child when the restaurant went under, remembered the following ten years fondly. "Before the bankruptcy, he was so busy. I remember the restaurant and the hill tribe activities, about twenty minutes from town, out in the country, and his antiques store. He never felt stretched, he liked to do many things. He moved faster than anyone. He walked ten steps for every one of ours, and he was always thinking."

With fewer enterprises, he slowed down a bit and was around more, though he sometimes traveled to Nan Province to tend to his teak plantation there. He also became obsessed with planting rare tropical trees on his Chiang Rai property. "In my primary school years, and the first two high school years, Dad wasn't so busy," Kwan recalled. "We lived in a house by the Mekong River, where for us kids Dad built what we called our Tarzan House, a tree house with a sliding board." Together they often went to their small farm twenty minutes away to pick ripe red lychee fruits, which Kwan sold out of the back of their truck. "Many people Dad had helped in the past came to the house to give us money and food, though we never felt we wanted for money, ever in our lives. We grew vegetables, and people who had cows or chickens gave us meat."

Kwan loved the times when rock musician Surachai Jantimatorn, whom she called Uncle Nga, came to visit Wicha, still one of his best friends. "About fifty musicians would come. They set up tents, and some slept in the Tarzan House. Dad would play harmonica, guitar, and flute."

Wicha eventually bounced back. "I was born to make money," he explained. He also spent his bahts easily, giving to people in need, as his father had done before him. He was dismayed by the treatment of the hill tribes and appalled at the massacres, forced village relocations, burned homes, and sexual slavery. He once led a raid on a brothel in order to free twelve-year-old girls.

Coffee Renaissance

THUS, BY THE TIME Adel came down the mountain from Doi Chang to ask for help in 2001, Wicha had already led an incredible life. He knew the jungle, knew the hill tribes and their plight, knew how to research new crops—and knew how to make money. He also loved a challenge.

Now he found himself sitting around a fire in a small hut in Doi Chang, talking late into the night with a group of desperate Akha and Patchanee Suwanwisolkit, the agronomist from Chiang Mai University. There was no electricity in the hut, which sat on one rai (a little over a third of an acre) that the Akha had purchased for 50,000 baht (less than $2,000) on the road to the village, just as it crested a hill and was descending into the small valley where most of the houses in Doi Chang were located.

The agronomist, who had been extremely nervous about coming to this notoriously drug-ridden, violent, remote village, forgot all her apprehensions as she saw the eager, receptive faces turned toward her. She talked about how to prepare seeds for new trees—choose ripe coffee cherries from the healthiest trees that bore the most fruit, then strip the skin off and dry them in the shade, not the sun. "Then you can plant them right away, or they will keep up to three months," she explained in Thai. She waited while Wicha translated her words into Akha.

"Before planting, soak the seeds in water overnight. Plant them in sand mixed with dirt. It takes six weeks for them to sprout. They will send out two butterfly wings at first—two leaves." At that point, she explained, they had to transfer the seedlings to individual pots filled with rich soil. "You can't expose them to full sun—they need about 50 percent exposure—so put black semi-transparent screening over the plants. Leave them to grow for six to eight months. A month before you're ready to set them out in a field, prepare the soil, exposing it to the sun to bake out impurities. At the same time, take the black screening off the seedlings so that they begin to adjust to the sun."

Adel's older brother Leehu, younger brother Ayu and brother-in-law Akong were also present. As Patchanee explained each process, from seedling to mature, producing tree, Wicha and the others asked questions. Wicha scribbled notes, but the Akha, with no written language, simply took it all in. With their astonishing memories, they had no trouble recalling the details later.

Charmed by Wicha and the receptive, hospitable Akha farmers, Patchanee agreed to help them, returning every weekend on her own time. The timing couldn't have been worse in terms of the world market. Because Vietnam had begun to flood the world with poor-quality robusta coffee beans, the price for coffee on the C-market in New York had dropped precipitously. The years 2001–2003 were the nadir of what came to be known as the Coffee Crisis. The good news for the Akha was that they were already in crisis, and the low prices did not discourage them.

Over the next three years, with advice and hard work, the Akha began to grow more coffee, and this time they knew better what they were doing. Nonetheless, they faced a steep learning curve and many unforeseen problems.

CHAPTER 4

Doi Chaang Coffee

URING THE FIRST YEAR of his coffee tutelage, Wicha read everything about coffee he could find, starting with the book Patchanee loaned him. He found that the material written in Thai was contradictory, ill-informed, and poorly translated from English, German, or other languages. So he read most of the material in English. "It was very hard for me and took a long time, but I did it," he said. Gradually, he learned about coffee—its history, cultivation, economics, and market. True to form, he immersed himself in his topic.

Coffee was first identified as a medicinal plant that grew wild on the mountainsides of Ethiopia, but no one knows exactly when or by whom. Of the various legends, the most appealing involves dancing goats. An Ethiopian goatherd named Kaldi allegedly noticed that his goats were behaving quite strangely, running about, butting one another, dancing on their hind legs, and bleating excitedly. The goats were chewing the glossy green leaves and red berries of a tree. Kaldi tried some of the berries himself. The fruit was mildly sweet, and the seeds that popped out were covered with a thick, tasty mucilage. Finally, he chewed the seeds themselves, but they were too hard, so he spit them out, then popped another berry in his mouth. Soon, according to legend, Kaldi was frisking with his goats. Poetry and song spilled out of him. He felt that he would never be tired or grouchy again.

There may be some truth to the story, since goats will eat almost anything and they do wander at will in the Ethiopian mountains. At any rate, coffee became an integral part of Ethiopian culture. By the time Rhazes, an Arabian physician, first mentioned coffee in print in the tenth century, the trees probably had been deliberately cultivated for hundreds of years. It is likely that, as in the legend, the coffee cherries and leaves were initially chewed, but the Ethiopians then learned to brew the leaves and berries with boiled water as a weak tea. They ground the beans and mixed them with animal fat for a quick energy snack. They made wine out of the fermented pulp and made a sweet beverage, kisher, out of the lightly roasted husks of the coffee cherry.

Finally, probably in the fifteenth century, someone roasted the beans. When roasted, they blew up to twice their size and turned brown, blackening if roasted too long. The Ethiopians ground these aromatic roasted beans and put them in hot water for a few minutes to make an infusion. Coffee as we know it had arrived.

Once the Ethiopians discovered coffee, it was only a matter of time before the drink spread through trade with the Arabs across the narrow band of the Red Sea. The Arab Sufi monks adopted coffee as a drink that would allow them to stay awake for midnight prayers more easily. Initially regarded as a medicine or religious aid, it soon slipped into everyday use. Wealthy people had a coffee room in their homes, reserved for social imbibing. Coffeehouses, known as kaveh kanes, then sprang up, allowing the less wealthy to indulge. By the end of the fifteenth century, Muslim pilgrims had introduced coffee throughout the Islamic world in Persia, Egypt, Turkey, and North Africa, making it a lucrative trade item.

As the drink grew in popularity throughout the sixteenth century, it also gained its reputation as a troublemaking brew. Various rulers decided that people were having too much fun in the coffeehouses. When Khair-Beg, the young governor of Mecca, discovered that satirical verses about him were emanating from the coffeehouses, he determined that coffee, like wine, must be outlawed by the Koran, and he persuaded his religious, legal, and medical advisors to agree. Thus, in 1511 the coffeehouses of Mecca were closed. The ban didn't last long.

Coffee drinking prevailed partly because of its addictive nature, but also because coffee provided an intellectual stimulant, a pleasant way to feel increased energy without any apparent ill effects. Coffeehouses allowed people to get together for conversation, entertainment, and business, inspiring agreements, poetry, and irreverence in equal measure. The brew became so important in Turkey that a lack of sufficient coffee was an acceptable reason for a woman to seek a divorce.

The Arabs tried to maintain a monopoly on coffee cultivation by parboiling the seeds to make them infertile. But some time during the 1600s a Muslim pilgrim named Baba Budan smuggled seven fertile seeds out by taping them to his stomach and successfully cultivated them in southern India, in the mountains of Mysore. In 1616 the Dutch, who dominated the world's shipping trade, managed to transport a tree to Holland from Aden. From its offspring the Dutch began growing coffee in Ceylon in 1658. In 1699 another Dutchman transplanted trees from Malabar to Java, followed by cultivation in Sumatra, Celebes, Timor, Bali, and other islands in the East Indies. For many years to come, the production of the Dutch East Indies determined the price of coffee in the world market.

Europeans eventually became enamored of the social and medicinal benefits of the Arabian drink. By the 1650s coffee was being sold by Italian street vendors. Venice's first coffeehouse opened in 1683. Named for the drink it served, the caffè (spelled café elsewhere in Europe) quickly became synonymous with relaxed companionship, animated conversation, and tasty food. Even Britain welcomed coffee, although tea would later supplant it as the favored caffeinated beverage. By 1700, there were 2,000 coffeehouses in London alone, each specializing in its own clientele, and called "penny universities" because of the stimulating conversation to be had for the price of a cup of coffee. Some coffeehouses were for actors, others for writers, businessmen, or sailors.

It could be argued that coffeehouses affected European culture by helping to sober up its citizens. Until the late seventeenth century, alcoholic beverages were widely and heartily consumed, from breakfast until the nightcap at bedtime. Coffee contributed to the advent of modern science, commerce, and industry by making clear thought much more common. It also unquestionably helped to spawn revolutions. The American and French revolutions were both planned in coffeehouses, and many Americans switched from tea to coffee after the Boston Tea Party protest of 1773.

Coffee cultivation spread to the western hemisphere in the eighteenth century. In 1714 the Dutch gave a healthy coffee plant to the French government, and nine years later a French naval officer named Gabriel Mathieu de Clieu introduced coffee cultivation to the French colony of Martinique after nursing a coffee seedling during a perilous transatlantic voyage, later referring to "the infinite care that I was obliged to bestowe upon this delicate plant." Once it finally set down roots in Martinique, the coffee tree flourished. From that single plant, much of the world's current coffee supply probably derives.

In the early eighteenth century, coffee arrived in Brazil and made its way through Central America and Colombia. By 1750 the coffee tree grew on five continents. The semi-tropical arabica coffee plant grows best at an elevation of 3,000 to 6,000 feet in a girdle around the equator, between the Tropics of Cancer and Capricorn, where the temperature never gets too hot or too cold, hovering around 75°F. The beautiful locations are also among the world's poorest and most violence-prone areas—in part because of the way coffee, a labor-intensive crop, was grown.

The Dark Side of Coffee

UNFORTUNATELY, COFFEE BECAME associated with slavery and oppression. Slaves had initially been brought to the Caribbean to harvest sugarcane, and the history of sugar is intimately tied to that of coffee. Sugar made coffee palatable to many consumers and added a quick energy lift to the stimulus of caffeine. When the French colonists first grew coffee in Saint-Domingue (Haiti) in 1734, it was natural that they would require additional African slaves to work the plantations.

By 1788 Saint-Domingue supplied half of the world's coffee. The slaves on the island lived in appalling conditions, housed in windowless huts, underfed, and overworked. They revolted in 1791 in a struggle for freedom that lasted twelve years, the only major successful slave revolt in history. Most plantations were burned to the ground and the owners massacred. Haitian coffee eventually reentered the international market, but it never regained its dominance.

The Dutch jumped into the breach to supply the coffee short-fall with Java beans. Though they did not routinely rape or torture their laborers, they did enslave them. In Brazil, slavery was not abolished until 1888, later than any other country in the western hemisphere, because of coffee. Although some Brazilian plantation owners treated their slaves decently, others felt free to do as they pleased. Slaves were regarded as subhuman, "forming a link in the chain of animated beings between ourselves and the various species of brute animals," as one slaveholder explained to his son.

In Central America, the indigenous peoples such as Mayans were not technically enslaved, but the system of forced labor (*mandamiento*) and debt peonage amounted to the same thing. For a Mayan in Guatemala in the 1800s, for instance, the only alternative to being dragged off to work on a farm (or to the army or gang labor on a road) or to going into debt to a coffee farmer was flight. To maintain order, the government instituted a large standing army and militia. Thus, coffee money funded a repressive regime that fostered smoldering resentment among the indigenous people. Sometimes they rebelled, but such attempts only resulted in massacres. Instead they learned to subvert the system by working as little as possible, by taking wage advances from several farmers simultaneously, and by running away.

So, in the history of the coffee industry, oppression and poverty have been associated with coffee cultivation, and inequities remain embedded in the global coffee economy, with most of the profits made near the consuming end in wealthier countries, not in the countries where coffee is grown.

The Blight and the Boom-Bust Cycle

BY THE LATE nineteenth century, coffee had become a global, semi-industrialized industry. Green coffee beans from remote areas around the world arrived via steamships in major consuming countries in North America and Europe and were roasted in factories, then sold in branded packages. The ground canned coffee wasn't great, since it had to be exposed to oxygen and pre-staled before packaging. Because freshly roasted coffee produces carbon dioxide, it cannot be put immediately into an airtight container—the releasing gas would cause a rupture. Still, the canned coffee was convenient and well advertised.

The market dominance of coffee from the East Indies was broken by a fungus, Hemileia vastatrix, the coffee leaf rust blight, which first appeared in Ceylon in 1869. It was called rust because of its initial yellow-brown stain on the underside of the coffee leaf, which eventually turns black, producing the spores of pale orange powder that rub off and spread. The blotches gradually enlarge until they cover the entire leaf, which then falls off. Finally, the entire tree is denuded and dies. The fungus effectively destroyed the coffee plantations of Indonesia for many years. Eventually, many farms in the East Indies began to grow robusta coffee (Coffea canephora), an inferior variety native to West Africa. It can withstand greater heat in the lowlands and is resistant to rust, but it has a harsher taste and contains twice the caffeine of arabica. Consequently, it has been used primarily in cheap blends, instant coffee and in many espresso blends to produce a foamy crema on top.

Various theories held that the coffee leaf rust was caused by the shade trees then in use, or that too much dampness encouraged the disease. It does appear that the fungus thrives in moist environments. The real villain, however, is monoculture. Whenever man intervenes and creates an artificial wealth of a particular plant, nature eventually finds a way to take advantage of this abundant food supply. The coffee tree is otherwise rather hardy.

The decline of coffee in Indonesia coincided with its explosive growth in Brazil and elsewhere in Latin America. Three importers in the United States, a syndicate nicknamed the Trinity that had controlled the majority of the crop from the East Indies, struggled to keep coffee prices high, even as Brazil flooded the market with beans. Finally, in 1880, they were unable to maintain the artificial price, and the market fell disastrously. "There was no attempt to do business, everyone being suspicious of his neighbor," recalled one veteran coffee man. The losses for coffee amounted to nearly $7 million in 1880.

In an attempt to stabilize the market, a coffee exchange was begun. Though complex in execution, a coffee exchange is a relatively simple concept. A buyer contracts with a seller to purchase a certain number of bags at a specified time in the future. As time goes by, the value of the contract changes, depending on market factors. Most real coffee men used the contracts as hedges against price changes, while speculators provided the necessary liquidity, since every contract requires a willing buyer and seller. While a speculator may profit, he also may lose his shirt. Essentially he provides a form of price risk insurance for coffee dealers.

But the C-market, as the exchange has come to be called, has not stabilized prices to any great extent, and various coffee quota schemes in subsequent years all failed as well. The crash of 1880 was the beginning of a boom-bust cycle that continues to this day.

The Specialty Coffee Revolution

WICHA LEARNED ALL of this rather disturbing history as he read and talked to Patchanee and her colleagues. And in 2001, the world was in the middle of the worst bust cycle ever experienced, due in large part to overproduction of cheap robusta in nearby Vietnam. Yet there was hope. He also learned about the specialty coffee revolution.

In the USA, by the 1960s, coffee had become a mediocre product, blended with inferior robusta beans, and served diluted in bottomless mugs to make it palatable. Per capita consumption declined, as baby boomers turned to soft drinks for their caffeine hit. In 1966, however, Alfred Peet, a Dutch immigrant and coffee trader dismayed by what had happened to his favorite beverage in the United States, opened Peet's Coffee and Tea in Berkeley, California. He soon had a cult following for his dark-roasted single-origin arabica beans. This was the start of what came to be called the specialty coffee movement.

Throughout the country a scattered, disparate band rediscovered or maintained a tradition of fresh-roasted, quality coffees. Many had roots in small, old-style family coffee businesses. Others were hippies who had hitchhiked through Europe and discovered the relaxed pleasures of café life and decent coffee. In 1971, three such men, inspired by Peet's, founded Starbucks Coffee in Seattle. It was just one of many such grassroots roasters. Starbucks eventually came to dominate the new specialty movement, although some critics complained that the chain was too big, slick, and standardized. Nonetheless, Starbucks was astonishingly effective at reintroducing coffee as a high-end product, similar to wine in terms of its *terroir* the unique taste that results from a particular microclimate and type of plant.

At the same time, consumers became more aware of the inequities built into the coffee system, where the laborers who did the hardest work often received the lowest pay. In November 1988, Max Havelaar Quality Mark coffee was introduced in the Netherlands. Taking its name from the 1860 Dutch novel that protested the inhumane treatment of Javanese coffee growers, this Fair Trade coffee garnered enormous publicity and grabbed a small but significant market share. Within a few years, the Max Havelaar seal had appeared in Switzerland, Belgium, Denmark, and France. In Germany, Austria, the US, Canada, Japan, and other countries, where the Dutch name did not resonate, it became Transfair or Fair Trade coffee.

The bureaucratic headquarters moved to Bonn, Germany, and the Fair Trade Labeling Organization (FLO), was established, later renamed Fairtrade International. In order to qualify for Fair Trade status, farmers had to own only a few acres, join together in a democratically run cooperative, and pass an annual audit. In return, beans labeled Fair Trade were guaranteed a minimum selling price set somewhat above the C-market—if they could find a market for them. Critics of Fair Trade pointed out that its certification did not cover well-intentioned estates that treated workers well, because by definition they were too large. As a result, the US organization split off from FLO in 2011 in order to redefine the guidelines and accept larger farms. Regardless, Fair Trade beans came to represent an important principle: people should be concerned about the farmers who were producing the product they drank every morning.

Coffee in Thailand

BY THE TURN of the twenty-first century, the specialty revolution had spread around the world, including the Pacific Rim. Starbucks opened its first store in Tokyo in 1995 and in Bangkok in 1998. While mostly tourists were attracted to upscale cafés at the onset, the coffeehouses also became trendy, hip destinations for businessmen and young Thai, for whom they symbolized one of the good things in life appreciated by Western culture.

Arabica coffee cultivation had been introduced to Thailand in 1954, when the Thai Department of Agriculture brought in several varietal lines from Brazil, but they suffered from leaf rust. In 1961, Baptist agricultural missionary Richard Mann gave the Karen tribe of Huey Haum village in Mae Hong Son Province enough Caturra and Catuai coffee hybrid seedlings for commercial production. Although more tolerant of the fungal blight, they were still affected by it. Huey Haum farmers were able to sell their beans for a small profit and so continued to grow coffee. Mann worked with UN crop replacement programs for the next two decades, encouraging coffee cultivation along with other fruits and vegetables.

In 1991, Richard Mann's son, Mike, also a Baptist agronomist and missionary, started the Lahu Irrigation Project in Chiang Mai, which soon expanded into the Integrated Tribal Development Program (ITDP). "At first we focused on family gardens, latrines, water supply and irrigation, and a few crops, including fruit, coffee and macadamia trees," Mann recalled. "But we didn't do any marketing, and we weren't thinking that coffee would take off as a cash crop."

That changed in 1997, when Richard Mann notified his son that a Japanese Christian organization, the Wakachiai Foundation, was interested in helping hill tribes market their coffee. With funding from Wakachiai, Mann organized a coffee cooperative, the Thai Tribal Arabica Coffee Production and Marketing Cooperative, and, using the foundation's connections, got the first Fair Trade certification in Thailand through Transfair Japan. The first few villages Mann recruited included Huey Haum, as well as Goshen and Payang, two villages on the mountain of Doi Tung in the north of Thailand near the Burmese border. By the next year, two dozen villages had joined the cooperative, which sold beans to Japan and the Netherlands.

That Doi Tung villages were growing coffee was thanks to King Bhumibol's aging mother. A Bangkok slum orphan who became a nurse and married a king, Princess Sangwal Mahidol, known as the Princess Mother, had a long-standing concern for the hill tribes. She had established a program for medical volunteers, landing with them in remote villages in helicopters, which earned her the nickname Mae Fah Luang—Royal Mother from the Sky—among the tribes. She had also helped sell tribal crafts in Bangkok.

The Princess Mother used to visit Switzerland every year for a ski trip. When she could no longer do so, she identified Doi Tung, which she had visited with her volunteer doctors, as an alternative vacation spot. The Doi Tung Royal Villa was built there, but she also wanted to help reforest the area and relieve tribal poverty. Thus began the Doi Tung Development Project under the direction of the Mae Fah Luang Foundation. Three Akha and Lahu villages had to relocate nearby, but otherwise the villages in the area were able to remain where they were.

The Princess Mother died in 1995, around the time that Nestlé, the Swiss-based largest coffee roaster in the world, donated coffee seedlings to the project. A coffee expert from the Kona region of Hawaii was hired to help launch the project. At first, the Mae Fah Luang Foundation tried to grow and market coffee on government-owned plantations, but things worked better when farmers owned their own trees (though they didn't own the land). Doi Tung eventually became a well-known Thai coffee brand, sold in Doi Tung coffeeshops in Bangkok, Chiang Mai, and Chiang Rai.

Creating Doi Chaang Coffee

BY 2001, when Wicha focused on it as the possible salvation for the village of Doi Chang, coffee was becoming more popular in tea-drinking Thailand. He thought how great it would be if he could help position Doi Chang as the premier source of top-notch coffee in Thailand, produced and roasted inside Thailand. Not one to limit his vision, Wicha concluded that the name Doi Chang would come to stand for quality coffee and for the Akha tribe. In 2001, he made a research trip to Italy, home of espresso. At the Thai

Embassy, an employee told him, "Oh, you must see my friend Chai in Bangkok." So Wicha sought out Phitsanuchai Kaewphichai, a consultant to hotels and restaurants, who became "Brother Phitsanu," a friend and advisor to Wicha, though he consistently turned down Wicha's repeated offers to take an official position in the new business.

Wicha's vision continued to grow. Not only would the Akha grow superior coffee, eventually, the beans would become as well known and sought after worldwide as Hawaiian Kona and Jamaica Blue Mountain beans. The Akha would not be subservient peons working for others. They would not be like the coffee slaves of the past. They would take charge of their own coffee, their own destiny.

Wicha now lived much of the time in a small thatched hut built for him in Doi Chang, as he and the Akha created their coffee enterprise. His wife and children, down in Chiang Rai, missed him, but they had grown used to his long absences.

Discussing his vision with Adel, Miga, Lipi, Akong, and the other young Akha, Wicha waxed lyrical, and his enthusiasm was catching. The Akha could do this! They were hard workers. They just needed to know the right way to do things. First, they needed a name. That didn't take long. They would call their coffee Doi Chaang, adding an "a" to the village name to make it distinctive and to imply that the coffee was of double-A quality. It was also common for the Thai to double vowels to indicate that the syllable would be drawn out, pronounced "Doy ChAAHng." Wicha and the small band of Akha registered the Doi Chaang Coffee Company Original on March 11, 2003.

On the package they decided to put a line drawing of Adel's father, Piko, wearing a traditional turban. Piko looked like a respected elder statesman, with his rugged, handsome features and the determined set of his mouth. It was appropriate to honor him, because he had stuck with coffee after most other farmers had given up on the crop. The Akha were still an egalitarian society, but Piko was nonetheless pleased at this honor.

Doi Chaang
C O F F E E

The next problem concerned how the coffee would be grown. Wicha hated the chemical pesticides and fertilizers that the Akha had been sold to grow vegetables, because such products put them into an endless cycle of debt and harmed their health and the environment. The chemicals also flowed in water down the mountain and affected other villages. He wanted the Akha to grow organic coffee. Patchanee taught them to plant taller shade trees among the coffee plants not only to provide the shade required to allow the beans to develop properly, but also to "fix" nitrogen by taking it from the air and converting it to ammonium to enrich the soil. The falling leaves from the trees would provide humus, and many of them, such as macadamia or banana trees, were themselves cash crops.

The coffee had to be carefully harvested, with only the ripest red or yellow cherries picked, and then processed that same day or the next. Patchanee emphasized that the wet process method generally yielded superior, reliable results with fewer defects, producing a drink with bright acidity and full, clean flavor. It is also far more labor-intensive and requires sophisticated machinery and infrastructure and an abundant supply of fresh running water at each processing facility. The springs on the mountain above Doi Chang provided plenty of water, but there was obviously no processing machinery.

Consequently, the Akha initially pursued the wet process by hand. They removed the skin from the ripe coffee cherries with a mortar and pestle, then put the pulp-covered beans in a bucket full of water to ferment for up to forty-eight hours, checking them frequently, since it was important to stop the process at just the right point to prevent over-fermentation. As the mucilage decomposed, it loosened from its sticky binding on the parchment. The process also gave a subtle flavor to the inner bean. Then the farmers took the beans, still covered in parchment, and spread them out to dry in the sun on clean surfaces (some farmers built small bamboo platforms), turning them every few hours. They threw out any beans that were cracked or discolored.

Wicha drove the dried beans to Chiang Mai, where a small coffee business removed the parchment and roasted the beans in a machine that held only one kilogram (half a pound) at a time. When properly roasted and brewed, the beans made superb coffee—a sweet, balanced cup, with a hint of roasted almonds, chocolate, and jasmine, and a syrupy-smooth mouthfeel. In terms of balance and versatility, the Doi Chaang offerings were comparable to the best Kona or Costa Rican beans, and they could be roasted medium or dark for different characteristics. The small Chiang Mai roaster wanted more, although its roasting methods were uneven.

The hand processing was inefficient, so with the initial coffee profits and loans from friends, Wicha bought a small depulping machine. It could run by hand crank or electricity provided by a generator or truck engine, and in an hour it could process 200 kilograms (around 440 pounds) of coffee cherries.

Wicha carried 5 kilograms (11 pounds) of roasted coffee everywhere he went—Chiang Rai, Chiang Mai, Bangkok. Before going into a retail store or coffeeshop, he threw the beans into cheap paper bags with the Doi Chaang Coffee label glued on them. "Please just test this coffee. If you like it, I will send you some every month," he promised. He began to build a market for Doi Chaang Coffee. Even with Phitsanu's encouragement and advice, however, Wicha's attempts to help get the village beans into upscale hotels failed. The Doi Chang beans were superior, but the Chiang Mai roaster produced an uneven quality, and the packaging was amateurish. Hotels preferred Boncafe, a well-run company that leased espresso machines and provided Thai blends. It became clear that the Akha needed to roast their own beans and put them in well-designed, professional-looking bags.

Roasting Their Own

WICHA WANTED TO borrow a small roasting machine, but he couldn't get permission from the Thai Food and Drug Administration (FDA Thailand) to roast. "I got mad," he recalled. He filled out the FDA paperwork but decided that he would go ahead and find a used roaster, assuming that the FDA would either approve the project by the time he managed to find a roaster and get it up the mountain, or approve a *fait accompli*. So he asked everyone he knew to help find a big, cheap, used roaster. He wanted one large enough to handle all the business he had so optimistically assured the Akha they would secure.

In the meantime, the Akha hired a backhoe to flatten the land they had purchased up the hill from Doi Chang village. With the money from the coffee they sold, they bought cement blocks and concrete to build a small warehouse, where they could store beans and later house their own roasting machine. "People thought we were out of our minds," Adel recalled. Akong and Lipi, Adel's young nephew, made multiple trips to the lowlands to bring back building materials one pickup load at a time.

Patchanee explained how best to nurture seedlings, prune trees, pick only the ripest cherries, and process them using the wet method. She told them how to dry the beans on concrete patios. She brought other professors and engineers to advise on constructing a processing station, with its diverted flow of water and holding tanks. The Akha then began to build a small processing facility. They constructed several adjacent vats where the freshly pulped beans could first be washed (the unripe beans floated off) and then transferred to a fermenting vat to complete the wet process. They poured a concrete slab to serve as a drying patio.

The villagers were intrigued but mystified by all this activity. Why were Wicha, Adel, and their group doing all this construction when they would never sell coffee for much money? "They called us the Crazies," Adel said. "We had no electricity up there, nothing."

As they were building the small processing facility, Phitsanu called Wicha to tell him that his business partner, Khun Pisan, had an antique German-built coffee roaster in a warehouse in Korat, in northeastern Thailand, that he might want to look at. Pisan had bought it five years earlier at an auction, but his plans for it fell through, so it was just sitting there. When Wicha saw the rusting hulk, he was enchanted. "I want it in Doi Chang," he told Phitasanu and Pisan.

Doi Chang village had electricity from lines run from a substation down the mountain, but the transformer was not high capacity, since little current was needed. Still, Wicha figured there would be enough power for the roaster if they ran a line up from the village. But first he needed to get the huge roaster from Korat to the top of this remote Thai mountain in one piece.

It turned out that he couldn't. Instead, it had to come up the mountain in many pieces. Pisan accompanied the 6-ton roaster on a semi-trailer to Mae Suai, the city at the bottom of the mountain, along with his friends Poom and Yut. Then Wicha, Pisan, and the others, referring to the German-language manual that none could read, disassembled it, piece by piece. It took a convoy of sixteen pickup trucks to get the roaster up the mountain to Doi Chang in July 2003, at the height of the rainy season. Pisan slipped and fell down the mountain, breaking his leg, ending up in the hospital. He refused to return to the project, but he arranged for an Australian engineer to come help.

It took over a month for Akong, Adel, Wicha, and others to put the roaster together again inside the small concrete block enclosure they had built for it. Anuchit, an Akha who had worked as a mechanic in Chiang Rai on rice processing machinery, was particularly helpful. "Every time there was a problem," Wicha recalled, "we had to call someone else for advice, and when we were missing a piece, even a small screw, we had to go back to Chiang Rai or Bangkok to get the piece." Yut recalled that he thought Wicha was obsessed with a wild, unworkable idea. Nonetheless, he helped fix a faulty starter ignition. "We had to find a Bangkok machinist to make a new part," he said.

Finally, after the machine was assembled and a line had run electricity up to the building above Doi Chang village, the grand day arrived when they were to fire up the roaster. Hundreds of villagers assembled, dressed in their traditional Akha costumes, to watch as the vintage machine roared to life. As it did, it blew all the lights in the village. Wicha poured in a bag of beans and adjusted the air intake. *Ingang, Ausgung*, which one should he pull? Instead of limiting the airflow, he ended up maximizing it. The machine overheated and set fire to the beans. Smoke billowed, choking everyone in the small building. They unplugged the roaster, rushing to throw buckets of water on it.

They eventually learned how to make the roaster work, and with a new transformer they got sufficient electrical power without interrupting service to the village. Akong became the master roaster, adjusting the temperature, finding that it worked best around 200°C (392°F). That gave the beans a slow, even roast in about seventeen minutes. Patchanee wasn't surprised. "After seeing how hardworking and focused they were, I knew they would succeed."

In 2003, the Akha processed 7 tons of coffee beans. Most were sold as green beans to traders, but now that they could roast their own beans, sales to lowland coffeehouses grew steadily. Following Patchanee's advice, they had begun to cultivate seedlings and plant them to replace tomatoes and cabbages, along with shade trees to protect the coffee trees from direct sun. They used no chemical fertilizers or pesticides. The 200 acres of original trees had now swelled to several thousand acres, and for the first time in many years, the sound of birdsong returned to the hills of Doi Chang.

That same year, in February 2003, Wicha and the Akha opened their first small Doi Chaang Coffeehouse in Chiang Rai. It had four tables and was run by Wicha's wife, Nuch, with help from Akha youngsters and her own children after school. They faced a steep learning curve, and so did their customers. "When we first started," Wicha's daughter Kwan remembered, "there were few coffeehouses in Chiang Rai, and people were used to paying 7 baht for Thai-style coffee with condensed milk and lots of sugar. We were selling a small espresso for 50 baht, and no one knew what we meant when we talked about *real arabica coffee*." On opening day, they gave away free drinks, but people said they tasted too strong and bitter.

Over time, however, people began to appreciate the Doi Chaang beans for their high quality, especially when the espresso was used as the base for cappuccinos and lattes. Wicha brought in a Korean barista to teach them how to make beautiful designs in the milk atop the coffee drinks. *Farang* tourists were excited to find good coffee so far from home, and many of them came behind the counter to offer tips on how to tamp and draw espresso and steam milk properly. Nuch and her children also learned to bake scrumptious coconut, chocolate, and espresso cakes and to make passion fruit, mango, vanilla, strawberry, and coffee ice cream to accompany the coffee.

As 2003 progressed, the whirlwind of activity made it clear to Wicha that he needed help. He was good at starting new enterprises, but he was a visionary, not a details man. Someone needed to keep the books and handle correspondence. Since most Akha were illiterate—with no written language, literacy had rarely been an issue for them—that posed a problem. Then he thought of Miga, Adel's younger sister, who had just returned to China, where she was studying Mandarin.

Miga, then twenty-eight, was the youngest of seven surviving siblings and the only one in her family to attend a university, near Chiang Rai, where she earned a degree in accounting. In 1998 she had gone to China on vacation, where she had been cheated out of her money because she didn't understand the language. Taking that as a challenge, she went back to China to study Mandarin.

In August 2003, Wicha called her back, after she had paid her non-refundable tuition and school was about to begin. She returned to Doi Chang just in time to see the German roaster engulfed in flames. "There was no office," she recalled, "and there were no files." She began to put some order into the stacks of paper Wicha handed her, as she sat in her father's house in the village, surrounded by piles of coffee bags. "We had no money. Every baht we made was put back into improvements. But the company really had nothing at that time. Where would we get money from? Not from Wicha—just look at him!" she said, referring to her scrawny, somewhat disheveled mentor. "But I had to believe in him. I really had no choice, he was the leader."

When asked when she knew that the business would succeed, Miga could not identify a turning point. "It wasn't something I ever thought about. We just processed, roasted, transported, and sold coffee. There were seven of us, working all day. I never thought about where it was going. We just had to show everyone we were working hard."

Soon afterward, they opened a small Doi Chaang coffeeshop near the roaster on the mountaintop to educate themselves and villagers about the taste of their own coffee, to impress potential buyers, and to sell to the occasional tourist. "We didn't know how to make coffee. We didn't start from zero, we started from somewhere negative," Miga said. As happened in the Chiang Rai shop, the kindness of interested strangers gave them a boost. Dr. Joanna Critchly, a Scottish coffee-loving philosopher who was backpacking around Thailand, stayed with them for a few weeks and gave them tutorials in brewing methods. She also told them about the Specialty Coffee Association of America (SCAA) and its emphasis on quality.

Meanwhile, at the end of 2003, Wicha opened the Doi Chaang Coffee House in Bangkok, an elegant affair that also served as an office. There he and Phitsanu drew up business plans, met buyers, and developed operating procedures for other coffeehouses they planned to open.

By 2004, optimism and coffee momentum were growing in Doi Chang, and not just from Wicha's efforts. Mike Mann's Integrated Tribal Development Program (ITDP) had reached the village in 2002, when he facilitated the formation of an Akha coffee cooperative with other local farmers, helped them with an irrigation project, and sold some of their beans to Japan. Then Mann decided that if Starbucks was operating coffeehouses in Thailand, why weren't they sourcing beans there as well? He persuaded the American chain to test samples from ten villages. Five types of beans, including beans from Doi Chang, were chosen to be included in a Starbucks blend called Muan Jai, which means "wholehearted happiness." In September 2003, when the blend was introduced, a few traditionally clad farmers from Doi Chang and Huey Haum were brought to Bangkok for photo ops. Mann considered this exploitation, but it helped put Doi Chang on the coffee map.

Sandra Joins Wicha

IN MARCH 2004, Kornkranok "Sandra" Bunmusik, the owner of a competing coffeehouse in Bangkok, met Wicha at a food exhibition. This meeting would have a dramatic impact on Doi Chaang Coffee. As a child, Sandra, whose father was a Thai government bureaucrat, had moved every few years as he was shifted to a new post. She learned to adapt and make new friends quickly and also became adept at learning new dialects and languages. At Khon Kaen University in northeastern Thailand, she majored in English but also studied Buddhism, which became an important part of her life. After graduation, secretarial work in a furniture factory bored her, but she then became a well-paid executive at a large insurance firm. That led in 1997 to an MBA program in the United States at Western Michigan University. "I planned to work in development administration with UNICEF," she said.

While studying, Sandra discovered the joys of specialty coffee at Starbucks and other coffeehouses. "In Thailand, I had drunk instant Nescafé with tons of sugar and milk. I had never had really good coffee, and in the usa I learned to love it." When she returned to Thailand in 2000, she decided that at thirty-five maybe she was too old to start at unicef or another development agency, and besides, she had fallen in love with coffee. She opened her own small coffeeshop in Bangkok. While she had been in the United States, Starbucks had opened its first Thai outlet, and now a few other independent cafés were also opening in Bangkok. With a four-person staff, Sandra was open from early morning until 9 p.m., serving three simple meals along with the coffee. She got her single blend from Aroma, a city roaster. "I had no idea where the beans came from, and I had never seen coffee growing," she recalled.

Then she and a friend attended a business exhibit, where she had a booth to sell her coffee. While she minded the booth, her friend, who had been walking around, came running back. "Sandra! You've got to go see this guy. He's selling coffee grown in Thailand, and he says it's the best in the world." Leaving the booth with her friend, Sandra went to see for herself. "Just try it!" the little man with the scraggly beard was saying. "You'll see. Doi Chaang Coffee is the best." Sandra sampled a cup. It was indeed superb. Entranced, she listened as Wicha told the story of the poverty-stricken Akha, how Adel had come to him, asking for help, and the extraordinary transformation that the village was undergoing. "You should visit, you'll see," he said.

The next month, Sandra flew to Chiang Rai with a friend and rented a truck. It took five hours to drive up the muddy road from Chiang Rai to Doi Chang. "If he had told me what it would be like to get up there, I wouldn't have come." She arrived, exhausted, at 7 p.m. Wicha and the Akha had had no idea they were coming (there was no cell phone reception in those days), but they made the newcomers welcome as best they could. They sat around a campfire, talking and gazing up at the stars, then slept in a small hut on the floor, covered by a blanket. Sandra wasn't used to bugs crawling on her and didn't get much sleep, but in the morning, she loved the mountain views and the glossy green leaves of the coffee trees, and she was impressed with the old German roaster and processing facility. The Akha were friendly and enthusiastic. She knew she would return.

Back in Bangkok, Sandra switched from Aroma to Doi Chaang Coffee. Wicha gave her advice on how to make good coffee, how to draw the best shots of espresso, and how to make lovely latte art with steamed milk on top. In 2006, he asked her to join Doi Chaang Coffee to help him expand sales and marketing in Thailand. Wicha was boundlessly and infectiously optimistic and ambitious. Sandra eventually closed her own coffeeshop to devote herself full-time to Doi Chaang.

Wicha was still not content, though, despite how well things were going. He wanted to export Doi Chaang beans. He wanted them to be recognized throughout the world. But how?

CHAPTER 5

Khun John from Canada

PONDERING HOW SHE might help Wicha Promyong introduce Doi Chaang Coffee to the rest of the world, Sandra Bunmusik thought of her old friend John Darch, whom she had met in 1997 when she worked at the Thai insurance agency. Darch, a former banker who had become a Canadian mining entrepreneur, had been coming to Thailand for years as part of exploration efforts that discovered a huge potash deposit in the northeastern part of the country. His company, Asia Pacific Resources, had tried in vain to get a green light from the Thai bureaucracy to begin operations. In June 2006, control of the Asia Pacific potash concession was bought by Italian-Thai Development, a huge Thai construction company, for over $80 million.

Sandra had kept up her friendship with John Darch over the years, and now it occurred to her that, as an internationally savvy businessman, he might be able to advise Wicha. Shortly before the sale of Asia Pacific, she called to see if he was at his Bangkok office. He was. "Khun John," she started, using the common Thai honorific that goes beyond "Mister," implying far more respect. "Khun John, there's someone I would like you to meet here in Bangkok.

Wicha is this wonderful man who is helping a hill tribe to produce really great coffee. He isn't looking for funding, just international contacts. Could you meet with him?"

Darch listened politely, and just as politely agreed to meet Wicha. He knew nothing about the coffee business and suspected that Wicha was indeed fishing for money, but he trusted Sandra, who was an intelligent, self-assured woman, behind the shy courtesy required in Thai women. Besides, when a friend asked something like this of you in Thailand, you agreed, but that didn't mean anything had to come of it. He would probably give this man a small donation, and that would be it.

Sandra brought Darch to Wicha's small Bangkok office, hardly bigger than a closet, where a small, wiry man sat cross-legged on a pile of cushions. He wore loose-fitting clothes with a sash around his waist and had a raggedy beard, earrings, and a shaved head, other than the multiple little pigtails held by colored ribbons. "Khun John," Sandra said, "I am pleased to introduce you to Khun Wicha." After indicating that her friend should take a seat in a chair opposite the little man, Sandra sat to one side on the floor.

As John Darch seated himself, he thought, *This guy looks like a cross between a monk and a hippy.* He half expected to be offered a joint, but Wicha disarmed him by asking, "Would you like some of my special green tea?"

"I thought you would offer me coffee," Darch said.

"I don't actually like coffee that much," Wicha admitted, "but it's good for my people. I drink many cups a day anyway, just to make sure of the quality. But let me tell you about the Akha and their coffee."

Over the next several hours and more tea, Wicha told the story of the Akha. As Darch listened, he thought about his own limited encounter with hill tribes. When he had first come to Thailand, he had taken part in all of the expected tourist activities, joining other *farangs* in temple tours, shopping for jade and clothes at the floating market—and visiting a Hmong hill tribe village near Chiang Mai. Such forays to carefully staged hill tribe villages were the second-largest tourist attraction in the country. "They took us on buses," Darch recalled, "so we could see these quaint people living in grass huts with naked children running wild with pigs and chickens. The tourists could take snapshots of smiling village women with elongated necks, their teeth blackened from betel-chewing." He had been mildly embarrassed, uncomfortable at the zoo-like atmosphere, but he gave a few coins to the children, as did many other tourists. Now he was hearing a riveting story about a particular tribe and place.

Wicha went on to explain how Adel had come to ask for his help, how he, Wicha, had spent many years roaming through the mountains, getting to know the hill tribes, and becoming increasingly outraged by the way they were treated. Young people were leaving their home villages because there was no future for them there other than grinding poverty. In the cities, lured by promises of a better life, they found themselves a despised minority, forced to take the most menial jobs. The girls frequently ended up as prostitutes. When they were mistreated, they had no one to turn to, not even the police, who were often bribed by Thai brothel owners.

Finally, Wicha told the story of the last few years and the remarkable success of Doi Chaang Coffee. Young people were beginning to return to the village, now that coffee might provide some kind of future for them there. "We grow the best beans in the world," Wicha said. "We need to find a way to export them for what they are worth. We are not asking for gifts. We don't want charity. The Akha are not beggars. Sandra said that you might have connections or suggestions." He explained that organizations from Korea, Japan, and North America had come to Doi Chang and offered to invest, but they all wanted at least 51 percent, a controlling interest. "The Akha came out of 200 years of slavery," Wicha said, "and I am not going to put them back into it."

Darch was impressed. Wicha had not asked him for money after all. He was not trying to sell him anything, either. He portrayed the Akha as dignified, hardworking people who just needed an opportunity. Darch was relatively wealthy, having done well in the stock market, selling shares of Asia Pacific Resources and other enterprises he had promoted and managed. He had promised his wife, Louise, that he would retire, but no one who knew John Darch believed that for a minute. He had come to love Thailand and its diverse peoples and environments. Maybe this was a new opportunity for him to use his business skills as well as his interest in making the world a slightly better place.

In the same way that Wicha's life could be seen as preparing him for the moment Adel asked for his help, John Darch's life might be seen as a similar preparation for his meeting with Wicha. The two men couldn't have looked less similar. Wicha, the slightly built Thai Muslim, had lived a vagabond existence. Darch, three years older than Wicha, was much taller, solidly built, and slightly overweight, and he had pursued a career as a banker and mining venture capitalist.

Yet there were uncanny similarities between Wicha Promyong and John Darch, and the two men who had grown up in such different cultures on opposite sides of the world seemed destined to form a close friendship akin to a brotherly bond and a partnership that would pioneer an alternative form of capitalism. This kind of enterprise would make sure that the profits flowed in an equitable way back to those who did the most important work.

Back to His Youth

AS HE LISTENED to the story of the Akha, John Darch thought back to something his mother had told him when he was growing up in a solid middle-class household in Weymouth, England. His parents owned, lived in, and worked in an old converted four-story hotel. On the first floor, Francis and Elizabeth Darch, his parents, presided over F. Darch Cycles and Motorcycles. His father worked in the back, repairing bicycles and motorcycles and making toys and clocks. His mother ran the front of the shop, kept the books, and served customers. "Mum was the real business lady, the driving force who dealt with salesmen and bankers," Darch recalled. "Dad was a gentle soul who would have been happy to drink tea and talk with his brothers all day if not for Mum."

His parents raised their five children to value honesty, hard work, and compassion. "One day I was playing with the toys and bicycles in the store, and my mother noticed some little kids staring in the shop window." They were obviously hungry for the goods that their parents could not afford for them. "John," his mother said, "you must never forget that the only difference between you and those children is an accident of birth. You didn't do anything special to deserve to be on this side of the window, playing with these toys. It doesn't make you any better or them any less deserving."

Elizabeth was also something of a risk taker. She liked to tell the story of how, during World War II, an unexploded German bomb was wedged in the floorboards, and she was about to hammer to dislodge it when horrified soldiers stopped her. Her son apparently inherited her appetite for risk, as his career would eventually demonstrate.

At the age of eighteen, Darch married his girlfriend Dorothy. "I knew it was a mistake," he recalled, "but I did not have the courage to back out." The couple had four children—John Alexander, born in 1966, Robert, in 1968, Katharine, 1970, and Sophie, 1972. Darch joined the Weymouth branch of National Westminster Bank in July 1965, four months before his wedding. Banking might appear a rather staid occupation, but for Darch it held the promise of change and possible adventure. "I knew the bank would move me every few years. The thought of walking down the same path to the same job for the next forty years was like going to prison." Still, joining a bank was akin to a career in the armed forces—it was regarded as a lifetime commitment, with a slow, steady progression up the ladder until retirement.

Darch became a loan officer in 1973, and although some parts of banking were mundane, he enjoyed the challenge of qualifying applicants, combining number crunching with character reading. At age twenty-seven, he was transferred as assistant manager to the bank's area office in Bournemouth. His new boss took every opportunity to belittle him, but fortunately he soon retired. He was replaced by David Giddings, who encouraged Darch's creativity and initiative. If a loan had been turned down at the branch level, Giddings suggested that Darch should look for a way to turn it around and make a deal after all. Giddings treated his staff well. He became an important mentor for the aspiring young banker, and when Darch applied for a job at the Royal Bank of Canada, Giddings congratulated him on his sense of adventure.

Though Darch didn't get that job—he was seen as overqualified for the position—six months later the Canadian bank offered him a better job at the head office in Ottawa at a salary four times what he was making in England. When Darch told the branch chief that he would be departing for Canada, the chief reacted badly. "How could you do this after all the bank has done for you? You're burning your bridges, young man. Don't think you can ever come crawling back here." Undeterred, Darch sold his home and all his possessions and left for Canada with his wife and children in January 1977. He was twenty-nine years old.

A Canadian Banker

PART OF THE reason John Darch decided to try life in a new country across the Atlantic was to save his marriage. "I kept thinking,

If only I do this or that, if only I move to a new place, if only I make more money, things might get better," he recalled. "But it never was better, regardless of what I bought or did." Because of his failing marriage, Darch focused his love and passion on his children and his work.

After serving a probationary period in Ottawa, he was assigned to the Peterborough branch of the Royal Bank of Canada, four hours to the southwest, as an assistant manager. He stayed in a motel during the week, driving home to Ottawa on weekends. He missed his children. Relations with his wife were volatile. He hated the frigid weather. He had been thrust unprepared into a position of authority over his seniors, who resented him, regarding him as an immigrant who had displaced a more deserving Canadian. Maybe this had been a huge mistake. One cold November day, he found himself overwhelmed, sitting in the bank parking lot, crying uncontrollably.

His weeping proved to be a pivotal catharsis. "It was like flipping a switch. After I dried my eyes, all my apprehension was gone." His family moved to Peterborough soon afterward, where they stayed for two years, but Darch never got used to the cold or to driving in blizzards. He told the bank executives that he had to be transferred to the coast or he would return to England. They finally obliged him.

In April 1979, Darch moved his family to Vancouver, British Columbia, where it was far more likely to rain than snow, and where the rugged mountains swept down to the sea. "I thought it was heaven." He quickly settled into his job at the Vancouver branch of the Royal Bank of Canada as a senior commercial loan manager, supervising a staff of fifty. Vancouver was the world headquarters for start-up mines and risk-taking entrepreneurs, who made and lost millions, apparently without batting an eye. Darch didn't get along with his immediate boss, but he took to the high-rolling scene, quickly getting to know clients who referred other hopeful borrowers to him. He enjoyed putting likely bank clients together to work on projects. "I just liked networking, looking for opportunities," he recalled.

Darch particularly appreciated getting to know on a personal level some of the characters he had for clients. One, Gerry Wright, a hard-drinking Irish engineer for whom he arranged a car loan, would feature strongly in his life. "Gerry was great fun and kept me in fits with his jokes at our lunches."

In 1980, one of Darch's bank clients introduced him to Gary Crawford, an Australian gold miner. Crawford wanted to restart placer mining operations in the Yukon area of Bear Creek and Fraser, to look for gold in the alluvial (sand) deposits. Darch authorized a $50,000 loan, and at Crawford's invitation, flew up for a few days that July to take a look. He invited Wright to come along. Wright, who had a doctorate in water resources, had been working on drainage for a mine in Jakarta, so it seemed logical that he should help with the placer operation, which was all about controlling water flow while separating gold nuggets from sand and dirt.

Darch loved the romance of the wild Yukon, much preferring its rugged vistas, adventure, and miners' bars to his coat-and-tie bank office and conservative boss. He pondered how he might continue to have such exhilarating experiences periodically, while being his own boss.

Blarney, Bluster, Adventure

OVER BEERS, DARCH and Wright talked about all the money they saw thrown around in the mining world. "Many of these guys were successful despite themselves," Darch observed, "so we figured we could do better." What if they combined their talents and struck out on their own as consultants to snag some of those dollars for themselves? Darch, with his British accent, well-researched sales pitch, and banking background, paired well with Dr. Gerald Wright, the engineer who could charm clients with his Irish jokes while explaining the nitty-gritty of the geological exploration. Their long-time mutual lawyer, George Brazier, explained: "John was gentle and could get things done without causing too much disturbance. Gerry was more hit-you-between-the-eyes to get his point across. He's Irish, you know. They were a good team; they complemented one another." Or as Paul Royce, their accountant, observed, "John was the ideas man, Gerry more the front man."

As they were discussing what to call their new enterprises, Wright looked out the window and saw a sign for Cypress Street. He became Cypress Consulting. Darch settled on Western Investments, since they were located on the west coast of Canada.

With great hopes and bravado, Darch resigned from the bank in the summer of 1981, but he soon found that many of his great friendships were really client relationships that cooled when he no longer had the bank's money to lend. He did get a lead through his association with Gary Crawford, though. Gold Sciences, an American corporation, was looking for mining projects to serve as assets behind their gold bond portfolio, and they had struck a deal with Crawford to buy Bear Creek and Fraser, along with another nearby property. Gold Sciences wanted Darch to monitor the books, pay the bills, and file reports.

They didn't need Wright, so Darch spent the summer of 1982 in the Yukon, where he got a good dose of local life during the long days and nights when the sun never set. Miners blew all their pay once a month in Dawson City on women and booze. Once, when Gold Sciences failed to send money, a miner threatened to kill him. Darch became friendly with the local police.

The gold operation was "so basic and fundamental," Darch recalled, as he observed the water from roaring creeks being diverted in channels to wash out the gold. At one spot, he and a miner saw a worker attempting to steal gold by placing a chain across a river. Darch had to prevent the miner from shooting the worker.

At that point, the price of gold had dropped to $300 an ounce from its high of around $800 two years earlier, but it was still profitable if you could find the nuggets without too many expenses. In this case, the profits couldn't justify the expense, and on Darch's advice, Gold Sciences closed down. When the season ended, Gold Sciences was unable to settle its bills, so Darch borrowed money from the bank to do so, using a large Caterpillar bulldozer as collateral.

In December, Darch and Wright heard of a promising project in Atlin, in northern British Columbia, on Otter Creek. It had produced very large nuggets but was difficult to mine because it lay beneath 200 feet of dirt. The partners agreed to pay $100,000 for the prospecting rights to the two owners, Ken O'Connor and Ken Watson.

For seed capital, John Darch called his old boss, David Giddings. "Have you got any money, Dave? I need some," Darch began. "Well, don't we all?" Giddings laughed. "I've left the bank," Darch continued. "Gerry and I are going up to the Yukon to work on a placer deposit, and we need some seed corn." Giddings sent him £4,000 to help him get started. "I thought they would do well," Giddings said. "John was a good talker, quite a charmer, and he understood money."

They came up with a $50,000 down payment for the Atlin claim, agreeing to pay the balance in three months. "We got along with O'Connor," Darch recalled, "but Watson saw us as suckers who would never come up with the rest of the money." So Darch struck an ingenious deal with O'Connor. "Ken, you lend us the $50,000, and we'll pay off the debt. You'll get $25,000 back immediately, with the other half going to Watson, and we'll still owe you the full $50,000. Plus, you'll be out of your partnership with Watson." O'Connor agreed, and he also agreed to take the Caterpillar, worth $40,000, plus $10,000 in cash to pay off the debt.

That winter, Darch and Wright hired Leo, a former mine manager, to drive his big truck with them up to Dawson City to retrieve the Caterpillar. Once there, Leo went off with his buddies, leaving Wright and Darch with the truck. They had a few drinks with Darch's police officer pals, then drove for dinner and more drinks with friends up the hill. By the time they left, they were quite drunk. As they drove around town, they decided it would be a great lark to knock down all of the stop signs. Amazingly, though the police caught them, they got away with only a fine, and they paid Leo for the damage to his truck.

In retrospect, it's astonishing that Darch and Wright eventually became millionaires, because in the early 1980s they lurched from one unsuccessful venture to another, albeit still somehow making money. "That's the nature of venture capitalism, though," Darch observed, "where the odds of success are a million to one."

They acquired the Atlin claim but needed to raise money to develop it, so they hired a geologist to review their leases and write a report, which showed that the mine did have real potential. It also revealed that there was a 3-meter gap between the two leased properties, so Wright went up and staked that sliver of land as well. After failing to raise sufficient development money, they ended up selling the Atlin rights back to Ken O'Connor, including $80,000 for the new "spoiler" claim. O'Connor went on to develop the placer mine profitably.

During that same period, a friend introduced Darch to Orville Gillespie, the president and majority shareholder of Caroline Mines, once known as the "princess of Canadian gold mines." The share price having dropped from $50 to $8, operations had ceased, and Gillespie needed money for redevelopment. Agreeing to work on a contingency fee basis, with Gillespie covering their expenses, Darch and Wright flew to London, where they knew no one, but as Canadians (albeit with English and Irish accents), they had the advantage of being seen as swashbuckling entrepreneurs. Through Lions Mining, a fledgling British company, Darch and Wright were introduced to James Hamilton, who worked for an Australian brokerage firm, and other London brokers who pledged $20 million to Caroline Mines, with the condition that Orville Gillespie step down as president. Gillespie refused, but since the partners had secured the money, they were still paid their fee of $50,000, even though the deal fell through.

And so it went. Darch and Wright fell into one complex international deal after another, creating a network of useful contacts, and as their reputation for fund-raising grew, people sought them out. "By the mid-eighties," Darch recalled, "we were the flavor of the week." It was at this point that Darch, looking back, compared the growth of his multiple enterprises to branches beginning to sprout off the trunk of a tree.

For their joint ventures, Darch and Wright created Canadian Crew Energy (later renamed Crew Development) in 1985. That same year, James Hamilton called from London. "I have a client in Australia buying a mine in Aurora, Nevada, looking for a Canadian shell company and investors. Can you help out?" Darch knew that there were innumerable "shell companies"— the remains of failed public ventures that still retained a legal status as businesses— available for a song, since Vancouver mining ventures suffered a huge casualty rate. He and Wright found such a shell, renamed it Nevada Goldfields Corporation, and became directors and officers in October 1985, holding 10 percent of the shares from the shell corporation. A prospectus featuring a youthful-looking Darch as vice president and Wright as a director boasted: "With three precious metals projects on the verge of production—all in the heart of America's historic gold mine country—Nevada Goldfields

Corporation has, in less than a year, succeeded in fulfilling its plan to become a significant contributor to the world's gold reserves." Investors pledged over $20 million.

Also in 1985, Darch and Wright were approached by employees of BC Hydro about a geothermal project in northern British Columbia called Meager Creek. During the oil crisis of the 1970s, BC Hydro had drilled several deep test wells that found temperatures of up to 275°F. But with declining oil prices in the mid-1980s, BC Hydro abandoned the project and planned to plug the hole. Darch thought, *This is the way the world will go, with alternative energy like geothermal power.*

As part of the deal, Canadian Crew Energy owned half of the shares and persuaded the Canadian government to grant a thirty-year renewable geothermal lease in 1987. New development began in 1991, but was suspended in 1995, then resumed in 2001, with drilling on three more test wells in 2004 and 2005. Darch's company sold the South Meager lease to Ram Power Corporation in 2010. Although the geothermal resource had yet to be successfully developed, he made money on the venture by judiciously selling shares along the way, as he did with many other enterprises.

Darch's personal life was also evolving at this time. He divorced Dorothy in 1986, and in February 1987, married Louise. The day the couple closed on their new home, the stock market collapsed. It was October 19, 1987, which came to be known as Black Monday. By the end of October, stock markets in North America had fallen by a fifth of their value. "I was lucky I had to sell a lot of my shares in Nevada Goldfields in order to buy that house, just before the crash," Darch said. "God must have been looking after me."

The consulting partners' next adventure took them to Texas, where an investor and gas operator named Michael Gustin persuaded them to help raise venture capital for an oil and gas project. Darch and Wright pulled in Brian Johnson, an Australian billionaire who agreed to help fund the Texas project.

The investment failed to flourish. The gas and oil never flowed, Gustin couldn't account for much of the money, and Brian Johnson's other projects went belly up at the same time. He went from being a billionaire to bankruptcy in three short years, but the two Canadian partners survived without much damage. "It's always better to do business with other people's money, I've found," Darch's banking mentor David Giddings wryly observed. Darch and Wright specialized in "junior" mining operations that were in the exploratory or development stages, and as one of their documents for potential investors warned, "Few properties which are explored are ultimately developed into producing mines... Mining operations generally involve a high degree of risk."

Anyone who invests in penny stocks has to understand that start-up mining companies have a high casualty rate. "Generally, there is a one in a thousand chance of going from a discovery to taking it to exploration," Darch observed, "and then one in another thousand to become operational. You could call it legalized gambling, if you look at the odds. All such young companies will disappear—either because nothing will come of them, or because they will be taken over by a larger corporation. My investors hung in with me because they knew that if I fell over, I'd get up and continue with something else. So you may have invested in Crew and it didn't work, but the shares were not just wallpaper. I'd be looking for something else." Also, share prices would go up as well as down, and wise investors who sold at the right time could make a handsome profit.

Fortunately, Darch and Wright had been careful to insulate themselves from personal risk. They had also invested in a shell company called Asia Pacific Resources that Brian Johnson had begun and put $5 million into because he was interested in the region and wanted to explore possibilities there. "We did a deal with the receiver for Brian Johnson's company to buy their controlling shares of Asia Pacific in 1988," Darch said, "and now we were not just consultants but majority shareholders of a shell company."

But what could they do with it? The year before, Robert Anderson, a geologist, had approached Darch and Wright, looking for a job. Having once worked for Broken Hill Proprietary Company (BHP), one of the world's largest mining enterprises, Anderson knew that there was potash potential in Thailand. "You fellows need a world-class project," he said, "not these piddly bits you've been dealing with." Now, with Asia Pacific Resources, they had an appropriate name for an operation in Thailand.

The Potash Project

MINED POTASH IS the primary source for the potassium in chemical fertilizer, the "K" in NPK (nitrogen, phosphorous, potassium). Before the industrial mining era, potash was made by soaking wood ashes in water, which explains why it was called "pot ash" (and it's the source of the word "potassium"). Until the late nineteenth century, much of the world's potash came from Canadian ash-leaching processes, but then German mining of mineral salts containing potassium chloride superseded the ash process. In the 1950s, a major potash deposit was discovered in Saskatchewan, putting the Canadians back into competition.

Most of the world's potassium was deposited when seawater in ancient inland oceans evaporated, leaving a mixture of sodium chloride (table salt) and potassium chloride (potash ore). As the millennia passed, these deposits were covered with dirt, so that many deposits are far below ground level. Consequently, most potash mines feature shafts going down thousands of feet.

Potash deposits have been found around the globe, most notably in countries such as Canada, Russia, Belarus, Germany, China, Chile, and Brazil. With China's economy and population growing, it was clear that there was a market for Asian potash. While China had some deposits of its own, it had to import most of its potash, primarily from Canada, Belarus, and Russia. A cheaper source in nearby Thailand would find a ready market.

Darch, Wright, and Anderson flew to Thailand for the first time in 1987 and met Dr. Anant Suwanapal, who had been working to develop potash and other rock salts in Thailand for ten years. Dr. Anant suggested that they talk with the principal executives of the Metro Group, a conglomerate of 200 prestigious Thai companies. The group was active in numerous areas, including steel, flour, agro-chemicals, and fertilizer, and was part of a partnership that had secured the only concession from the Thai government for a potash mine. In 1992, Darch and Wright finally acquired a 62.5 percent interest in the project in return for raising the necessary money.

"By 1996 we had raised $70 million," Darch said, "but of course it didn't all happen at once." First, they had to prove that there were indeed major potash deposits in Thailand. They conducted a test drilling program in the Udon Thani province of northeastern Thailand, with some hundred drill holes proving that there was a continuous bed of potash deposited there. Not only that, it wasn't several thousand feet below ground but a mere 300 meters, about 1,000 feet, and it had a billion ton potential. At the beginning of the project in 1992, Asia Pacific was a typical penny stock, selling for 15 cents a share. As the test drilling proceeded, the price climbed to $4 in 1994, shooting up to $11 by the spring of 1996.

As the stock price rose, Darch and Wright prudently sold what Darch called "bits and pieces" of their shares, building their cash portfolios. That turned out to be a good thing. In early December 1996, the bottom fell out of the Asian stock market, starting in Thailand. The value of the Thai baht collapsed when it was unpegged from the US dollar. The Metro Group, with its 25 percent interest in Asia Pacific Resources, held $500 million in international debt—due in baht. Consequently, the Metro directors were eager to liquidate their assets. Darch and Wright saw an opportunity to improve their holdings from 62.5 percent to 90 percent of Asia Pacific, with the Thai government holding the other 10 percent, as arranged by Dr. Anant. He also instigated changes to Thai laws, which took effect three years later, so that mines 100 meters or more below the surface were not required to purchase surface land, only to pay compensation in the event of damage on the surface.

Darch and Wright could have raised the necessary $40 million to buy out Metro in 1997 by issuing more shares of stock, but that would have diluted the value of their own shares. Instead, they took a convertible debt loan from the Olympus Group, based in Hong Kong, which meant that Olympus retained the right to purchase Asia Pacific shares for a set price, even if the share prices declined. But Darch and Wright were sure that wouldn't happen. Besides, they were negotiating with Norsk Hydro, a huge Norwegian conglomerate, to acquire an equity position in order to get the Thai potash for its fertilizer.

A senior executive for Norsk Hydro signed a contract with Asia Pacific to purchase equity in the joint venture, subject to board approval. Then, to everyone's shock, in March 2001, after more than two years of discussion and planning, the Norsk board members nixed the deal, saying that they did not want to be involved in potash mine development in Asia after all. They thought it was too risky.

In the midst of this tumult, six of the eight board members of Asia Pacific, on which both Darch and Wright served, approached Darch and demanded that Wright resign because his behavior had become erratic and he had become "impossible to deal with," as one board director said. Reluctantly, Darch agreed, and on March 21, 2001, Gerry Wright resigned. The previous year, Wright had also resigned as cochairman of Crew Development, as part of the deteriorating partnership/friendship between Darch and Wright.

In 2002, when the Olympus Group took over management of Asia Pacific, Darch resigned from the board but retained 2.5 percent of the shares.

In the Meantime, Diamonds, Tin, Gold, Nickel...

DURING 1992–2002, John Darch had been busy with other mining and energy ventures around the world, in addition to Thai potash. In 1997 the partners changed the name of Canadian Crew Energy to Crew Development, because the focus was changing to include exploration, development, and income properties, which would lead to investments in gold in Greenland, tin in the United Kingdom, nickel in the Philippines, and diamonds in Botswana and South Africa, among other ventures. "It was the period when my former partner Gerry and I were most active," Darch recalled. "For me it was a very exciting, challenging, and rewarding time. When people asked me why and how I did all these things, my honest reaction was that I never thought I could not." Although it may be hard to believe, he asserted that his primary motivation wasn't money. "I truly believed in the projects and what they could be. I could visualize them up and running."

Sometimes his visualizations came true, but often they did not. There were moments of controversy and one horrific tragedy. In 1993, Darch and Wright became involved in diamond exploration in Botswana with geologist Norman Lock, who had grown up in Botswana and had previously worked for De Beers, the venerable diamond firm. Together, Darch, Wright, and Lock formed a new entity called Botswana Diamondfields. But exploratory drilling failed to find diamonds. Consequently, in 1996 they acquired the Rovic mine in South Africa, which had begun as an open pit operation in the early 1900s, then became an underground mine. With Lock's advice and leadership, they engaged Metorex, a South African mining company, to manage Rovic, with the intention of upgrading the mine to increase production. Initial results were encouraging. By summer's end, a large 17-carat diamond had been found.

Darch and his wife, Louise, flew to South Africa in early November 1996 to examine the Rovic mine and meet with Norman Lock and the Metorex executives. Darch remained aboveground to talk to the mining manager, while Louise donned coveralls, boots, gloves, and a hardhat to go down 200 meters into the mine. "I wasn't afraid," she recalled, "but the enclosure we were in rattled all the way down." She and other visitors were escorted by miners, who wore helmets but no shirts, down a ladder from which she could make out huge holes leading to offshoots.

Two weeks later, a main beam in the Rovic mine collapsed, flooding the mine with an avalanche of water and mud. Twenty miners were trapped inside. Only four of the bodies could be recovered. The other sixteen victims remained entombed in the mine, which was sealed and never reopened. Darch's company agreed to a million dollar settlement. "Those deaths haunted me for years and years," Darch said. "Metorex, our subsidiary, had fine people who had intended to improve the mine. So it had nothing to do with reckless exploitation of the workers. Of course, I would never have allowed Louise or anyone else to go down there if I had had any idea of the danger." The experience did not put him off mining, however. "It didn't make me think that mining was a terrible thing. It just made me aware of how fragile life is, and how little control you have over it."

Darch was not involved in any other such mining disasters. In early 1997, Crew Development acquired half-ownership of Metorex, which went on to develop several other successful, money-making mining ventures in copper, coal, zinc, fluorite, gold, antimony, and cobalt, all in southern Africa. In 2002, Crew Development sold some of its Metorex shares for $12.6 million, while retaining 21 percent of the mining company.

Darch and Wright also invested in South Crofty, the last tin mine in Cornwall, England, in August 1994, hoping to make it a profitable venture and keep much-needed jobs there. They were hailed as saviors. The worldwide price of tin had collapsed in 1985, when the International Tin Agreement lapsed, and it had never fully recovered. In mid-1995, the price of tin rose sharply, inspiring hope, but then fell again. Drilling to find more tin in the South Crofty mine uncovered ore of a lower grade than anticipated.

Darch asked David Giddings, his old bank mentor, to go to Cornwall to assess the situation. Giddings had retired from banking and was then a "company doctor," specializing in turning around troubled businesses. "I was horrified by the whole thing," Giddings said. "A third of their expenses were for overtime." To keep the half-mile-deep mine dry, 2 million gallons of water a day had to be pumped out of it. The ore contained 1.4 percent tin, which had to be crushed and separated. At the same time, the British pound strengthened in relation to the US dollar. Having to pay expenses in pounds, while taking income in dollars, was crippling them. "The operation was losing two million pounds a year," Giddings reported, and the mine had to be closed down. "It was very sad."

Fortunately, Darch and Wright also made a successful investment, assuming majority ownership of Nalunaq, the first gold mine in Greenland, discovered in 1993 and located on the southern tip of the island. The Greenland gold venture came about in 1999, when Crew Development merged with Mindex, a Norwegian company that also held mining interests in the Philippines and West Africa. By that time, Darch and Wright had raised a total of $170 million for various potential projects, and Crew Development was internationally known. The Norwegians approached Darch and Wright, who saw the merger as a way to increase their holdings and gain access to wealthy investors in Norway. The merger contract contained some fine print, however, saying that once the deal was 94 percent financed, the balance had to be paid.

"I received a short e-mail," Darch recalled, "saying that we had reached that minimum and that $4 million was now due in cash. I flew to London, drove to Capital Group, and explained the situation, asking for half of the money. I told them that I had someone else putting up $2 million." After receiving a stern lecture, Darch got their pledge. Then he went to Equitable Life, where he explained that Capital Group had put up half of the required cash, and he got the balance a few days before Christmas 1999. "So you see, I never told a lie," Darch explained, "but at times I shaded the truth a bit."

The deal left the Mindex investors with 75 percent control of Crew Development, but Darch wasn't worried. "We were in a glorious situation, with projects all over the world. The Norwegians were hungry for our company, with exciting prospects. We were making acquisitions. If we needed $10 million, it could be done within days."

As the gold mine in Greenland prospered, the plans for mining in the Philippines ran into trouble. Despite having obtained a mining license from the Philippine government and having spent a great deal of money and time planning the project, the mining venture was halted before it really began by protests from a coalition of environmental groups, church organizations, politicians, and local activists.

Plans had called for nickel and cobalt mining in the central mountains of Mindoro Island, where eight indigenous tribes, collectively called the Mangyans, lived. Like the hill tribes of

Thailand, they practiced subsistence agriculture and hunting, and until recently they had had little contact with lowland civilization. In 1997, Mindex received an exploration permit; two years later, the company agreed to pay a royalty of 2 percent of sales to the Mangyan community. Striving for environmental and social acceptability, the company also paid for a free local medical clinic, road maintenance, and the construction of culverts, bridges, and schools. Crew/Mindex paid for plant nurseries to cultivate 10,000 seedlings of hardwood and fruit-bearing trees and bamboo, while supporting local cultural and sporting activities. Nonetheless, protests led the government to cancel the company's mining license in July 2001.

Soon afterward, John Darch went to the Philippines. He and the Canadian ambassador to the Philippines were flown by helicopter to a mountaintop village, in hopes of explaining the benefits of the mine. Promising to mine only 10 hectares at any given time, Crew also planned to replace topsoil, replant trees, supply cheap fertilizer and power, and dispose of the tailings far off, deep in the ocean.

Inside the jam-packed assembly hall, the moderator told Darch, "Just explain your position to the people." For ten minutes, Darch tried to do just that, but the crowd shouted over him in various languages, including English, "Give us back our land! We don't want you here!" The ambassador whispered to Darch, "Let's leave. Don't stop walking." The crowd parted, and they were able to depart safely, but it had been a tense and hopeless meeting. Back in Manila, Darch met with Philippine president Gloria Macapagal-Arroyo, who was sympathetic but said she could not reissue the mining license, since she would be accused (unjustly) of corruption.

At the next annual general meeting of Crew Development, a group of Norwegian shareholders tried to oust Darch and move the company to Norway. In 2002, he bowed to the inevitable and stepped down from the Crew Development board, though he continued to run a subsidiary, North Pacific Geopower, which held the South Meager geothermal project. He sold his shares in Crew over the next few years, but he continued to pursue other, unrelated projects.

"From 1997, when we first started Crew Development, to 2001, Crew was massively successful," Darch said in retrospect. The company had projects on which the sun never set, and they were diversified. "We had raised $44.3 million, had $40 million cash in the bank, and an income stream from South African subsidiaries. That's not bad for a four-year-old concept." Years later, it still pained him that the new management dismantled much of what he had accomplished.

The thought of what might have been in the Philippines was particularly galling to Darch. "That nickel mine would have helped the Mangyans, the indigenous people. We would have created wealth, employment, and given them new opportunities to elevate their lives. The project would have brought much-needed infrastructure, health, and education. It's a myth to think that poor people in those remote areas enjoy their poverty, ill health, and early death. They do want improvements. Our goal was the opposite of exploiting the local people."

Deciding to Help the Akha

BY THE TIME he drank green tea with Wicha Promyong in Bangkok in 2006, John Darch was fifty-nine years old and had lived a full life, but he still had more to give. Before she gave up keeping a calendar, Louise documented that he had once traveled for 300 days in one year. She may have missed him when she wasn't traveling with him, but she had nothing but admiration for him. "John is the most compassionate, gentle, positive, honest, intelligent, caring individual I have ever known," she said. Her only complaint: "I wish I could get him to retire."

The Akha are not beggars. What Wicha said to Darch that day stuck with him. "That tied in with my idea that charity, while absolutely necessary in an emergency, doesn't really help anybody in the long run." The Akha were not begging for money. They wanted an investment. It was similar to mining in a way, Darch thought. They had a promising idea, but until someone spent the money to explore and develop the idea and bring the product to a broader market, it would remain just a promising idea. He told Wicha that the next time he was in Thailand, he would go up to Doi Chang and have a look.

CHAPTER 6

The Creation of a Canadian Coffee Company

AFTER HIS MEETING with Wicha, Darch flew back to Vancouver full of excitement. He called Wayne Fallis, who had served with him on the Crew Development board of directors for many years. Fallis, then in his early seventies and retired from a career as a grocery importer, assured Darch that he could help him with the new coffee venture and might even be interested in investing.

Darch talked to various other colleagues and friends about the coffee project, and one of them, Jeff Weaver, put him in contact with a roaster in Calgary named Shawn McDonald. Darch asked him to test some of the Doi Chaang green beans he had brought back.

McDonald was, fortuitously, already familiar with decent arabica beans from Thailand, having previously imported some from Paradise Mountain, a coffee farm to the northwest of Chiang Mai. He had by then sold his roasting business, so he called a former competitor, Jeff Farris, who owned Joffee Roasters, and arranged to do the sample roast there. He was pleasantly surprised and called

Darch with the good news. "They're really top-notch," McDonald said. "I thought maybe they were Kona beans. They've got that same kind of high overall quality and balanced acidity and flavor."

Darch wanted a second opinion, just as he would have wanted for a new mining prospect. McDonald recommended Kenneth Davids of Berkeley, California. He ran an online outfit called Coffee Review, which billed itself "The World's Leading Coffee Guide," and he had also written three books about coffee. Davids validated McDonald's opinion in his review: "A quiet but interesting coffee: soft, low-toned, with hints of cedar, warm spice, chocolate, and a low-acid fruit that suggests banana. The chocolate notes become more explicit in the impressively long, resonant finish." He gave it a score of 89 out of a hypothetical 100 (few beans hit the low 90s), which was not off the charts but still well above the score of 80, the accepted cut-off point for what would be considered specialty coffee. Doi Chaang was, Davids noted, a "coffee that rewards patience and attentiveness."

First Time up the Mountain...

WITH THESE ENCOURAGING assessments, Darch returned to Thailand in June 2006, with his eldest son, John A. Darch.* When they arrived in Doi Chang, they were astonished at what they saw. "I couldn't believe what they had done," Darch Senior recalled. A small cement building held the ancient German roaster, with an adjoining room that served as both office and packing area. On the right side was a small bamboo hut with a thatched grass roof, in which a small fire had been set, with a pot simmering a dinner of

---

* John M. Darch is the father, John A. Darch the son. For convenience, they will be called Senior and Junior, though that is not technically the case.

rice, greens, and chicken, with sauces in small bowls ranging from mild to fiercely hot.

Just below the roasting hut, a small plot of land had been cleared for a drying patio. A group of Akha was pouring the concrete for it when they arrived. Nearby was a small wet processing facility, where the freshly harvested coffee cherries would be pulped and fermented, then spread to dry on the new concrete patio.

Just after a downpour (this was the rainy season), Wicha and Adel took the Darches for a tour of the coffee fields. As they drove slowly along the muddy road through the trees, they saw men wielding machetes, pruning the coffee shrubs. Others were climbing the shade trees to lop off a few limbs, allowing the proper amount of sunlight to filter down. Further along, still others were spreading rotted compost made from fermented coffee pulp.

They stopped the truck and got out. They ventured off the road, down a steep hill, to talk with some of the men who were pruning. Adel translated from Akha to Thai, and then Wicha told the Darches in English what the worker said. "Yes, of course, we have to be careful with the machete, or we can hurt ourselves. But few get hurt. We cut off this part here," he said, indicating a sucker growing between two sturdier branches, "so that the tree will produce more cherries."

Clambering back up to the road, Darch Senior had to pull himself up by the trunks of the trees and found himself out of breath. He thought about how difficult it must be to harvest all these cherries. They were small and green now but would swell and ripen by the fall. He pondered all the labor involved, even in the off-season. *But look at where they get to work*, he thought, as he caught his breath on the road, looking out over the valley to the surrounding mountains. This was one of the most beautiful places he had ever seen. Yes, the people were poor—beyond poor, according to Wicha, since you had to have *something* in order to be poor—but they were obviously intelligent, hardworking, and incredibly friendly. *I'm going to do this*, Darch thought. *I'm going to get involved.* He thought of the poster his mother had given him, and that he still kept on his office wall: "I shall pass through this world but once. Any good therefore that I can do or any kindness that I can show to any human being, let me do it now. Let me not defer or neglect it. For I shall not pass this way again."

Over dinner in the grass hut, he told Wicha that he wanted to be a part of the initiative, that Wayne Fallis knew how to import and sell grocery items, and that Shawn McDonald would roast the beans. He proposed that he start a Canadian roasting company especially for the Doi Chaang beans.

"That sounds wonderful, Khun John," said Wicha, "but we've had others, Japanese and Koreans, who wanted to go into partnership with us, and we've turned them down because they wanted to own 51 percent or more of the company. The Akha will not give up ownership. They want to keep control."

"That shouldn't be a problem," Darch said. "How about if we give the Akha 50 percent of the roasting company? We would make no demands on you to change your operation here in Thailand, and we would pay a good price for the green beans we import to Canada. In return for that, we would have the right to purchase up to 75 percent of your premium coffee beans and to have exclusive rights to them in North America and Europe." It was an extraordinary, unique offer, allowing the Akha farmers to keep full ownership of their Thai operation, while receiving half the equity in the prospective Canadian firm. The Akha would not share in any losses the Canadians might sustain, but they would reap half of the profits.

And so it was agreed, around the fire under a thatched roof on top of a mountain in northwestern Thailand. "We will be like a family," Wicha said. "It's beautiful. But—" he paused dramatically. "We must stand strong together. Are you strong enough?"

He grasped Darch Senior on the shoulder. "If not—" he said, and dragged his finger across his throat. "If not, we all die." Then he laughed and slapped Darch's leg.

That night, the Darches slept in a grass hut a mile or so up a mountain road, as strange insects explored their bodies. The next day, they met with the village elders, including Adel's father, Piko, to formally cement the deal, which seemed to meet with universal approval. Darch Senior had seen Piko's turbaned visage on the Doi Chaang Coffee packages, but now he and the other elders were wearing what appeared to be fedoras. They looked quite dapper, Darch thought. Yes, this was a good thing. He would help the Akha by selling their fantastic coffee in Canada, then he would expand into the United States and Europe. No problem.

A Family Business

BACK IN CANADA, Darch Senior contacted his lawyer, George Brazier, and told him to begin drafting papers for the incorporation of the Doi Chaang Coffee Company, to be funded privately but with half the ownership going to the Akha farmers of Doi Chang village through a shareholder arrangement in which they were represented in several loosely organized associations.

"Are you sure that's the way you want to do it?" the astonished lawyer asked. "Yes, that's exactly the way I want to do it," Darch said in his mild but definitive manner. Brazier shrugged and drew up the papers. Darch had had enough of public companies, share price swings, and boards of directors, so the new entity was a private corporation. It was also a family affair. Darch Junior, a former banker and professional photographer, signed on to the new project as the chief financial officer, although he recalled, "My title was somewhat deceiving. I did take care of the books, but I also did a little of everything else. We all did."

His younger sister, Katharine Darch Regan, also joined them, coordinating the first marketing strategy and developing their website. Politically, she and her father had their differences, but she recognized that he had a big heart. And he had taught her two important principles, both of which he was now putting into practice: 1) *The best investment you can make is to create a healthy society;* and 2) *Question everything. Just because someone says that's the way it is, doesn't mean it is necessarily so.*

Katharine had plenty of questions for her father. "He was a mining executive who had raised tons of money for new operations. But this was a grassroots effort, not some big boardroom deal. And Dad didn't know anything about coffee." Still, after asking many questions about Doi Chang and doing extensive research on the hill tribes and their problems, Katharine joined the effort to help create a healthy Akha society halfway around the world. Working part-time as a young mother, she would create the firm's website and coordinate marketing efforts.

The new company, officially launched in April 2007, had a main office in Vancouver, where the three members of the Darch family worked with Danielle Bower, Louise's niece, who handled sales and marketing, and Tanya Jacoboni, a receptionist with no family connection. The separate roasting facility remained in Calgary, 600 miles to the east, where Shawn McDonald supervised a staff of four at the Joffee Coffee roasting facility, two sales people, and a delivery vehicle.

Calgary Conundrum

WITH GREAT ENTHUSIASM—and what turned out to be profound naïveté—Darch committed to buying four containers of Doi Chaang green coffee beans from the 2006–2007 harvest season (November–February). "I asked Wicha what price he needed in order to move forward with all the programs he envisioned," Darch remembered. Wicha not only had ambitious plans to buy a new roaster, he also wanted to create an Academy of Coffee, where the Akha farmers could learn about agronomy and other subjects, and eventually he wanted to build a school where hill tribe children from surrounding villages could learn, regardless of whether they had a Thai ID card or not.

Wicha had asked for $6 per kilo, or $2.73 per pound—well above the C-market rate of $1.00 a pound. The C-market was the price for average coffee, and Doi Chaang beans qualified as specialty gourmet beans that should command a premium, but that was still a very high price, especially for unknown beans that were just being introduced into an established market.

In addition, Darch Junior had advised his father that for environmental, social, and marketing purposes, their beans should be certified as both organic and Fair Trade. "We knew that the beans were truly organic, since the Akha used no chemical fertilizers or pesticides," the younger Darch said, "so it was just a matter of getting certified." Fair Trade guaranteed a base price of $1.26 a pound for green beans at the time, so the certification would make no difference to the price. But being certified as Fair Trade was becoming increasingly important in the specialty coffee market, where the logo signified that the coffee farmers were being paid a fair wage.

Pursuing both certifications meant that the new roasting company would have to pay to permit auditors to visit the farms and make sure that the Akha farmers of Doi Chang qualified. That brought Darch Senior's costs to almost $3 per pound.

The first four containers of coffee that shipped from Thailand to Vancouver carried a total of 150,000 pounds of beans. When roasted, coffee beans blow up to twice their size but lose about 20 percent of their weight, so that translated to 120,000 pounds of roasted coffee, or the equivalent number of retail units if sold in traditional one-pound bags. But because they had decided to sell Doi Chaang in half-pound bags (to keep the retail price of the unit lower), they would have to sell 240,000 bags. They planned to retail each bag for $10, which would yield gross sales of $2.4 million dollars, if they could sell them all. Of course, there was also a great deal of overhead.

The new company sponsored motivational speaker, educator, and author Stedman Graham to give inspirational speeches to launch the coffee product at gala events in Calgary and Vancouver. Graham, who was on a book tour, was a powerful speaker, focusing on how determined, resourceful underdogs (the Akha among them) could achieve greatness. He didn't drink coffee, but his partner, Oprah Winfrey, did. Darch hoped she would sample it and promote Doi Chaang in the United States, but although she apparently enjoyed the coffee, she never promoted it.

To cover the initial costs, John Darch Senior and Wayne Fallis each invested a million dollars in Doi Chaang Coffee. Fallis had assured Darch that he could handle imported coffee beans, just as he had sold containers of imported oranges, but McDonald warned Darch that they had committed to an extremely ambitious amount of coffee to start with. "Coffee is not a short-term business," he warned. "It's going to take at least three years for you to turn a profit. It's not easy to launch a new coffee brand." Fallis remained optimistic. "I've been doing this for fifty years, kid," he told McDonald. "You just watch."

Darch Junior designed new bags, modifying the Thai version. He retained Piko's face as the logo and put it on a handsome black plastic one-way valve bag, explaining the story of the Akha on the back. Even though the beans all came from the same place, there were varied offerings: dark- or medium-roasted, "signature" (a combination of dark and medium), decaf, and peaberry (single rather than double beans).

McDonald had a network of loyal customers in Alberta from the time he owned Planet Coffee Roasters (his former company, with six associated coffeehouses), and he was able to get roasted Doi Chaang beans into prestigious places like the Banff Springs Hotel and Lake Louise Ski Resort. Sysco, the giant food distributor, agreed to carry Doi Chaang, and the Darches also hired a broker, SunOpta Grocery West, to help place the coffee in new outlets. However, a broker takes anywhere from 10 percent to 25 percent of the profits depending on the service level.

But as 2007 bumped along, it became clear that Wayne Fallis had been overly optimistic, to say the least, and McDonald couldn't begin to sell that much roasted coffee. Calgary wasn't a thriving coffee hub, and McDonald's hordes of customers never materialized. Even after an expensive, time-consuming penetration of two Costco outlets in Calgary, the Darch team was able to sell only a tiny percentage of the beans they purchased. "It was like getting pregnant, and now what do we do with the baby?" Darch Senior recalled. They were forced to dump the remainder of the green beans at a loss. That first year was a disaster, with gross sales of only $73,000. "The reality was that I knew zero about coffee," Darch Senior admitted. "I didn't really care if we were selling tea or cacao or something else. I just wanted to help the Akha. We didn't know what we were doing." As Darch Junior had realized and had been frantically trying to tell his father, coffee wasn't like oranges or many other commodities. You couldn't just sell it straight from the container in bulk. And the overheads were significant.

So were the marketing challenges. They were a new company trying to introduce an expensive new coffee brand called Doi Chaang, which sounded more like Chinese tea to most consumers. No one had heard of good coffee from China (or Thailand, for that matter), and the picture of Piko, which they kept on their bags, didn't help. Who was this severe-looking man with the turban? They could attract attention if they could get people to read the story of the Akha on the back of the bag, but how to get them to pick up the bag in the first place?

Katharine stepped in. While she was developing the marketing material for the firm, her father told her that he wanted to get the coffee certified as Fair Trade to help promote sales. Katharine wasn't convinced. "This coffee is way beyond Fair Trade. We're offering a real partnership, not just a higher price for their green beans. In addition, we're paying much more than Fair Trade requires." Thus was created the slogan for the Doi Chaang brand: *Beyond Fair Trade*.

That helped to entice customers to pick up and sample the product, but it also created a new problem. The beans were certified as Fair Trade by the Fair Trade Labeling Organization (FLO), and FLO managers told Darch Senior that he was infringing on their trademark by calling his beans "Beyond Fair Trade." He had to take it off the label and throw away all the bags featuring the phrase if he wished to continue to use the Fair Trade mark on Doi Chaang beans.

Outraged, Darch Senior e-mailed back. It was rather ironic, he noted, that the Fair Trade movement was created to make sure that impoverished farmers were paid a reasonable amount for their hard work. Now he was being punished for doing exactly that—for going *beyond* the Fair Trade criteria to help the Akha farmers. He agreed to change his logo if FLO would put in writing what it was requiring, and why. He promised to then publicize this letter widely in order to embarrass them. No letter arrived, and Doi Chaang Coffee continued to proclaim that it went *Beyond Fair Trade*.

Nearly Pulling the Plug

AT THIS POINT, near the end of 2007, Wayne Fallis balked at putting more money into the venture. Coffee was a complex business, and he was over his head. He told Darch Senior that he was bailing out, chalking it up as a lost cause. Darch consequently contemplated the unthinkable. He might have to fold the company and renege on his commitment to the Akha. He had never believed in charity. He had thought of himself as a pioneer of a new form of sustainable capitalism. He would prove that profits could be equitably shared across continents. Although it might lose money for the first few years, Doi Chaang Coffee could be a thriving enterprise in the long run.

But his usual self-confidence was shaken. He realized now how naïve he had been, thinking it would be simple to launch a new brand, and that the Akha's story would ensure large sales. Katharine had also told him that she wouldn't be working on the project much longer for personal reasons.

Darch Junior, who had been trying for so long to get his father to face the complex, challenging realities of the specialty coffee business, surprised him now. "Of course we're going to lose money at first, Dad. But we've actually done an amazing thing. Starting from scratch, we've created a new brand, and you haven't given it time to gain traction." He wanted to keep the company going, and he was willing to buy out Wayne Fallis's share at a discount. Encouraged by his son's commitment, Darch Senior agreed to keep going, though it would mean investing more of his own money.

The next two years saw a few positive developments on the Canadian side. The Darches managed to get bags of Doi Chaang onto the shelves of a few gourmet food stores like Meinhardt Fine Foods in Vancouver. Gross sales increased to $336,000 annually—but profits still came nowhere near expenses.

In April 2009, Darch Senior missed the third anniversary celebration of the Academy of Coffee in order to attend the annual convention of the Specialty Coffee Association of America (SCAA), held in Atlanta that year. The SCAA, founded in 1982, had grown from a tiny fledgling organization of coffee quality-obsessed rebels to a large, respected rival to the older National Coffee Association, which represented the huge traditional roasters selling Maxwell House, Folgers, and other canned products.

Darch spent little time roaming the aisles, where a veritable United Nations of coffee countries were represented, choosing instead to remain in the little Doi Chaang Coffee booth he had rented. He felt like a rather small fish in a huge pond, and it was difficult to attract the attention of the crowds wandering by. His British reserve prevented him from yelling out or seeking attention. But one particularly friendly man stopped to sample a cup of Doi Chaang and was impressed. He had seen Doi Chaang bags back in Vancouver in the Meinhardt coffee section and thought that the slick black presentation was "fabulous packaging." He was intrigued by the Asian slant.

Now he introduced himself. "My name is Eric Lightheart, and we're neighbors. I work for Canterbury Coffee, the largest roaster in British Columbia. Here's my card." Darch was polite but confused. He had never heard of Canterbury Coffee. Lightheart explained that Canterbury, based near Vancouver, BC, started in 1977 as a small office coffee supply company, founded by Murray Dunlop, who began roasting his own coffee in 1981. Now Canterbury supplied the private label roasted coffee for giant outfits in Western Canada such as Safeway, Costco, and London Drugs, while providing coffee service for major universities, hotels, and restaurants, accounting for $60 million a year in sales. The company was known primarily as a "toll roaster" in the trade. It didn't have its own brand, which is why few people had heard of it.

Lightheart listened to Darch tell the story of the Akha and their coffee. He was impressed. "Here was the owner of the company, manning his own booth," he recalled. "John was warm and gracious. I could tell he had heart."

Darch presented a positive front, but it was obvious that the young firm was struggling. Lightheart offered his opinion: "You need better distribution. You need to get Doi Chaang out there into more avenues. We could help you. We've got seven branch offices. We could get you into more food service, grocery, and offices. I've been wanting to find a coffee to buy directly from the farm, with a great story behind it and a brand name we could promote. With our great distribution and your great brand and story, we could work well together. In fact, we could roast your coffee for you."

Darch explained that he had already committed to a roaster in Calgary and didn't want to move the business, but he was interested in working out some kind of arrangement. Back in Canada, Darch Senior took Darch Junior, office manager Tanya Jacoboni, and Shawn McDonald to visit the Canterbury roasting facility. At that point, McDonald could see the writing beginning to form on the wall. Darch Senior asked him if he would consider moving to BC to work with Canterbury, but McDonald had no interest in uprooting to work for a larger outfit. Darch Junior, uneasy about pulling out of Calgary, procrastinated. His father continued to pump money into his fledgling coffee venture, fulfilling his promise to buy another three containers of Doi Chaang beans for the same price of approximately $3 a pound, paying up front and then hoping to sell them.

Meanwhile, Back in Thailand...

MEANWHILE, WICHA AND the Akha were working diligently to expand the coffee business. In the spring of 2007, with the new income from sales to the Canadians, they built the imposing Academy of Coffee, harvesting teak poles from Wicha's property in Nan Province, to the east of Chiang Rai. They used fifty-seven poles to represent the fifty-seven generations recited by the elders in their oral history. The 3,000-square-foot building had a roof of thick thatched grass, and in the middle of the office on the left-hand side there was a traditional fire pit. The smoke from the fire helped to cure the roof and discourage insects from eating it. Patchanee Suwanwisolkit from Chiang Mai University taught agronomy classes in the classroom area and brought colleagues for other educational offerings.

In the middle of the building there was room for a coffee-soap-making venture that a young Akha woman named Nuda began, with Wicha's encouragement. Nuda started with a "soap base," purchased in Bangkok, then shaved off pieces and put them in the top of a double boiler to melt, along with coffee pulp, honey, and olive oil infused with a fragrant local flower. She also made espresso soap, with concentrated brewed espresso added, along with some very finely ground coffee that acted as a kind of pumice to scrape off dead skin. Three people could make a thousand bars of soap in one day, to be sold in the coffeeshop and other outlets.

On April 16, 2007, the facility opened, with John Darch Senior and Wayne Fallis in attendance as honored guests and partners. Both of them struck the ceremonial gong. The Akha women had donned their silver-laden headdresses and brightly embroidered clothing. There were speeches, music, and dancing. This celebration would become an annual event that drew thousands of Akha from many other villages, even from China, Laos, and Burma.

In September 2007, with money from the Canadian venture, the Akha bought a new ultra-modern Brambati roaster, manufactured in Italy, to replace the ancient German one. Paolo Fantaguzzi, an Italian machinist, took fifteen days to install the roaster for Wicha, who later convinced him to move to Bangkok to build coffee roasters and brewers in cooperation with Doi Chaang. The Brambati roaster featured a computer screen so that Akong, the roastmaster, could monitor every aspect of the process.

The coffee was harvested and prepared with obsessive care, then sorted several times to make sure that any defective or imperfect beans were removed. The Doi Chaang Coffee Original (the name of the main Akha company) processing plant wasn't big enough to handle all of the coffee, so twelve loose associations were formed by other Akha (including Adel's older brother Leehu and cousin Apa) in the village to receive the ripe coffee cherries and supervise the processing and drying, for a small fee of 2 baht per kilogram. Then they would deliver the beans in parchment to the main Doi Chaang Coffee location where they were again sorted and eventually hulled.

During the sorting, the Akha women also separated "peaberries" from the regular beans. Most coffee beans grow in facing pairs, but peaberries, shaped like tiny footballs, sometimes grow alone in a coffee cherry. They are prized for their rarity and supposedly more concentrated flavor. In April 2008, Kenneth Davids gave Doi Chaang Peaberry an extraordinarily high score of 93 along with high praise: "Pure, refreshing coffee. Sweetly acidy and honey-toned in the aroma, with floral and coffee fruit (tart cherry) notes. In the cup softly acidy, delicate in mouthfeel, crisp but very sweet in structure, with continued notes of tart coffee cherry, honey and flowers, together with a slight, deepening butterscotch-like pungency. In the finish the sweetness fades, but the fundamental flavor notes persist far into the long finish… A pure, lyric, light-roasted breakfast coffee, gently exotic."

Wicha was a bundle of creative energy. To display and sell their coffee in the village, he had a coffeehouse built near the Academy, where Akha women pulled shots of espresso and steamed milk for cappuccinos and lattes. He encouraged Lipi, one of Adel's nephews, in his efforts to grow blue oolong tea to complement coffee sales. The tea, processed in a Chinese factory 40 kilometers to the west in the town of Wawi, was of a high quality, but it couldn't compete with cheaper Thai teas, and it was also too pricey for the export market. Nonetheless, Doi Chaang tea was sold in the coffeeshop.

To take advantage of the annual March coffee-blossom season, with its jasmine-like fragrance and explosion of white flowers, the Akha became beekeepers and sold delicately flavored coffee-blossom honey in the coffeehouse, along with the soap and tea. The hives were then trucked to the lowlands, where the bees collected pollen from flowers and orchards for standard (but still delicious) honey.

Already a seasoned traveler, Wicha began a series of promotional trips for John Darch Senior and his Canadian company. In May of 2008, Wicha flew to Canada, where he charmed the Doi Chaang staff with his charismatic enthusiasm and humanity, although the doorman at the elegant Terminal City Club, where he was staying, at one point refused Wicha entry because of his odd garb. He appeared on several local radio and television shows, which temporarily boosted sales. Darch also took Wicha to the annual Specialty Coffee Association of America conference held in Minneapolis that May, where he won the distinction of being named "the best authentic character" at the event.

In his suitcase, Wicha had brought what appeared at first glance to be Oh Henry! candy bars. "This is kopi luwak, civet cat coffee," Wicha said. "Will you try it?" The agglomeration turned out to be coffee beans that had been eaten and excreted by wild civet cats in the coffee groves of Doi Chang. Wicha knew that such beans from Indonesia fetched a ridiculously high price in some countries.

Darch took the beans to John Gilchrist, a Canadian gourmand and food writer, who told him, "John, I've tried this civet poop coffee before, and it's terrible stuff." Yet when he washed and roasted these beans, he loved them for their mellow, lingering honey flavor. Darch took them back to Vancouver and arranged for six chefs to test the civet coffee, with positive results. Finally, he sent a sample to Kenneth Davids, who gave the civet beans a score of 90, along with flavor notes: "Intriguing mid-tones throughout the profile:

mainly a sort of orangy, floral citrus with a backgrounded complex simultaneously suggesting fresh earth, mushroom and decomposing leaves. All of this takes on a vaguely chocolaty tone in the finish. Gently smooth acidity, medium body."

Wicha returned to Doi Chang brimming with ideas for new products, but mostly the Akha would grow more and more coffee. From the 200 acres originally growing in 2002, in 2009 there were nearly 2,000 acres, with plans to plant up to 8,000 acres. Some of those trees were starting to produce cherries, having been planted as seedlings three or four years previously. Others would come into maturity in the next few years. While the Thai market for Doi Chaang beans was growing—there were now a dozen Doi Chaang coffeehouses in Chiang Rai, Mae Suai, Bangkok, and elsewhere—Wicha and the Akha were counting on the Canadians to buy most of their premium beans for high prices.

2010: The Crucial Year

FINALLY, IN 2010, Darch Senior and Junior concluded that they could not continue with the Calgary operation. Their primary potential market was in Vancouver. It made little sense to pay for the beans to be shipped from the coast inland to Calgary, where McDonald's team roasted and packaged them, then shipped most of them back to Vancouver. Eric Lightheart was eager to have their business at Canterbury. Thus, the Darches made an orderly transfer of their business to Canterbury in July 2010. It was a two-part deal. Canterbury would serve as a toll roaster for accounts that Doi Chaang Coffee found on its own. Using the specified roast profile for the beans, the huge roaster would charge a toll fee to roast, package, distribute, and invoice customers for Doi Chaang Coffee. It was a fairly expensive option in some respects, but it saved the salary of several people, plus the cost of a roasting facility and delivery truck. Darch Junior, who had been advocating such a change, was able to implement a switch from the half-pound bags to one-pound offerings, which put them in the same size as their top competitor, Kicking Horse Coffee. A new broker, Cyba Stevens, helped get Doi Chaang beans into IGA grocery stores as well as London Drugs.

The second part of the deal had Doi Chaang Coffee give Canterbury the exclusive right to handle its food service coffee. Canterbury would purchase the green beans at a small mark-up and then pay Doi Chaang a 5 percent royalty on all sales to its institutional customers. Not all of these 6,000 customers would order Doi Chaang, but gaining access to such Canterbury clients would instantly and dramatically expand the market for the Thai beans. Canterbury provided all of the coffee brewing equipment and service to these customers as well—something that tiny Doi Chaang could never do. In return, the deal gave Canterbury a distinctive brand and story to offer that no one else had.

In the competitive world of specialty coffee, Lightheart argued that this special deal with Doi Chaang would be advantageous to Canterbury. He encountered some resistance, though. "Explain again why we want to promote someone else's coffee?" founder Murray Dunlop asked. In the end, he grudgingly agreed to the deal, though he groused that Canterbury made less profit on Doi Chaang beans than any others they handled.

The move to Canterbury eventually saw Doi Chaang beans move into Safeway and more Costco stores, as well as over 200 coffeeshops, restaurants, and hotels. Getting onto more Costco shelves proved to be challenging. At Darch's expense, Doi Chaang and Canterbury had to put on a "Costco road show" in eight stores in Alberta and BC. That meant bringing two skids of coffee (pallets holding over 400 two-pound bags) to each store, paying for a presenter to offer free samples of brewed coffee all day, and hoping that enough customers would buy the coffee. If accepted in the store, sales of Doi Chaang had to reach at least a skid-and-a-half per week in order to stay there. Costco eventually accepted the beans in fifteen locations.

Eric Lightheart visited the village of Doi Chang that fall. He was impressed with the whole setup, including the latte art in the shape of a dragon atop his cappuccino, and he was particularly taken with Wicha, whom he described as "a lovely guy, humble, outgoing, passionate, and dying for more coffee knowledge, asking lots of questions."

Back in Canada, Lightheart was delighted with the sales to institutions. "I told the story of the Akha and their coffee," he said. "Everyone wants to hear a good story that rings true. They are leery of American big business hype, but this was completely real. I had seen it for myself, and I told customers." Other than Kona and Jamaica Blue Mountain beans, he sold more Doi Chaang Coffee than any other brand.

Documentary Evidence

THREE MONTHS AFTER the momentous switch to Canterbury, Doi Chaang Coffee got another crucial boost: Darch Senior (and Wicha, when he visited Canada) had appeared on local television and radio shows. The story about the extraordinary coffee from northwestern Thailand was beginning to percolate but had not yet achieved national recognition. In October 2010, Darch got a call from producer Linda Aylesworth of Global Television Network, which had twelve owned-and-operated stations across Canada. Aylesworth wanted to arrange a visit to the village of Doi Chang with a film crew. Could Darch perhaps facilitate that?

Yes, indeed, he could, and he and his son would accompany her. Because of the success of Doi Chaang coffee, earlier in 2010 the government had finally paved the road up to the village. Because it was seen as being for the benefit of the hill tribes, the road was sub-standard, without proper foundation, and the asphalt was too thin, so that potholes almost immediately appeared, but it was still a vast improvement on the previous mud road, and now it took only an hour to drive from the city of Chiang Rai instead of four or five hours.

Aylesworth was enchanted by what she found. She was charmed by Wicha and the Akha. What had originally been planned as a three-minute segment on the news turned into four consecutive nights, showing audiences the miracle that was occurring on this remote mountainside, in large part because of the Darches and their Vancouver coffee company.

The first show aired on Monday, November 22, 2010, introduced by an anchorwoman: "It's been said that the only thing that keeps people awake more than coffee is your conscience. Well, what if your conscience could be eased by the perfect cup?" Then she turned the show over to Aylesworth, who said, "Canadian coffee lovers are increasingly demanding more than a heady aroma and full-bodied taste. They want to know that the people who grow their beans are being paid fairly—people like the Akha of northern Thailand…"

With that, the camera zoomed in on a traditionally dressed Akha woman, singing in her native tongue as she picked coffee. The scene was exotic, enticing—and almost realistic. It was true that Akha women did the bulk of the coffee harvesting, but they no longer wore their elaborate headdresses, except on special occasions. Apparently a television documentary was one of those occasions. "In spite of their hard work," Aylesworth said, "discrimination and unscrupulous coffee brokers have kept them from rising out of poverty."

Then Wicha appeared on camera, with his earring, beard, and earnest manner, explaining: "These people have nothing, [treated] worse than a dog. OK, they look down [on them], that's why their children are not to go to school. Even teachers, they just look down at our people." The camera turned to cute little children running down a broken concrete village road.

Aylesworth then introduced Darch Senior, shown drinking coffee with Wicha at the café in Doi Chang. "He's good, he's a kind man," Wicha said of Darch, who then explained in his calm, measured British accent, "I wanted to see if, by taking the coffee to North America and introducing it, that I would be able to add to what Wicha wanted to do." He would pay "beyond Fair Trade" prices and give the Akha half of the company. With that money, Aylesworth explained, the Akha had been able to expand production, which the camera documented by showing the newly constructed wet processing plant and huge concrete drying patio, where a worker was raking beans to turn them.

The program did not explain why the new processing plant had been necessary, or what a rift it had caused in the village. The success and fame of Doi Chaang Coffee, and the higher prices it commanded, had tempted some of the Akha processors to buy inferior beans from lower elevations and mix them with the locally processed beans. As a result, some of the Doi Chaang green beans had been rejected. Adel and Wicha decided to stop using the twelve Akha associations and their processing stations. Instead, they would build a larger, faster facility and buy just-harvested cherries directly from the farmers. But this move to cut out the middlemen infuriated some of the Akha who had run the processing facilities.

Aylesworth continued: "This year 800 tons of premium beans will be shipped to Richmond, BC, where they will be roasted and distributed to Canadian buyers, who with every purchase help the Akha to help themselves." The figure was inaccurate (only 200 tons would go to Canada), but otherwise Aylesworth had it right.

"After decades of being paid a pittance for their beans, the Akha are at last getting what they deserve," she concluded. "We never beg," said Wicha on screen. "We want to work for whatever we want to see." Darch wrapped it up: "I was living a comfortable life. I could have retired. But there's a much greater feeling and passion toward this project than anything else I've done before." The program closed on a shot of Akha children laughing.

That first night, 250,000 people watched the Global TV news show with this segment. By the time the fourth segment aired three days later, viewership had risen to 750,000. Aylesworth took the rest of her footage and turned it into a half-hour documentary, televised over the Christmas holidays of 2010 and then posted on YouTube.

Because of the switch to Canterbury and the media bonanza from Global TV, Doi Chaang sales hit $1.3 million for the year 2010.

Growth, Awards, and Profits in Sight

THE DOCUMENTARY WON the award for the best long feature of the year from the Radio-Television News Directors Association of Canada and launched a string of other awards and media that followed in 2011 and 2012. The Thai-Canadian Chamber of Commerce, based in Bangkok, named Doi Chaang Coffee its "Company of the Year 2011." The Canadian Association of Food-service Professionals gave the firm its "Outstanding Community Development" award, while Asia-Pacific Economic Cooperation, covering twenty-one nations with borders on the Pacific, from Peru to Russia, from Canada to Thailand, awarded Doi Chaang Coffee third place in its "One Village One Brand" contest. The firm was short-listed to the top ten Small-Medium Enterprises at the United Nations Conference on Sustainable Development in Rio de Janeiro in June 2012—the only coffee company and sole Canadian company to be so ranked.

The media fell in love with the story of the plucky, thriving Akha of Doi Chang village, their coffee, and the Vancouver firm that was roasting it. *Mutineer Magazine*, which covered all "fine beverages," alcoholic or not, ran a long encomium to Doi Chaang Coffee in its May 2011 issue. "The Akha seem to possess an uncanny ability to learn by doing," wrote author Chris D'Amico. "They've mastered complex agricultural practices as well as mechanical and civil engineering."

The June 2011 issue of *Sawasdee*, the inflight magazine of Thai Airways, featured Doi Chaang in "Coffee Quest," an article by Matthew Kadey, with the subtitle, "A mountain community in northern Thailand is brewing a success story in coffee, tea, and agro-tourism." Kadey, who bicycled up the mountain to the village as part of a ten-week cycling adventure through Laos and Thailand, declared the strenuous effort worthwhile once he got to the top and got an iced coffee from Adel and a tour from Miga.

Global Coffee Review, in its September 2011 issue, featured a photo of Wicha and Darch with hands clasped in solidarity in an article by David Swinfen, headlined "Business Thais." Wicha, who had grown into his role as a media star, told Swinfen, "I live for Doi Chaang, and it's 24 hours. I sleep for two hours sometimes, but I work at night, in the day, whenever there is anything the village requires me to do." One could doubt whether Wicha really slept only two hours a night, but there was no question that his mind was racing with new plans, and he seemed unstoppable. Darch told Swinfen, "I met with Wicha out of politeness, but I was overwhelmed by the commitment that I saw [in the village]."

Darch explained that the Fair Trade coffee certification had "done a wonderful job in terms of raising public awareness about the need for a decent and reasonable wage for growers," but that the Fair Trade price was really equivalent to a minimum wage. "It does little to break the cycle of poverty for many coffee farmers."

That was why he had gone "Beyond Fair Trade" in his business model. By that time, 2,000 acres of coffee trees in Doi Chang were producing 640 tons of green beans annually. Another 5,000 acres had been planted with coffee seedlings in various stages of growth. Each year, the Akha planted another 100,000 shade trees, including macadamia, plantain, plum, and peach trees, as well as nitrogen-fixing trees that were particularly good for the soil.

"Until you establish a brand which is recognized internationally," Darch said, "there is no demand other than for your [bulk commodity] green beans." Now that the brand was getting attention around the world, sales were growing in Thailand, where pride in being recognized outside the country translated to better domestic appeal. Luxury Thai malls such as Siam Paragon and Emporium were begging for the beans. Thai sales had reached 200 tons, with the same amount sold in Canada.

In the article, Darch Junior noted that they were selling at select stores in the UK, including Harrods of London, where Doi Chaang was the most expensive coffee. Darch Senior's younger brother, Terence "Terry" Darch, who still lived in Weymouth, had taken on the task of promoting Doi Chaang coffee in the UK, at first selling roasted beans he got from Canada. He carried samples to London and the Midlands, spreading the Doi Chaang gospel and persuading Harrods to sell the beans. He then contacted DRWakefield, a British coffee bean importer, where Simon Wakefield had taken over the business his father had begun. Wakefield began to buy a container of Doi Chaang beans annually to supply the UK specialty market.

Canadian sales were growing as well, surpassing $1.8 million in 2011, though the company had yet to turn a profit, and Darch had now sunk nearly $4 million into the enterprise. All the articles mentioned that the Akha owned half of the Canadian coffee company and were entitled to half of the profits—but they did not mention the inconvenient fact that there *were* no profits yet.

Regardless, the Akha shared in the equity and goodwill of the company, and the Canadian company's marketing, including the widening press coverage, proved invaluable.

As 2012 rolled around, the media attention continued. Miles Small of *CoffeeTalk Magazine* visited Doi Chang village and was blown away by the coffee and the place. He wrote an article in which he called Wicha "this quiet, peaceful, and wickedly intelligent man." He also injected a little romance when he wrote that Darch first rode up the mountain on a mule—not true, but not that far in comfort level from the actual jarring trek in a four-wheel-drive truck that Darch had taken up the rutted dirt road.

The coverage just kept coming. In March 2012, *Stir*, a coffee industry periodical, published a feature article, followed the next month by a long article in the *Tea & Coffee Trade Journal*. Kenneth Davids made a pilgrimage to the Thai village and wrote about it in *Roast* in the October 2012 issue. At first, he wrote, Wicha seemed too good to be true, "with his endless energy, open, innovating spirit and part hippie, part Buddhist idealism. But he ultimately convinced me, thoroughly." He was impressed that Wicha, Adel, and the farmers had "tirelessly worked almost every possible angle to increase the Akha cooperative's coffee volume, coffee quality, revenues, and general well-being."

By this time, there were twenty Doi Chaang coffeehouses that were fully owned by the cooperative, and nearly 300 other Thai cafés that exclusively served the Doi Chaang brew, so that they were essentially franchises. Doi Chang village had running water, a rudimentary sewage system, electricity, and paved roads. Thai officials who had once scorned the ignorant, lazy Akha now proudly took visitors up the mountain to show off an example of their successful development efforts. In April 2012, Darch Senior was invited to accompany Canadian Prime Minister Stephen Harper to Thailand on a goodwill trip. Though his roasting company was tiny compared to the other corporations whose CEOs came along, his was the only Canadian venture that actually partnered with people in Thailand—and with marginalized hill tribes at that.

A Family Feeling

OVER TIME, Darch Senior and Junior assembled a tight-knit young office staff in Vancouver. "We try to run it like an extended family," Darch Senior said. "Everyone here is involved and passionate." He became chairman in 2012, while his son, elevated to president, was more active in day-to-day nitty-gritty details. Tanya Jacoboni progressed from receptionist to office manager and then vice president of business development. "I always laugh at titles here," she said, "because we all do so many things."

Danika Speight joined Doi Chaang in January 2011 as an accountant, taking over the bookkeeping from Darch Junior and gradually handling receivables and payables, then doing the firm's financial statements. When Darch Junior became president of the company, Speight was named chief financial officer.

Anand Pawa, who had been born in Bangkok and moved to Vancouver with his family when he was in Grade 8, joined the company in 2011 and quickly became a key employee. During his interview with Darch Senior and Junior at a Vancouver restaurant, Darch Senior told him that he wanted someone with extensive experience with media contacts. Anand Pawa, who had earned a degree in marketing from Simon Fraser University, admitted that he didn't yet have that specific expertise, but he could learn. He pointed out that he was fluent in Thai. "That's nice," Darch Senior said, "but Wicha and Sandra both speak English, so I don't think we'll really need that skill."

To his great disappointment, Anand Pawa wasn't initially offered the job, but the Darches called back in March to offer a three-month trial period. He quickly proved to be invaluable, especially after he visited Doi Chang in October 2011 with Jacoboni and Darch Junior. Anand Pawa discovered that every piece of information about the village he'd been given back in Canada was incorrect, including how the coffee cooperative functioned and how the coffee was processed. "It was all lost in translation," he said. He quickly bonded with Adel and Miga, translating for Darch Junior. They negotiated prices for the next harvest, a process that went smoothly for the first time.

The next hire, in November 2011, was receptionist Jacquelyn "Jackie" Kingston. She was followed by Sanja Grcic, a native of Bosnia, who became vice president of sales in the grocery division in February 2012, and Katharine Sawchuck, who was hired in October 2012 as public relations director.

Darch continued to travel extensively, not only for Doi Chaang Coffee, but also for his other business ventures. He may have sold the first potash development company he helped to start, but now he was working on six other Thai potash deposits in the same northeastern region, as well as having part-ownership of Waste Energy, a Thai firm that would burn waste to produce sustainable energy, IMS Global Corporation, a Canadian firm providing safety systems to mining companies, and a few other ventures. His daughter Katharine was back as his main assistant.

Thus, by the end of 2012, most of the Vancouver Doi Chaang staff were in their twenties, excited to be pioneering the new coffee venture that was helping the Akha tribe halfway around the world. Each would get to visit the village of Doi Chang three years after joining the firm.

Despite his travels, Darch Senior kept close tabs on the Vancouver roasting business. Gross sales crested $2.3 million in 2012, finally netting a small profit of $145,000 for the year.

CHAPTER 7

Learning Curves in Vancouver

Y JUNE 2013, the coffee company that John Darch Senior and Junior had launched in 2007 with such optimistic naïveté had gone through a series of trials, tribulations, and growing pains. The idealistic, energetic young office staffers were working smoothly together, but trying to increase sales of Doi Chaang Coffee remained a challenge, particularly because the name sounded so strange to Canadian ears. Even when consumers realized that these were coffee beans from Thailand rather than tea leaves from China, they often didn't know why they should choose Doi Chaang over other coffees.

The fact that they were labeled "Beyond Fair Trade" was a nice touch, but what did that mean? The story of the Akha tribe, its transition from trading in illegal opium to specialty coffee, and the impact that coffee sales had had on life on a remote mountainside in Thailand were difficult to convey on the side of a bag of coffee. And getting consumers to first pick up the bag and read it was even more challenging.

Doi Chaang bags were jostling with competitors for shelf space in the coffee section of several Vancouver stores. At Meinhardt

Fine Foods, a small upscale store where Doi Chaang would seem a perfect fit, the Doi Chaang single-origin beans sold in one-pound bags for $16.99, but they were up against more established names, including Ethical Bean, 49th Parallel, Piccolo Brothers, Salt Spring Coffee, Caffè Umbria, Level Ground, Commercial Drive, illy, Starbucks, and JJ Bean, Meinhardt's house blend. Many of these coffees sold in 340 gram (12 ounce) bags for $13.99 or less, and while the price per gram for Doi Chaang was competitive or even cheaper, many customers made purchasing decisions based on the sticker price of a bag. They didn't see much visual difference between the 12 ounce bag and a full pound.

Another problem Doi Chaang faced was that all its beans came from just one place, so that its different offerings were really just different roast levels or permutations of what were essentially the same beans. The company offered a Dark and Medium Roast option, as well as a Signature Blend, combining Dark and Medium. And there was the Doi Chaang Peaberry, with mutant round beans that grew singly rather than two facing seeds inside a coffee cherry, the Doi Chaang Espresso (at a real disadvantage for making a good crema, without blending with other origins), and a decaf version.

All of these options were available through the Doi Chaang website, but each item also had its own SKU (stock keeping unit), and in the fierce grocery business, companies often had to pay an initial "slotting fee" for each SKU taking up shelf space. Small stores such as Meinhardt did not charge a fee, but shelf space was still limited, so Doi Chaang sold only Dark, Medium, and Peaberry there. In larger stores, the slotting fee could range from $5,000 per SKU for twenty stores up to $40,000 for a national chain. This one-time fee was no guarantee that the store would continue to stock Doi Chaang if it didn't meet their sales targets or if the store reconfigured its shelves. At Save-On-Foods, for example, Doi Chaang's bags had been displayed on the bottom shelves and were subsequently ousted by the store's new house brand, also sold in a black bag.

At Meinhardt, in a section labeled "Locally Produced," only 49th Parallel was on display, even though Doi Chaang, Ethical Bean, Salt Spring, Piccolo Brothers, and Commercial Drive were also local. Of course, no coffee trees grow anywhere in North America other than the Hawaiian Islands, so the "local" character stemmed from where the imported beans were roasted. It was a constant battle to get store managers and consumers to understand that Doi Chaang was a local, family-owned business, despite its exotic-sounding name. Darch Junior commented wryly that some consumers thought that Salt Spring Coffee was actually grown on Salt Spring Island, just to the west of Vancouver.

The other challenge was to convey the Doi Chaang story so that people understood the company's unique character. The company was half-owned by Akha farmers in a mountaintop village in northern Thailand, and they were paid better than Fair Trade prices for their beans. The Akha had been marginalized and oppressed, and now they were self-reliant and thriving, and without the Vancouver company's sales and publicity efforts, it is doubtful that the Thai operation would have been the incredible success that it was. But that story was not breaking through to most people who needed to hear it, despite the earlier media exposure.

Doi Chaang beans brewed a terrific cup of coffee, but so did many other beans from many other companies. Doi Chaang was certified Fair Trade and organic, but so were many other coffees. On its website, for instance, Ethical Bean describes itself as "one of Canada's leading suppliers of 100% Fairtrade Certified Organic coffee. The Vancouver, BC, based company prides itself on being both just, and better, in everything that they do. Whether through programs that respect the earth and its farmers or by leaving a minimal environmental footprint, Ethical Bean is constantly seeking new ways to do the right thing." Ethical Bean offered blends called Rocket Fuel, Bold, Lush, and Mellow, with beans from places such as Sumatra, Bolivia, Ethiopia, Nicaragua, and Guatemala.

And Ethical Bean wasn't even the biggest competitor. That was Kicking Horse Coffee. Like Doi Chaang, Kicking Horse sold its blends in one-pound bags at comparable prices, with funky, aggressive names such as Kick Ass, Grizzly Claw, Kootenay Crossing, and Cliff Hanger Espresso. Founded in 1996 by Elana Rosenfeld and Leo Johnson in their garage in tiny Invermere, British Columbia, west of Calgary, Kicking Horse developed a loyal following across Canada. It was purchased in 2012 for multiple millions by New Jersey–based Branch Brook Holdings, with Elana Rosenfeld remaining as CEO. "We're the underdog in the coffee world," Rosenfeld claimed after the sale, but Doi Chaang had a more legitimate claim to that title.

The Whole Foods Flap

IN JULY 2012, Doi Chaang Coffee had been kicked out of seven Whole Foods stores in British Columbia in an exasperating illustration of the crazy politics of the specialty coffee business. Given the fact that Whole Foods promoted itself as a socially responsible supplier of organic, sustainable products, and that its Canadian stores also sold Ethical Bean and Kicking Horse, Doi Chaang would seem to be a natural choice for the chain's shelves. But when a Canadian distributor asked why Doi Chaang had mysteriously disappeared from the shelves of local Whole Foods, Bonnie Meyer, the Whole Foods coffee coordinator for the Pacific Northwest, e-mailed from her office in Bellevue, Washington: "Most of the stores are dropping them, since they made the decision to go into Quick Marts (not sure if this is the name, but the gas station guys).

They have been doing massive advertising around this and we just don't feel this is our type of product any longer."

Meyer was referring to a promotion the convenience store chain 7-Eleven was running across Canada. In an effort to go a bit more upscale and appeal to socially conscious consumers, 7-Eleven managers, who bought their coffee from Canterbury, had been attracted by the "Beyond Fair Trade" slogan. Consequently, for three months they brewed Doi Chaang coffee in their Canadian stores, while providing valuable free advertising to the struggling young coffee company.

In response to Meyer's e-mail, which the distributor forwarded, Darch Junior exploded in an internal company e-mail: "This is hypocrisy! A grocery chain that is supposed to support small farmers and organic and sustainable farming would drop a product that moved mainstream." Instead of condemning the benefits of promoting a sustainable product, Whole Foods should be congratulating Doi Chaang. "I am appalled. It's just plain snobbery!"

Darch Senior wrote a carefully considered official response, pointing out that Doi Chaang was not being sold in gas stations, that it was a small, local, family-run business with an "equal direct partnership" with the Akha hill tribe, and that 7-Eleven had approached them and had paid for a short-term promotion that was soon coming to an end. "We remain a small *barely* for-profit business committed to the growers of Doi Chang village and to our Beyond Fair Trade structure," he wrote. "The core values of Doi Chaang Coffee Company are very much in line with Whole Foods Market and the suppliers it partners with. We too strive for wealth through profits and growth yet ensure our business practices better our communities and environment." He concluded by saying that he hoped Whole Foods would reconsider its decision. "If not, then hopefully in the future we may have the opportunity to re-establish our business relationship."

No one from Whole Foods responded.

A Canterbury Tale

THE DOI CHAANG beans were still being roasted by the Canterbury Coffee Corporation in the city of Richmond, just south of Vancouver. Housed in a large metal building in an industrial park, Canterbury was founded in 1977 by CEO Murray Dunlop. After earning his MBA, he had taught briefly in a business school. "But all my life I wanted to have my own business," he said, and as he searched for options, coffee was appealing because it didn't require a whole lot of capital. His initial strategy was to supply coffee and brewers to offices and institutions, getting his beans from various roasters in Canada and California, but the quality was variable. "I had a lot of complaints, so I decided to do my own thing."

In 1981, when he started to do his own roasting, the specialty coffee movement was just beginning, and he realized he could fill a niche, providing small lots of fine coffees. From initial gross sales of $100,000 a year, he grew the business to $60 million a year in sales, offering not only coffee and its accessories, but tea, chocolate, smoothie concentrate, energy drinks and bars, mineral water, and flavored syrups.

Dunlop was impressed with Doi Chaang coffee and its unique relationship with the Akha farmers, but he complained about the high cost of the green beans, which limited profits. "Most roasters don't take instructions from their green bean suppliers. Of all the products we do, we probably make the least amount from Doi Chaang." Dunlop had been astonished when he visited the village of Doi Chang during the April 2013 celebration. "I was absolutely flabbergasted by the rapid expansion of facilities and the wealth transfer to the farmers. In 2001, there were only fourteen cars in the village, but now there were close to 300 vehicles, including SUVs. You would never see that on farms in Central America, where there are just beat-up pickup trucks."

Dunlop observed in June 2013 that in the past eighteen months, green coffee prices on the C-market had declined from close to $3 a pound to $1.28, but that John Darch's company had continued to pay the same high rate for Doi Chaang beans. "The world does not start and end in Doi Chang," he said. Other organic Fair Trade beans didn't cost as much, and already he was seeing a 15 percent decline in Doi Chaang sales because of noncompetitive retail prices.

He was pleased that "Doi Chaang is getting a reputation in British Columbia, and we're trying to help them. We hope they will be a good long-time customer." But it was clear that at Canterbury, Eric Lightheart was Doi Chaang's real champion. "Eric is passionate about it," Dunlop said. "He likes the concept of helping regional people."

Since his first visit to Doi Chang village in 2010, Lightheart had returned several times, and he had also spent time with Wicha in Vancouver. "I fell in love with the whole scene," he said, and he was able to sell Doi Chaang to food service accounts such as the University of Victoria and the Blue Parrot Coffeehouse on Granville Island by telling the Akha story. Canterbury was also able to get the coffee into chains such as Save-On-Foods (for a while) and Urban Fare. Lightheart likened the Doi Chaang brew to Hawaiian Kona coffee: "very smooth and balanced, with low acidity, winy notes, just a great cup of coffee."

He admitted, however, that with the C-market coffee price down, Doi Chaang had a "much bigger hill to climb" because Darch continued to pay the same high price for the green beans. "I keep saying that gold goes up and down, and so does the coffee price. You have to adjust to reality."

In the last few years, the single-serve revolution had surprised many in the specialty coffee industry. Aside from all the other bagged coffee competition, store shelves were now displaying boxes of capsules that fit into Keurig machines, owned by Green Mountain Coffee Roasters (later renamed Keurig Green Mountain) in Vermont. K-Cups and other compatible products were becoming popular in homes and offices as a quick, simple way to brew a good cup of coffee, despite greater expense and throwaway, non-recyclable plastic cups. Canterbury had just purchased an Aroma Cup machine, which would produce innovative Keurig-compatible capsules with soft mesh bottoms. Unlike the K-Cups, they were 90 percent compostable and held a bit more coffee as well.

In June 2013, John Gray, Canterbury's chief coffee cupper and blender, was busy creating and testing a prototype Aroma Cup capsule, carefully spooning in ground coffee and using a soldering iron to attach the film. He had worked for Canterbury since 1983 and was mostly self-taught. He remembered attending the first Specialty Coffee Association of America Exposition in New Orleans in 1989, with only 200 people. In 2012, Gray passed a grueling SCAA cupping course to become an elite Q-grader.

Although he rated Doi Chaang beans highly, he believed they were too clean, too well-processed. It would be better to use the semi-washed process, leaving a little of the mucilage on the beans to dry, which adds complexity. Consequently, Wicha and Adel had agreed to provide semi-washed beans from the next harvest.

Father and Son

JOHN GRAY WAS also busy creating Doi Chaang blends that would be introduced before the end of 2013. The decision to depart from offering the single-origin beans from the village in Thailand had been difficult, just one of the contentious subjects that Darch Junior complained about when discussing the travails of working with his father. As with many sons who work with powerful, successful fathers, Darch Junior frequently chafed at what he viewed as his father's too conservative, less than flexible approach. "We are opposites," he said. "Dad is old school, with a top-down management style… I'm a team player, looking for more input. Dad just decides, *This is the way it will be done.*" He paused. "He'll say that's not true. We fight a lot about that."

Darch Senior was not generally regarded as a dictator. Rather, he came across as courteous, thoughtful, caring, and receptive to hearing other people's ideas—and his commitment to working with the Akha, rather than having them work for him, corroborates this. But it may have been true that he was used to having things go his own way.

"Dad's business is the Akha people," Darch Junior said. "He doesn't care about anything but their welfare, and he wants to give back to Thailand all he has gotten out of it. I have to be the pragmatic side of the partnership and make sure we work as a company. The Akha practice sustainable agriculture. We have to be sustainable as a business, too." He observed that the Canadian specialty coffee market was near saturation point. "We can't create a bigger pie than what is there, so we have to be competitive." The Akha story was not enough. "People are interested in what they get out of a product more than what they are doing for someone else. We need to convey that we are among the best coffees in the world, and on top of that, we are half-owned by the Akha farmers. Our coffee is better, but people don't know it."

Earlier in 2013, the Darches had hired Fluid Creative, a professional Vancouver marketing company. Darch Junior felt vindicated by their advice. *There should be a taste profile on the bags. The black bags are dull and should be livelier. The face of Piko as a logo looks unfriendly. Change the name from Doi Chaang to its English equivalent, Elephant Mountain. Offer blends, not just single origin. Sell 340 gram bags, not one pound.*

Darch Senior ultimately agreed to add blends in smaller, variously colored bags. Perhaps they could be called Elephant Mountain, but Doi Chaang and Piko's face as the logo were already established for the single origin and should remain the same. This decision was reinforced when Darch Junior met with Costco managers, who insisted that the name and large black bags remain unchanged. As the company's largest customer, Costco could not be ignored. Ultimately, the Darches decided that the Doi Chaang brand was too well established to change to Elephant Mountain in Canada, but they registered the English name in the United States, where they hoped to expand someday.

There were two US possibilities. Darch Senior owned a second home on the island of Lanai in Hawaii, where John Walton, a fourth-generation Pepsi distributor in Washington State, was a sometime neighbor. Darch talked to Walton about carrying Doi Chaang/Elephant Mountain beans on Pepsi delivery trucks. Washington State, just across the border from Vancouver, seemed a logical US entry point. But the Walton Beverage managers weren't so sure, and the deal stalled. Besides, as Darch Junior pointed out, just getting the coffee on US shelves wasn't sufficient. How would they advertise and sell them?

Another possibility arose when Todd Carmichael, the wildly adventurous CEO of La Colombe Torrefaction Coffee in Philadelphia, Pennsylvania, got in touch. Carmichael, who set a world record in a 2008 solo trek to the South Pole, starred in a Travel Channel show called *Dangerous Grounds*, which documented his trips to seek out great coffee on exotic mountainsides. In May 2013 he ventured to Doi Chang village for an episode called "Thailand's Hidden Coffee," in which he bought 5,000 pounds of Doi Chaang peaberries for special distribution in cafés in West Elm stores across the country. In the show, Wicha was unfortunately reduced to a cameo appearance, while Darch Senior did the talking. To add drama, Carmichael was shown hauling himself out of the steep coffee fields on a rope ("Just call me Spiderman," he said) to reach the village. In reality, the rope was tied to a truck bumper. Although the show provided good publicity and a one-time sale, it did not create a permanent US presence.

Darch Senior came across very well on the TV show, as he did whenever he represented Doi Chaang. "Dad is a great salesman," his son admitted. "He's good one-on-one." As a mining venture capitalist, he was best at convincing investors to fork over their millions. But it was quite a different matter to convince millions of consumers to spend their dollars on Doi Chaang coffee.

Roasting was another source of conflict between father and son. Darch Senior was happy with the arrangement with Canterbury, but Darch Junior agitated for establishing their own roasting facility, now that gross sales were approaching $3 million annually. The toll roaster's fees were eating up too much of the potential profits. Wicha, who had achieved near-complete vertical integration in Thailand, also thought the Darches should have their own roaster. "No problem!" Wicha would say. "I send Akha to roast, bag, and deliver to stores for you. They sleep on the floor." Darch Senior politely explained that Vancouver was a different world, and that this would be viewed as illegal labor and exploitation, but Wicha didn't really get it. The Akha were eager workers who took charge of all aspects of the coffee business—they could do the Canadian work, and the business would be profitable, he insisted. In the end, they agreed to disagree, and Wicha did not pursue his suggestion.

Darch Senior had one other reason to stick with the large toll roaster. Canterbury had just purchased the big old Kraft roasting plant in Toronto and planned to expand eastward into Ontario. Canterbury was a very big fish in the relatively small pond of western Canada. Now Murray Dunlop hoped to make his mark in the Canadian heartland, and Doi Chaang could come along for the ride.

The Terminal City Club Office

THE DOI CHAANG offices were on the third floor of the elegant Terminal City Club building, on Vancouver's West Hastings Street, where Darch Senior had overseen his mining ventures. It housed many financial and mining-related firms, but it seemed an odd place for a coffee company. Because the small staff didn't need to roast, package, or distribute the coffee physically, however, it functioned perfectly well. Executive assistant/receptionist Jacquelyn Kingston not only helped keep the coffee company in order but also served as John Darch Senior's Western Investments secretary. Darch Senior had the only separate office, with a door, which he shared with his daughter, Katharine. They multitasked on Thai potash projects as well as Doi Chaang coffee.

In the main room, John Darch Junior, Anand Pawa, Tanya Jacoboni, Danika Speight, Sanja Grcic, and Katharine Sawchuk occupied cubicles, where they could yell across partitions to one another, and they often sat around a table or on the couch in the common space for meetings or casual lunch conversation. Darch Junior, forty-six, established a relaxed, playful but hardworking tone, fitting in well with the twentysomethings who worked for him.

John Darch Junior and Anand Pawa, the marketing director, flew to Thailand every six weeks or so to visit Doi Chang and talk directly with Wicha, Adel, Miga, and the other Akha, making sure that they were on the same wavelength. Each side of the partnership had to deal with seasonal issues—coffee sales began to pick up in the fall in Canada, for instance, just when the harvest season got underway in Doi Chang—and each side of the business tried to anticipate the needs of the other.

John Darch Senior joined them several times a year to lend his support and fatherly advice, and he kept tabs on all major developments. He never wavered in his commitment to the Doi Chaang project, and those around him acknowledged this. His lawyer George Brazier, who had helped Darch with various mining deals and had helped incorporate Doi Chaang Coffee, commented, "I take my hat off to him for the coffee venture. Most people would have thrown in the towel long ago." His accountant, Paul Royce, called him a "big picture" type who didn't always have the details at his fingertips, "but if he didn't have the answers, he would get them."

Sharon Cramen, Darch's private banker, made the most interesting observations. "John is as honest as can be, his integrity is super important to him, and his word is everything. If things fall through, he'll try to back it up eighteen ways to make it come to fruition." Cramen's select clients were all quite wealthy—some were billionaires—and she said that they all share one characteristic: Money isn't what drives them. Their work is fun, it's what they do, it's a challenging game, and money is just a way to measure it. "They are all workaholics. Being successful in business, putting a deal together, it defines who they are. I have clients in their eighties." Even among such high-powered clients, though, Darch Senior stood out. "I have never seen anyone travel as much. He used to buy a one-way ticket around the world once a month. I told his wife, Louise, that she had better come to grips with the fact that he will probably never really retire."

The Canadian coffee company was still barely making a profit, but two banks had each made substantial loans to Doi Chaang Coffee. Greg Noda and Scott Bearss of Canadian Western Bank's branch in Surrey, BC, first agreed to a $500,000 line of credit. Both men had worked for much larger banks, which wouldn't have made the loan, but Canadian Western was smaller and more nimble—and could think outside the box. "We met with John and John Junior and were impressed," said Noda. "It's rare that you find deals in which there is a bigger emotional connection, where it's not just number analysis. We were impressed with their compassionate capitalism model." And they trusted Darch Senior. "For us, John being behind it was enough. If half a million goes sideways, a big bank would look for a building to take over as an asset. But John is passionate and he will stand behind it. Also, he used to be a banker, so we speak the same language."

Noda then called Robert Napoli in Langley, BC, at First West Capital, part of a large credit union. "I've got something a little different for you," Noda said. "You've got to meet John." Napoli remembered thinking, *Oh no*, but over lunch, when Darch Senior told him the story of the Akha and their coffee, he made a quick decision. "That was the only time I've gone to a meeting where I met a client and made an offer on the spot." First West Capital made an additional $500,000 five-year loan.

Expanding Ripples

DARCH SENIOR'S NEW approach to doing business was attracting attention outside the coffee world. In June 2013, he was asked to participate in a seminar at the business school at the University of Victoria, BC, in which several MBA students were trying out their presentations for the Nespresso MBA Challenge contest. The challenge focused on how to ensure long-term sustainability for Colombian coffee farmers, and Professor Matt Murphy hoped that aspects of the Doi Chaang experience might provide a model to emulate. The University of Victoria cafeterias brewed Doi Chaang coffee.

Darch Senior enjoyed this aspect of his business: "connecting the dots," networking, sharing knowledge, and seeing what happened. In Victoria, Darch Senior explained how he had been introduced to Wicha and the Akha, how impressed he was at their self-determination, and how he decided to start the coffee company as a result. He spoke simply and from the heart. "We are practicing an alternative form of investing. We want to elevate the tribal farmers, helping the schools, giving them choices. We are a catalyst," he said. "We don't tell them what to do." He emphasized that his company was neither a charity nor a religious organization, as many people often assumed.

Then Anand Pawa and Darch Junior took over to explain the details and challenges of the business. Darch Junior emphasized that inequality was still built into the coffee business. "If you paid the Canadian minimum wage to Thai coffee harvesters, you'd be paying $50 here for a cup of coffee." Nonetheless, the prices they paid for green beans, well above Fair Trade requirements, meant that it was challenging to thrive in Canadian supermarkets, where they had to remain competitive.

The MBA students presented their "Cooperative Incubator" plan for Colombia, which proposed the development of regional cooperatives to disseminate "coffee-centric knowledge" and help farmers secure capital and access technology through mobile phones and the Internet, while encouraging crop diversity. What they were suggesting was already happening in the village of Doi Chang, where it wasn't unusual to see a coffee harvester pause on a mountainside to check his cell phone, where the Academy of Coffee provided free classes and seminars, and where honey, macadamia, tea, soap, and cordyceps were providing diverse income streams.

Darch Senior also told the MBA students that his company had just facilitated delivery of medical supplies to the village. The story behind that donation provided another example of the ripple effect. One day Robert Denning had called Darch from Calgary. As a coffee aficionado traveling through Thailand in 2011, he had stopped at a Doi Chaang café, loved the coffee, and been surprised to see a sign about the Canadian company. Once home, he looked it up online and called the Vancouver office. It turned out that he and Darch Senior both grew up in the British county of Dorset, and they hit it off, talking about cricket and rugby.

Denning told Darch that he wanted to help the village of Doi Chang in some way. Formerly an airline transport pilot, when he was forty-five he had sustained disabling injuries when his car slid off an icy road in the winter of 2009. He had gone to Thailand for therapeutic massage, fell in love with Peetah, now his fiancée, and discovered Doi Chaang coffee.

Subsequently, Denning arranged for Doi Chaang Coffee to be served at GlobalFest, an international Calgary event, where in August 2012 Wicha, Piko, Adel, Miga, and Sandra came to speak at the human rights forum. Denning and his two sons served the coffee. He also raised thousands of dollars from Calgary businesses and individuals to pay for the container of used, refurbished medical supplies through Food for the Hungry Canada, including an ultrasound machine, dental equipment, beds, blankets, gowns, wheelchairs, and instrument and scrub kits. Darch's company helped pay for the shipping costs. Denning then worked with the Rotary Club to send another container of books and furniture for the school in Doi Chang, as well as physiotherapy equipment for the clinic. One day he hoped to move to the village to teach English and coordinate aid efforts.

Crisis upon Crisis

IN SEPTEMBER 2013, Doi Chaang Coffee introduced its new blends, all organic Fair Trade, which John Gray of Canterbury had created. Following advice from Fluid Creative, the Vancouver marketing company, they opted for trendy, hip-sounding blend names, with pastel-colored 340-gram bags replacing the stark, black one-pound packages of the old single-estate Doi Chaang. The dark roast (Doi Chaang mixed with Nicaraguan beans) was called Hardwired, light (Doi Chaang, Peruvian and Guatemalan) was Chillin', medium roast (Doi Chaang and Sumatran) was Social Medium, and the espresso blend (Doi Chaang, Brazilian, Sumatran, Nicaraguan, and Peruvian) Espress-Yoself!

Unlike the single-estate packaging, the blends featured flavor notes on the bags. Social Medium, for instance, offered this description: "Our whole bean medium roast blend. Download your daily dose with this sweet, earthy medium roast blend. A balanced interaction of Doi Chaang Thai and Sumatran beans for fine complexity and a high-grown clean finish. Life is good." The blends all referred to "Our Master Roaster" (i.e., the Canterbury roaster) who "picks only the world's best fair trade organic beans." The story of the Akha hill tribe, featured prominently on the single-estate pound bags, was notably absent from the blends. Piko's picture was still there, but it had been modified slightly to make him less severe-looking than he was on the original packaging. In keeping with the company's approach to business, Wicha and Adel were consulted about these changes.

In October 2013, the Darches and Anand Pawa went to Doi Chang to negotiate the price for fifteen containers of coffee for the

TOP This 1988 photo shows the denuded Doi Chang area before coffee and shade tree reforestation. (photo: Duangta Sriwuthiwong)

ABOVE Village of Doi Chang nestled in the morning mist. (photo: Mark Pendergrast)

TOP *From left to right:* Wicha Promyong, whose vision inspired Doi Chaang Coffee, Piko Saedoo, whose image is the coffee's logo, and John M. Darch, who founded the company and gifted half of it to the Akha.

ABOVE Wicha Promyong (second from right) with Akha, circa 2005. Adel Saedoo is farthest to the right.

TOP Akha on village swing in Doi Chang village. (photo: Adel Saedoo)

ABOVE Akha women dressed in their finery on the coffee drying patio. (photo: Linda Aylesworth)

TOP LEFT Casually dressed Akha women usually harvest Doi Chaang coffee, but they don traditional headdresses for formal shots such as on the cover of this book. (photo: Mark Pendergrast)

TOP RIGHT Coffee tree in Doi Chang. Note that coffee beans ripen on the same tree at different times. (photo: Mark Pendergrast)

ABOVE You can still see signs that anti-missionary Matthew McDaniel posted in Doi Chang. (photo: Mark Pendergrast)

TOP Nowadays most houses in Doi Chang have metal roofs. (photo: Linda Aylesworth)

ABOVE The old village gate in Doi Chang, seen here with male and female figures, is no longer kept as an important protective symbol. (photo: Mark Pendergrast)

TOP This holy well in Doi Chang is one of nine the king drinks from each year. (photo: Mark Pendergrast)

ABOVE Doi Chaang Coffeehouse in Chiang Rai, Thailand. (photo: Linda Aylesworth)

TOP One of the few remaining thatched houses in Doi Chang. (photo: Mark Pendergrast)

ABOVE Truck stuck during rainy season on new dirt road going up to Doi Chang, circa 1984. (photo: Bandid Prasong)

LEFT Wicha Promyong with his ever-present clippers. (photo: Mark Pendergrast)

BELOW John M. Darch (Senior), the Canadian who started Doi Chaang Coffee in Vancouver, on the right, with his son, John A. Darch (Junior). (photo: Rhonda Dent)

new harvest, asking for a slightly lower amount, given the global decline in coffee prices. "I love Wicha like a brother, but he lives in his own world," Darch Senior said. "Our relationship continues to evolve and move forward, but it has to be a true partnership. It won't work if they regard us only as buyers of their green beans at an unrealistically high price." Fortunately, the negotiations went surprisingly well, with Wicha and Adel understanding the challenge and agreeing to $2.93 a pound. But that price would remain in place for an entire year, regardless of the C-market. "Most commercial roasters shift all the risk to the farmers, but we want to give them some stability and share the risk with them," Darch said.

Yet another crisis had erupted in mid-September 2013, when the BBC (British Broadcasting Corporation) aired a disturbing television program showing Indonesian civet cats kept in cramped cages, where they were fed coffee cherries. "The cages are completely barren, they're filthy, there's nowhere for them to climb, there's nowhere for them to properly hide," said Neil De Cruz of the World Society for the Protection of Animals (WSPA) on the television program.

The same day, the *Guardian* newspaper published an editorial by Tony Wild, the British coffee importer who had introduced *kopi luwak* (the Indonesian name for civet cat coffee) into the UK in 1991. Now he was launching a "Cut the Crap" campaign. "Nowadays," he wrote, "it is practically impossible to find genuine wild *kopi luwak*—the only way to guarantee that would be to actually follow a luwak around all night yourself." Wild lamented the terrible conditions that some caged civets endured: "The naturally shy and solitary nocturnal creatures suffer greatly from the stress of being caged in proximity to other luwaks, and the unnatural emphasis on coffee cherries in their diet causes other health problems too; they fight among themselves, gnaw off their own legs, start passing blood in their scats, and frequently die." Consequently, he launched a boycott of all civet coffee, which he called a

"preposterous, utterly hideous trade." On his blacklist, he included
Doi Chaang beans.

"Check out this campaign," e-mailed Simon Wakefield of
DRWakefield, the green coffee bean importer who sold Doi Chaang
beans in Britain. "Means we have to stop buying your regular coffee if you still trade luwak! [coffee excreted by civet cats]."

Two Thai staff employees of the World Society for the Protection of Animals (later renamed World Animal Protection) made
a clandestine visit to the village of Doi Chang in October 2013,
where they apparently spoke to Miga. In their report, they noted:
"The woman spoke strongly about Doi Chaang Coffee's commitment to collecting and selling only wild-sourced coffee and
pointed out that caging civets is cruel." They found that some villagers were keeping caged civets, but they had no affiliation with
the coffee company.

Despite this exoneration, Lynn Kavanagh, the Canadian WSPA
director, refused to make the report public, writing: "We can't
endorse a company because doing so would then require that
we continue to do regular checks." But she did offer to put Darch
Senior in touch with Tony Wild and to let him know that "your
company is genuine in its claim about selling only wild-sourced
civet coffee."

In the meantime, some irate consumers blasted the Canadian
coffee company, as in this December 2013 e-mail: "There are several petitions going around that call for an end to the cruelties you
impose on these beautiful little animals that you seem to want
excrement from ... You say it is organic and fair trade, but what you
don't mention is how you steal the lives of sentient beings ... Wake
up and smell the coffee, you heartless, apathetic lunatics."

Public relations director Katharine Sawchuk wrote back: "We
truly understand why you are passionate about the welfare of
civets, and we believe they should not be caged or abused for
the production of coffee." She included links to documentaries

indicating that Doi Chaang's civet coffee was indeed collected from the village mountainsides. The angry correspondent was convinced and even wished the Canadian Doi Chaang staff a Merry Christmas. On January 6, 2014, Darch Senior had a good conversation with Tony Wild, who agreed to remove Doi Chaang civet coffee from his Cut the Crap campaign.

Then, just as one crisis ended, another began. At the end of February 2014, Vancouver truckers went on strike. The city's port was closed down for a month, leaving a container of Doi Chaang green coffee beans stranded. For three weeks, the company had nothing to roast. Darch Junior estimated that the company lost $300,000 in sales for the month of March. To add insult to injury, the port charged $300 a day for storage fees. "We have one [new] container arriving today," Darch told a reporter on March 28, 2014, a few days after the strike ended, "but the port won't accept it because they are backlogged, so that container has to be shipped for an extra $5,000 to Calgary."

Two months later, on May 22, 2014, the Thai government of Yingluck Shinawatra was overthrown in a bloodless military coup, following six months of protests. Yingluck was widely perceived to be a puppet of her older brother, Thaksin, who was ousted as the Thai prime minister in 2006, convicted of abusing his power, and now lived in exile. Some Thai felt that the Yingluck government had disrespected the king and had ruined the rice market by endorsing a poorly planned, corrupt stockpiling scheme. While many uninformed observers might hear the phrase "military coup" and assume the worst, most Thai experts thought that the coup, which the elderly king subsequently endorsed, was a reasonable solution to an untenable situation.

The coup had no discernable impact on Doi Chaang coffee, in Thailand or in Canada, but Darch Senior realized that the Canadian company he had started needed to assess its goals and trajectory. That May, he asked banker Rob Napoli of First West Capital to moderate a meeting about the future of Doi Chaang, seeking a long-term plan. "The Akha tribe in the village of Doi Chang is doing pretty well now," Napoli observed. "It feels like the goal of self-sufficiency is mostly accomplished. Where does that leave your company, what is its mission in life?" Should they extend the Beyond Fair Trade model to another needy community?

Maybe at some point that would make sense, but the staff consensus was that there was more to do for the Thai village, which still needed to build its new school and had yet to begin to take its own profits rather than plowing them all back into capital projects. Besides, the Canadian business was not in nearly as good shape as its Thai counterpart. It continued to struggle to establish itself as a strong contender in the specialty coffee industry, even in its home territory of British Columbia. What strategy did they want to pursue? They had begun to do some business in Ontario. Would they continue to push into Eastern Canada? Would they be able to penetrate the neighboring market in the United States? They had established a foothold in the UK. What was their ultimate goal in Europe?

"What do you want to be in five years?" Napoli asked, "and what are you willing to give up to get there?" No one had good answers to Napoli's questions. Everyone agreed that none of them were coffee experts. The Darches had launched a new company with great idealism but without really knowing what they were doing. Canterbury had been very helpful in reaching a certain level, but as Doi Chaang grew larger, the toll fees were eating up too much of the profits. While it might make sense to start their own roaster at some point, Darch Senior made it clear that he was not eager to throw more money into the venture until they had a clearer mission statement. He assigned Darch Junior to get the staff to come up with a strategic vision paper in the coming months. Then they would call Rob Napoli back for another session.

In the meantime, the Canadian company underwent some changes. Receptionist Jackie Kingston left, and Ksenia "Senni" Dempster replaced her. "What drew me to this job," she said, "was that it is an ethically focused, sustainable business. It makes you feel that you are working for a good cause."

In early August 2014, the company changed locations, moving to new offices on Powell Street, a few blocks to the east of the Terminal City Club. There Doi Chaang would have more space for less money in a grittier, industrial area not far from trendy Gastown and its restaurants, bars, and coffeehouses. It was a more logical location for a coffee company, with street-level access, and now the name Doi Chaang Coffee would be prominently displayed outside the building.

From a business perspective, the staff dedicated a great deal of attention to every account. In Costco, a TDP ("temporary price discount") for Doi Chaang was boosting sales of the two-pound black single-estate bags, but Starbucks overlapped with its own TDP, which was irritating to Doi Chaang staffer Tanya Jacoboni when she went to check the shelves in 2014. Costco had not yet added the new Doi Chaang blends, but some of those blends were doing well elsewhere, particularly Social Medium, the medium roast in the pastel blue bag. Chillin', the light roast, fared poorly, and London Drugs was phasing it out. Espress-Yoself, the espresso blend, wasn't selling very well either. There was also concern over the Safeway account, where sales of single-estate had been lagging. The company wondered if it should arrange a promotion and try to persuade the store to add the new blends. Conversely, things were going well at City Market, where the store was promoting Doi Chaang at a $2 discount, and the company had offered free brewed drinks during a "demo." And there was hope that Whole Foods would once again sell Doi Chaang, since the new coffee buyer was interested in new brands.

Public relations director Katharine Sawchuk had plans to promote Doi Chaang Coffee at Destination Thailand, an event to
be sponsored by the Thai Embassy in Toronto's Yonge-Dundas
Square in September. This was a chance for thousands to sample
Doi Chaang coffee, which was particularly exciting because Doi
Chaang blends were newly available in Longo's and Freshco chains
in Ontario. To capitalize on a forthcoming article on Doi Chaang
in Canada's *Financial Post*, Sawchuk planned to send gift baskets
to promising Toronto outlets, bloggers, and media. Another positive development was that Fair Trade Canada was becoming more
proactive, planning a Fair Trade promotion, "The Power of You," in
major grocery chains, and Doi Chaang would be prominent in the
Fair Trade literature.

At City Market, Doi Chaang blends were on sale for $10.49 in
the 340 gram bags, versus Ethical Bean's $12.99 sale price for the
same size bag—and the Doi Chaang bags were also positioned at
eye-level, thanks to Joe, the friendly store manager. Such personal
connections were very difficult to make, but they were worth pursuing because of the return on time investment. Doi Chaang had
therefore decided to hire a full-time merchandiser to keep tabs on
retail stores, making sure they were well stocked and the products
well positioned.

The new Doi Chaang Aroma cups were not selling well, though,
regardless of their positioning and competitive pricing. The
single-serve capsules worked in the current generation of Keurig
machines, but the Keurig 2.0 was due out soon, and it would not
accept anything but the company's K-Cups. Litigation against the
Keurig monopoly effort was pending. With the future of Aroma
cups uncertain, Doi Chaang was not going to spend its limited
marketing budget on trying to increase their sales.

Meanwhile, Darch Senior mulled over the future of the company. Following the staff meeting with Rob Napoli, he recognized

the importance of having a strategic business plan to look forward to the next few years. A chain of Doi Chaang coffeehouses in Canada was one possibility. "My talent is not on the operational side," he acknowledged, but he was good at overall vision and leadership. He regarded the coffee venture as similar to starting a junior mining company, which would be successful only if it found investors. "We need to find strategic partners to help us get to the next level. I don't have a short list yet. I don't know who we'll marry, but I can tell you the virtues of our future mate—a well-funded person who helped develop a successful coffee company, with experience in marketing and organization." But whoever came aboard would have to buy into the model of 50 percent Akha ownership. That part would remain nonnegotiable.

Anand Pawa felt the company needed a passionate specialty coffee person, perhaps a Q cupper. "None of us are really coffee people," he said. "We go to SCAA meetings, and people don't know what to make of us." In other words, they just ran an office. He thought they needed to have their own roaster by the end of 2015. They were losing money by staying with Canterbury because Canterbury charged too much for various services.

Darch Senior agreed that "we have reached the level of sales where it makes sense mathematically to roast our own, but math is one thing, and skill sets is another. For our growth, we have to reach outside our company for expertise in marketing, sales, and operations." Until then, he planned to stick with Canterbury.

The partnership forged by Wicha Promyong and John Darch seemed to be working remarkably well. But as I discovered during three research trips to the village of Doi Chang, tragedy and conflict might have derailed all the progress already made there. Since this book became a kind of personal odyssey for this coffee author, I have switched to the first person to write the final two chapters of this saga.

CHAPTER 8

An Outside Perspective

THE CANADIAN SIDE of the company went to great lengths to maintain a solid relationship with the Thai side. It was company policy to take the Vancouver employees (those who stayed at least three years) to Doi Chang to show them where the coffee they sold came from and why it was so important. I was invited to accompany some staff on one of these trips in March 2013 so that I could see for myself how the company operated and what changes it had produced in the village.

The rainy season hadn't yet begun, and as we drove up the mountain to the village, the hillsides, mostly barren of trees, were brown and unappealing. Some still smoldered from illegal fires set to clear the brush. On the side of the road, we saw garlic bulbs spread out to dry. As we neared the top, we entered a more forested region, with coffee seedlings by the side of the road, growing under black cloth screens to shade them. An off-shoot road forked left to the Akha village of Saen Charoen and another went right to the Lisu village of Doi Lan, but we kept straight on and crested a ridge near the top of the mountain. Now the landscape was completely transformed, with trees everywhere, some towering over us, others shorter, sporting the glossy green leaves I recognized as belonging to coffee shrubs.

We could see the village of Doi Chang tucked into the valley below, but before we got there, we turned off the road to the left onto what looked like a large concrete parking lot. It was, in fact, the drying patio for processed Doi Chaang coffee beans. The harvest had ended a few weeks earlier, so there were only a few remaining beans scattered near the big processing mill to the right, with its various concrete vats where the coffee cherries had been fermented for twelve hours, then depulped and fermented again in water—twenty-four hours for "semi-washed" and forty-eight hours for "fully washed"—before being demucilaged. A big conveyor belt at a 30-degree angle reached up from the processing plant. Below its highest point was a huge pile of cherry pulp. Worms and special bacteria had been added to help turn the new pile more quickly into fertile compost to spread beneath coffee trees.

Next door, women sat around tables, sorting the processed green coffee beans, removing any that were broken, bug-damaged, over-fermented, or otherwise imperfect. And next door there was a large warehouse with piles of burlap bags bulging with coffee. Many contained beans still resting in parchment, their papery outer covering. They would be hulled shortly before they were shipped out.

I was to discover all of this shortly, but first we got out of the van, stretched our legs, and walked left into the brand-new two-story coffeehouse, which would be dedicated that night. We ordered coffee drinks—I got a beautiful cappuccino—at the bar, then sat at tables made of cross sections of rustic logs. The chairs, too, were rough-hewn and solid.

I met Adel, a round-faced man with straight, silky jet-black hair and an engaging smile, dressed in conventional, comfortable slacks and a sports shirt. He looked much younger than his forty-three years. As a child, he spoke only Akha, but now he was fluent in Thai and could understand much of what I said in English. He was just uncomfortable trying to communicate in English.

Then a small man with a scraggly beard and loose-fitting clothes strode over the parking lot from the large Academy of Coffee building at the far end of the concrete drying patio, where Doi Chaang delivery trucks were lined up. Wicha Promyong greeted me with a firm handshake after shifting his ever-present clippers to his left hand. He later explained that he used the clippers to snip promising cuttings of unusual plants. The clippers were almost a security blanket for him. He even slept with them next to his pillow in his "palace," as he called the tiny thatched-roof hut where he lived in a small leafy glade to the left of the Academy.

Wicha spoke excellent English (he had lived four years in England, and his first wife was Scottish), so I didn't need a translator. Despite his maniacally busy schedule—he always seemed to be explaining something, planning a new project, or talking on his cell phone—he spent a lot of time with me over the next few days, explaining the operation, telling me about his childhood and remarkable life, describing the plight of the hill tribes, and outlining his vision for the future.

We piled into a four-wheel drive truck for a tour. Over time, I drew a rough map of Doi Chang and the surrounding area, reproduced at the front of this book, as improved by graphic artist Carol MacDonald.

We drove out of the Doi Chaang Coffee compound and turned left, passing A-Roy's noodle soup restaurant, a small office building, and the Doi Chaang Mart (which features the highest ATM machine in Thailand). We descended to a Y intersection where we turned left to go down to the village. The roads here were concrete, old and cracked, but more durable than the new asphalt. My first impression was that this was a sleepy, poverty-stricken area, with scruffy children and chickens in the road, red clay gashes, clothes hung on lines outside ramshackle homes, and vegetables drying on bamboo platforms. But then I noticed all the motor scooters and trucks, the satellite dishes, and some modern-looking homes amidst the shacks, and I realized that in its way, Doi Chang was a boomtown.

In the middle of the village, we turned right and started uphill. The road deteriorated quickly, then turned into rutted dirt, as we bounced higher and crested a ridge. We were surrounded by hundreds of acres of lush coffee trees in delightfully fragrant bloom. This was a critical time, when a severe storm and high winds could severely impact the next crop. The white coffee flowers last only a few days, though they bloom on the mountain in waves over a few weeks, during which the honeybees busily work to produce the special Doi Chaang coffee honey.

We lurched from side to side, then stopped to get out and explore. We walked down among the blossoming coffee trees, which enveloped us in their gentle, sweet odor. Wicha pointed out the macadamia shade trees as well as a white-flowering tree he called a siew, explaining that it fixed nitrogen to enrich the soil. A few workers were pruning coffee trees nearby. In his emphatic way, Wicha used the present tense, though he was talking about the past: "Many grow tomatoes and cabbage here. I hate that kind of crop. They cut down all trees, and they spray insecticides and chemical fertilizer. Then the price drop, no use even harvesting. And people get sick from the pesticide. You see this?" He swept his arm expansively. "Coffee is beautiful crop, no need for chemicals." Indeed, with the coffee and its shade trees, biodiversity had returned to the area. We could hear birds singing, insects thrumming. Snakes, deer, and civet cats had reportedly come back to the mountain, along with pythons and cobras.

We continued our drive to Ban Mai, which means "New Village," an outpost of raggedy-looking dwellings near the coffee fields, then looped back to the intersection where we had turned down to the village. This time we turned left to go up the mountain, past the Wawi Highland Agricultural Research Station and its thousand-plus acres that had been snatched from the Lisu and Akha back in the 1980s, past a few small Akha communities hanging onto the left side of the road, past the Royal Project on the right and the military outpost on the left, and up to a park owned by the research station, with a spectacular view of the mountaintop and valley. "You see?" Wicha said. "It looks like elephant's head with trunk curved back."

On the return trip, we stopped in the middle of a peaceful bamboo grove that featured multiple statues of Buddha, apparently over a century old, though no one knows who brought them there. We walked quietly through the grove and came to a swampy pond with lily pads, hanging moss, bromeliads, and croaking frogs. Around the far end, we came to a circular stone-walled well, one of the nine sacred wells from which the Thai king drinks once a year. A young monk, whom I later met, lives nearby in a small house with its own temple area. He walks down into the village every morning with his begging bowl, but few could blame him for hitching a ride back up the steep slope.

We drove back to the Doi Chaang compound. There I met Miga, Adel's younger sister, at her desk in the Academy, where she kept track of orders and maintained records. A short woman with a ready laugh, Miga was the one who worked most closely with Wicha, whose desk sat just behind hers. I also met Nuda, a niece of Miga and Adel, who made the Doi Chaang soap, and Lipi, a nephew, who grew tea as well as coffee.

That night we took part in a feast to celebrate the opening of the new coffeehouse, with many Akha men and women in attendance. The men looked debonair in their fedora hats and sober dark pants, with their brightly colored embroidered vests and bags hung from their shoulders. The women were decked out in elaborate leggings, skirts, and jackets, topped by extraordinary headdresses, dripping with silver coins, balls, colored feathers, and beads. They laughed and gossiped in Akha as they ate.

There was an extravagant amount of food, including lots of meat—beef, chicken, pork, duck—as if to make up for all the years of poverty on the barren hillside where game had disappeared along with wild edibles. Wicha told me that at one stage people had been reduced to eating fried banana flowers with salt.

To round out my first day, as the darkness fell, we gathered in the Academy of Coffee around the fire. (That fire was kept smoldering all day to cure the thick thatched roof and prevent insects from eating it.) Wicha and I sat against the wall, where he sipped his green tea and smoked a cigarette. I observed that he *really* ought to quit smoking. He just laughed. I said that his body was too small to abuse like that. Maybe that's why he was more tired than usual, he said. He didn't want to travel so much anymore.

I love to sing, especially old folk songs, and Wicha had told me he used to be a rock musician and protest singer, so I asked if we might sing something we both knew. It turned out he knew a lot of songs—Bob Dylan; Joan Baez; John Denver; the Kingston Trio; Peter, Paul & Mary; Hank Williams; Harry Belafonte; Nat King Cole; and other old tunes—so I harmonized above his sensitive, smoky baritone, sitting around a fire there on a mountain in Thailand. Then he broke into "Malaika," an African song. I pulled out my harmonica, on which Wicha played a lively version of "Oh! Susanna" and a soulful version of "There's No Place Like Home." *This man will be my friend,* I thought.

The Village

THE NEXT DAY Anand Pawa, Lipi, and I drove down into the village. I wanted to get more of a sense of who lived there and how coffee had impacted their lives. Coffee trees were growing in front yards, coffee beans drying on various patios.

In addition to those who called themselves traditional Akha in the village, there were a sizable number of Catholic and Protestant Akha—perhaps as many as 70 percent of the villagers. The Catholics had mostly been converted by Korean or Italian missionaries, and the Protestants (just called "Christians," as opposed to "Catholics"), had been converted primarily by American Baptists, Australian evangelists, or Aje, who all those years ago had convinced his father, Aso, to become a Christian. A small but growing number of Akha had become Buddhists. The remaining Lisu—many of whose relatives had left for the lowlands in the 1990s—lived on the high side of the village. There were a few Chinese families in the same neighborhood, and some Chinese had intermarried with Lisu. The old antagonisms seemed mostly to have been consigned to the past.

Near the main road, I saw a traditional Akha swing, its four tall posts tied with thickly twined vines at the top. It stood ready to carry boys, girls, and adults for three days the following August or September, during the annual fall Swing Festival. I asked where the upper village gate was, and Lipi led me to a small gate such as I had seen in books, with wooden birds atop it and a carved woman and man (with an oversized penis) outside it. But the gate was lost amidst a jumble of houses, as were the other two village gates. Doi Chang had spilled outside the gates, which had traditionally divided and protected the Akha from threatening jungle spirits and outsiders. No one had bothered to replace them annually, so they were slowly rotting. *This is a sad, symbolic commentary on fading traditions*, I thought.

The houses, mostly made of concrete cinderblock and lumber, with corrugated metal roofs, were jammed close to one another, with little room for vegetable gardens, which had been moved near the coffee fields. Land on the main road sold for $1.5 million baht ($50,000) for a hundred square meters (about a thousand square feet), while prime coffee-growing land cost 50,000 baht ($1,700) per rai (about 0.4 acres), putting it far beyond the reach of the average laborer.

No one knew exactly how many people lived full-time in Doi Chang. The official census, taken every ten years, is unreliable, because illegal immigrants from Burma and Laos are, of course, unregistered. There are probably 8,000 to 10,000 people living in Doi Chang, and during the coffee harvest, that number could nearly double with temporary workers. There were signs of new construction everywhere, with raw red clay cut away, rebar sticking up from concrete foundations. Almost all of this growth had taken place in the past ten years, with the pace increasing in the past five years, after the Canadians had begun to buy Doi Chaang beans.

A consumer lifestyle was becoming established. Somsak, a former village chief and another cousin of Adel, invited us into his spacious home, where we sat on a couch in his tile-floored living room on the second floor, which featured a large flat-screen television. The house was only a year old, with room for his three children, ages fourteen, sixteen, and twenty, but they were all in school down in Chiang Rai. He ran a business on the bottom floor of his home, bottling Ja Dae Water. The brand name came from the city of Ja Dae in Yunnan Province, from which the Akha had allegedly been forced to flee centuries ago. Water piped from a spring up the mountain was subjected to UV light and a reverse osmosis process. His sixteen-year-old son, home on vacation, was using a hair dryer to melt hygienic plastic over the filled bottles to seal them. Somsak said that the spring water coming out of his tap was perfectly safe, but he had to treat the bottled water to meet Thai FDA inspection criteria.

Somsak also owned a 30-acre coffee farm and his own brand, Ja Dae Coffee, which he roasted and sold in Bangkok, Chiang Rai, and elsewhere. The Doi Chaang trucks transported his coffee for a fee. Why would they help the competition? "We all help each other," he said, which is the same thing Adel had told me. There was a big enough market for everyone.

Everyone in the village now had income relating to coffee, one way or the other. This boom was bringing more and more people to Doi Chang, and there was some concern that the village was becoming too congested. While the growth meant more and varied jobs—for cooks, construction workers, fruit growers, motorcycle repairmen, for example—it was now harder for villagers to find room to grow vegetables near home.

We then stopped at a community gathering spot, where men, women, and children sat or reclined on a raised bamboo platform shaded from the hot afternoon sun by a makeshift roof, where I spoke to Boocha, a woman who lived nearby. She was a Catholic, she told me, along with everyone else there. There were ninety-six households in the neighborhood. She was converted twenty-two years ago by Italian missionaries from Mae Suai, down the mountain.

A young man leaning on his motor scooter seemed particularly friendly and interested. Unlike many of the older Akha, Worachit spoke fluent Thai. He grew coffee on 3 rai and sold his cherries to Doi Chaang. "Wicha is a good man," he said. "He helps people." He knew that some of his beans might go abroad somewhere for *farangs* to drink, maybe Canada, he had heard.

I asked if anyone still had a thatched roof, and Worachit surprised me by saying that he did, though he didn't like having to patch it, and he planned to replace it with metal when he could afford to. Intrigued, I asked if we could see it, so we followed his scooter far down a truly awful, narrow dirt road and stopped beside a tiny thatched hut with children's clothes hanging on a line in the back. His home had a bamboo floor and two rooms. He and his daughter, six, and son, four, slept together on one side, while his wife and eight-month-old daughter slept in the other room. On the rough wooden walls were pictures of Mary and the baby Jesus and, of course, the king and queen. On a shelf sat a very small television set.

Back in the truck, we drove back up to the main road, turned left, and soon turned off into a courtyard where we found the Lisu macadamia factory in full swing, since this was the harvest season. The round brown casings that contain the white nut meat grow inside something resembling a dark green walnut shell. A clattery machine took off the shells, and then the unripe "floaters" were picked from the surface of the water. The rest of the smooth round brown balls, which reminded me of giant gumballs, had to be slow roasted and dried at low heat for three days. Then they were cracked open one at a time by women operating a simple device that brought a sharp point down on each shell, cracking it gently without harming the gumdrop-shaped nut inside. The nuts could then be further roasted, sometimes flavored with honey or other spices.

The afternoon was waning by the time we found a Lisu man in his late fifties who was willing to talk to us as his grandchildren played nearby. I forgot to ask for his name. "Yes, I grow coffee," he said, on 5 acres. He used to grow rice, corn, and eggplant, but now, coffee and some macadamia and Chinese cherry. He sold his coffee to Doi Chaang, using the profits to improve his house, which was made of concrete blocks. He had been born in this location in a thatched hut.

He said that there was no longer friction between the Lisu and Akha. His nephew was married to an Akha woman. "It will be easier for my grandchildren, but I wouldn't be sitting here doing this

interview in my father's generation. They didn't talk to strangers."
It wasn't that the Lisu and Akha hated each other in years past, he
said. They just stayed in their own groups, that's all, with very limited interactions.

An Education in Coffee

ANOTHER DAY I was lucky enough to meet agronomist Patchanee
Suwanwisolkit, who had been so instrumental in helping the
Akha. From Chiang Mai University, she brought an expert, entomologist Professor Yaowaluk Chanbang, to teach farmers from
Doi Chang and nearby villages about how to control coffee berry
borers (Hypothenemus hampei, known as broca in Latin America), a
tiny black insect nuisance, without using chemicals.

The infestation had to be caught when the cherries were just
forming. It would be too late once the coffee beans were mature.
"Females can bore into cherries as small as 2.3 millimeters," the
entomologist said. They chew chambers in the coffee seed in
which they lay their eggs. The hatched larvae then feed on the
seeds. He recommended that each farmer get a magnifying glass.
All diseased cherries had to be picked off. He flashed photos of the
insect's life cycle—eggs, larvae, pupa, adult—all of them living
inside a coffee cherry. Then he demonstrated how to make a simple trap out of an empty plastic bottle, cutting a section from the
middle and hanging a small bottle of scented lure—three parts
methanol to one part ethanol—to attract the bugs. Drill a hole
through the bottle cap to hang it by wire to the tree, and put soapy
water in the bottom to catch and drown the insects.

As he explained all of this, I talked to a few visiting farmers. Sura Phon, a Lisu from Doi Lan, had started with a half-acre
thirteen years ago and now owned 30 acres of coffee. He grew

supplementary crops including cabbage, radish, and tomato and some fruit trees. Unlike most farmers, he drank his own coffee, he said. Yes, he had noticed a lot more birds now, and he planned to plant more shade trees, including some macadamia. I asked what he did for fun. "I am too busy to play."

Yi Pha, an Akha from Ban Mai, told me he had been growing coffee for eight years on 7 acres because it guaranteed a more stable income than the tomatoes he used to grow. As he spoke, I noticed his reddish brown teeth, stained from chewing betel nut. Yes, he said, he now had a Thai ID card, which Adel helped him to get when he was village chief.

I asked Wicha if there had been a turning point for the village. He explained how he had motivated two Akha brothers, Law Beh and La Cho, who own about 10 acres nearby. "I told them, trust me, follow me, you do the way I am teaching, you do pruning, mulching, fertilizer like this, I guarantee that you will get at least 80,000 baht. But whatsoever, if you make more money, it belong to you. The first year they follow me, they make more than 300,000 baht. That was ten years ago. Two boys start doing it. Some follow, more and more now, doing shade-grown, mulching, pruning."

I told him that I was confused about who owned the land, since I had read that, technically, the government had declared all of the northern mountains a national preserve. "In a sense they own their own land to grow coffee on, but they have no rights by law, no papers." But the government couldn't realistically confiscate the land, since it was doing too well already. "Instead, the government now brings people up here to show them what we are doing and to take credit for it. I don't care, as long as the way of life of my people is better," Wicha said.

He explained how he had studied the tea, honey, and soap businesses, and he hoped to expand into a line of cosmetics, having found that coffee oil was good for the complexion. He had also added a small line of Doi Chaang macadamia nuts. For three years, Doi Chaang had been the exclusive agent for small Colombian coffee pulpers. "We sell to Laos, Burma, Thailand, all over." He had convinced Paolo Fantaguzzi, the Italian who had installed the new Brambati roaster, to move to Thailand and start the Ital-Thai Service Company, to build and repair brewers and, eventually, to build their own coffee roasters. "I can't just keeping doing one thing, you know?" Wicha said. "We have to do everything by our own."

Wicha said that there were now some 300 coffeehouses serving Doi Chaang Coffee in Thailand, six in Australia, five in Japan, two big shops in Malaysia, and he had ambitious plans for 300 Korean cafés within the next two years. "They asked for 1,200 in Korea, but we don't have enough coffee yet to supply them," he said. That made me ask why he still needed the Canadians, if he could sell so much roasted coffee for a bigger profit right there in Asia. It was thanks to Darch and his company, he said, that Doi Chaang coffee had gained international recognition. "Don't forget that we start together, you know? People know the name Doi Chaang. That's from Canada. Ourselves, we know how to grow coffee, how to produce coffee. But to introduce to the market, they do it. We are family, we are family. We work together," he said, clasping his hands together. "Not just business."

I asked Wicha whether the sudden relative wealth from coffee might be too much for some of the Akha to handle. "Now everyone gets paid," he said. "Some want to show off, go to town, spend money like rich man, buy new truck every year, new house in town, gambling. These are mostly men in their forties and fifties." Yes, there were drug problems in Doi Chang, especially methamphetamines called Ya Ba. "To solve this problem, we asked the military to base here."

Still, he had high hopes for young people. He wanted the Doi Chaang Coffee Foundation to build a $2 million school for children from all twenty-five villages in the district. The school would have room to house one hundred children who came from too far away to commute. "All tribes will learn to be together."

Wicha still seemed to be the heart and soul of the operation. I wondered what would happen if he were bitten by a cobra? Would the business collapse? Would Adel and Miga be able to carry on without their visionary leader?

In Chiang Rai, before flying back to Bangkok, I met Wicha's charming daughter Kwan, my waitress at the Doi Chaang Coffee-house. This was the café's third location, larger and more central than the previous spots. With its trees and courtyard, it provided an oasis from the busy city street. Its menu extended beyond coffee, including goodies such as coffee fudge, coconut pie, and macadamia brownies, along with homemade ice cream flavors such as strawberry, green tea, and mixed berry. There were also light lunches to appeal to Western tourists, ranging from mushroom Panini sandwiches to a hamburger and fries. Although they may have faced a steep learning curve, it was obvious that Wicha's family, many of whom lived in the back of the coffeeshop, ran a sophisticated, popular operation that was attracting both locals and tourists.

Harvest Time in the Mountains

I RETURNED TO Doi Chang in November 2013, near the start of the frenetic harvest season. Every afternoon, pickup trucks laden with bulging burlap bags lined up near huge scales next to the processing station. Farmers threw the bags with freshly picked coffee cherries onto the scales, then anxiously awaited the results, before a team of Doi Chaang workers emptied the sacks into a huge vat of ripe cherries. The farmers received a chit to redeem for cash at the

ATM machine down the road. In 2013, with the C-market prices dropping, they received 18 baht per kilo early in the season, when there were more unripe berries in the mix. A week or two into the season, the price would go up to 20 baht.

With the cash flowing more slowly than it had in 2012, Wicha took a two-day trip to borrow money from a couple of banks in Nan Province. Despite the fact that Thai banks don't like to lend money on volatile commodities, Doi Chaang was now well known within Thailand, and the loans wouldn't be difficult to secure.

The previous morning in Bangkok, before flying to Chiang Rai, I had met John Darch Junior and Anand Pawa, who had been in Shanghai striking a deal with two young sisters whose father had begun Oro Caffè, based in Udine, Italy. Oro Caffè had ordered a container of green beans to roast or sell in Italy, Germany, and France. "If all goes well, this could be a big foot in the door in continental Europe," Darch Junior said.

Then we picked up a Rainforest Alliance auditor from Indonesia, who was joining us to explore certification for Doi Chaang beans. Darch Junior explained that Fair Trade certification was cumbersome and expensive, with a 20 cent per pound charge at both the green bean and roasted level. "Plus we have to pay the $4,200 annual auditing fee." Rainforest Alliance charged only for the audit, so many roasters were considering a switch away from Fair Trade.

We flew to Chiang Rai and drove up to Doi Chang. All seemed amicable at first, but talks with the Rainforest auditor soon turned tense. He wanted more information about the farmers than anyone could easily provide. Anand Pawa, Wicha, and Darch Junior explained that any village farmer could sell to Doi Chaang, but that they were also free to go elsewhere. Rainforest wanted a more formal cooperative arrangement. The next morning, the auditor left without any resolution of the issue.

Wild or Captive Civet Cats?

DOI CHAANG COFFEE had been cleared of any involvement of cruelty to civets, but I wanted to see for myself how the Doi Chaang civet beans were found and collected. The day after a heavy downpour, Lipi's brother Jay led me up into Lipi's steep acreage. I brought my small digital video camera to document the trek, which I undertook in my sandals, slipping badly and clutching onto coffee and shade trees to keep my balance. After a very challenging climb, we finally located a mound of civet-pooped coffee beans, clustered between the coffee trees. Jay explained that they wouldn't pick it up until the end of the harvest season, because a civet would return to the same place to defecate only if the site remained undisturbed. We climbed further up the mountainside and found several more civet cat deposits. We also encountered Jay's sister-in-law picking coffee cherries; she had told him where to find the deposits of civet coffee.

Jay said that he could tell the difference between wild and caged coffee poop, that the wild version was darker, with more variation in bean size. He had never seen a civet cat, since they come out only at night. As I clambered down the muddy mountainside, splashing over a stream, I considered that it would indeed be easier to feed caged civets, but I could now prove that the Doi Chaang civet coffee I witnessed was authentically wild.*

Later I found that some villagers were raising civets in cages, feeding them coffee cherries, and attempting to market them for a large profit. But none of them were trying to sell them to Doi Chaang. The caged civets I saw did not appear to be mistreated, and their owners were obviously unaware that they were doing anything wrong or controversial. The civets, which looked like

---

* On YouTube, search "civet cat Pendergrast" to see video I shot.

skinny raccoons, were kept in relatively large, separate cages, and were fed coffee cherries and bananas. Nonetheless, I agreed with Wicha and the WSPA that civets are wild animals and should not be kept captive.

Cordyceps

BACK FROM HIS trip to woo bankers, Wicha revealed that he had several new projects on the go. Eight types of edible and medicinal mushrooms from Hungary and Nepal were growing in moist test wood in plastic jugs, with a small building under construction for mushroom agronomy near the pulp pile. Wicha said that the mushrooms thrived using the pulp as a growing medium. "Just one hundred pots of mushrooms, it feeds like ten or twenty families, and you don't have to invest a lot," he explained. He planned to use it as a demonstration project for villagers, who could get a tenfold return by growing their own mushrooms and selling them fresh or dried. A Chiang Mai University professor would come every week to offer tutorials.

In the basement of the office building, Wicha was having equipment installed to process and bottle fruit and energy drinks he planned to make from the mushrooms and local wild fruits, as well as blue and green teas, along with bottled water. He created a new corporate name for each new business. Doi Chaang EcoZone would make the drinks, and Doi Chaang BioGrade the mushrooms. But the biggest and most exciting project was to grow cordyceps, a fungus that was gaining a growing reputation as an alternative medicine. The parasitic fungus grows in spectacularly ghoulish fashion from the bodies of caterpillars and spiders in the mountains of Tibet and Nepal, sprouting in stringy orange growths that kill their hosts. It has been used in traditional Chinese medicine for centuries and is supposed to prevent various types of cancer and kidney disease, strengthen the immune system, increase energy levels, and act as an aphrodisiac.

Over the summer, a Thai entrepreneur nicknamed Nong (Chayanin Sritisarn) had seen Wicha on a television program and contacted him. Having made a substantial amount of money from selling a chicken processing business, she was seeking a more life-affirming enterprise and had hooked up with Professor Tawat Tapingkae of Chiang Mai University, who experimented with various types of cordyceps. I met them when Nong and Professor Tawat drove up the mountain one afternoon to see how their new lab in the Academy of Coffee was doing. Nong and Professor Tawat explained that *Cordyceps sinensis*, the traditional Tibetan version, had to grow from a medium using ground-up insects, but that *Cordyceps militaris*, which contained even more of the active ingredients adenosine and cordyceptin, could grow in a medium of cooked rice. Professor Tawat turned out to be the mushroom expert Wicha had been telling me about, and he was also an orchid specialist. Wicha was sure he could sell a brand of Doi Chaang Cordyceps in the coffeehouses for a sizable profit.

That evening, Nong, a slim, lively woman in her forties with a ready smile, roasted sweet potatoes and coconuts for us over the fire, while Wicha and I grew mellow and sang folk songs, though he complained that he had trouble catching his breath. To end the evening we sang the old African peace anthem "Kumbaya." "We are hand in hand, Kumbaya, we are hand in hand, Kumbaya...Ah, good!" he declared. Then he retired to sleep behind his desk, having abandoned his hut after he found that he was about to share his bed with a python.

Over the next few days, I talked to several new people. Dawan, twenty-six, the third of five siblings, worked in the Doi Chaang office next to A-Roy's noodle shop, and she was the one who sat at the table handing out chits every day as farmers brought their coffee cherries to be weighed. She was yet another Akha relative,

Adel's niece. Lipi and Jay were her older brothers, and she told me that she was embroidering a traditional Akha shirt as a wedding present for Jay, who in January would be marrying a Thai woman who worked for a television station in Bangkok.

Dawan spoke good English, in part because she had spent three months in Panama City, Florida, part of a work/travel program sponsored by Chiang Mai Commercial College, where she earned a business degree. Her mother, Piko's daughter Misor, had married an Akha man from Chiang Mai, so Dawan had grown up in that city's suburbs, three hours to the south, but she frequently visited her grandparents in Doi Chang, living with Piko and his wife, Bu Chu, every summer. "I loved the Swing Ceremony," she said. "It was so much fun. You could see the whole valley, and I felt like I could fly."

Every Friday at her school was "culture day," when Dawan wore traditional Akha dress. When she was twenty, her mother made her a full Akha headdress, with tassels down the back to indicate that she was single. Like most younger Akha, she did not really believe in jungle spirits or divination, but she valued the Akha language and culture.

I asked her what she thought of Bangkok and other big cities, and whether she wanted to settle down in Doi Chang. "I like learning new things and meeting many people," she said, "so I enjoy Bangkok, and I want to explore the world. But when I am older, I want to settle here." The weather was nicer than in the lowlands, the coffee business was thriving, and most important, these were her people, her family.

I met A Sho, thirty-six, an Akha man who had worked in Taiwan for eight years in an automobile factory. He had returned to Doi Chang to care for his elderly grandfather, who died three years ago, and A Sho was now married, with an eight-month-old son. He had inherited 8 acres on which, of course, he grew coffee. "I know about the *pima*," he said, "but I know little about Akha culture really." He had become a Buddhist, the leader of thirty-five Buddhist Akha families in the village. "My grandfather felt that Buddhism was the same-same with the Akha Way. But when he got sick, he put the Akha string on his wrist." When A Sho's son grows up, he will not learn the Akha Way. He will be a Buddhist. I asked if A Sho thought other Akha his age would raise their children as traditional Akha. No, he said, maybe just 20 percent.

I had seen a slim Akha man with a ponytail and slight limp, who frequently hung out in the coffeehouse. I finally introduced myself and learned his name, Leebang. He had his own coffee brand called Doi Yama, and he drove me with his two cute little girls and baby boy in his pickup down a dirt road just behind the coffeehouse. The road dead-ended at his farm. An older girl was in school in Chiang Rai. He grew coffee on 20 rai but also purchased cherries from other Akha. He had created the Doi Yama brand two years ago. Before that, he sold to Doi Chaang.

His farm, which offered a stunning view down the valley, had its own processing station, drying patio, and roaster. He had just begun to grow strawberries as a supplemental crop. While I wandered around, his children watched a Thai translation of the *Flintstones* on a small TV in the warehouse.

Leebang was one of the processors who had initially supplied Doi Chaang, but whom Wicha and Adel had cut off in 2010 when they upgraded their processing station in order to buy directly from farmers. "All of these guys used to come drink free coffee here at the Doi Chaang coffeehouse and laugh at Wicha," John Darch Senior told me later, "because they were rebagging cheap coffee from down the mountain and calling it Doi Chaang. They thought Wicha was stupid for not doing the same thing."

This story isn't so simple, I thought as I climbed in bed in my little green cottage up the hill on the other side of the road from the Doi

Chaang compound. *Yes, it's an uplifting story showing the impact that an alternative approach to capitalism can have on an oppressed people. But they are still people, and human beings being human, there will always be conflict, greed, misunderstanding, and unforeseen consequences of change, even when the change is clearly for the better.*

Going to School

ONE OF WICHA'S big plans had been to make education equally accessible to all the children within the region of twenty-five villages. The Doi Chang primary school educated first through ninth grades. Nearly 600 children attended the school, though children without Thai ID cards would receive no graduation certificate and would be unable to pursue further education beyond Grade 9. In the library, which was funded by Doi Chaang Coffee, a group of girls were drawing and painting during an after-school program, and a boy was singing karaoke through a microphone attached to a computer.

I spent a morning in English classes for seventh, eighth, and ninth graders taught by Meeyae Saedoo, the only Akha teacher in the school. In the first class, most of the students were Akha, with a few Lisu and one Chinese. About half were Christian, with a slight Protestant majority. All of their parents grew coffee, some on small plots, others on up to 40 rai. Most of the students planned to go to Chiang Rai to attend high school, where they would rent rooms.

As much as I appreciated Meeyae's energetic teaching efforts, it wasn't clear how much English her students were learning, as she taught from curriculum-prescribed workbooks. She had them repeat words and sentences, such as "She is going to town at the present moment." Not only was the language stilted, it was incomprehensible when they repeated the sentences in their heavily accented singsong manner. I only ascertained what they were supposed to be saying by reading the workbook. Meeyae wrote the words living room, kitchen, and bathroom on the blackboard and had the students assign words such as sofa, armchair, fridge, coffee table, and toilet to the correct room.

Meeyae was an enthusiastic, supportive teacher, but I was saddened that she, the only Akha teacher in the school, was not teaching anything about the Akha way of life—nothing about bamboo platforms, men's and women's sides, of a home, ancestor shrines, hunting, gathering medicinal herbs, creation stories, spirits, divination, weddings, or funerals. Nothing about a rich way of life that was disappearing, although of course no one mourned the absence of poverty, malnutrition, and other problems of the recent past.

The Village Elders

ANOTHER DAY, I met with the traditional Akha village elders at Piko's house, a large modern tiled home on the main street. The older men, wearing their fedora hats, sat on rustic benches or cross sections of large trees. We drank tea, as Wicha translated.

All of the elders, who ranged in age from sixty-six to eighty-two, were part of the Saedoo clan that Piko belonged to, and they still performed important rituals. The pima, Akue Choemue, was right there, one of the elders. He was also the nyipa, the shaman. He killed water buffaloes as part of funeral celebrations and could recite hours of ritual poems and stories. He was training four younger men to be pimas and to carry on the tradition.

They expressed some concerns about the traditional way of life being eroded by television and increased contact with Thai culture. It was less of an issue with the older generations, but the younger Akha were vulnerable. Some of the elders attended meetings to discuss how to minimize the damage to their traditions. Some wanted to videotape the ceremonies to preserve them. I asked about a written version of the Akha language that Paul Lewis had created. They knew nothing of it and were not interested. Theirs was an oral tradition, and that was it.

With some trepidation, I asked whether they still killed twins at birth. No, there had been a meeting of Akha from China, Myanmar, Laos, Vietnam, and Thailand in 1998 to discuss many issues, and they had decided to stop the long tradition of smothering twins. No Akha twins had been born in the village since then. Other laws remained unchanged. Were they worried about Ya Ba and heroin use in the village? Yes, they never saw such problems in the past. What about the illegal mobile casinos? They hated them. In the old days, there was some small-time gambling, but not these high-stakes games for millions of baht. Many gamblers came from the lowlands, and they didn't listen to old people.

I asked what they used to eat. In the old days, when there was deep jungle, they ate many animals, but once they moved to Doi Chang, there was no more jungle and no animals to hunt. They had carp in a fishpond and grew vegetables. Now that the trees were growing back, wild boar and barking deer were returning. Yes, they sometimes ate dog during a ceremony. And they were fond of bamboo worms.

What about music? They carved Jew's harps and a simple flute out of bamboo and used big bamboo poles to thump rhythmically on the ground, along with gongs and drums, to accompany dances. During harvest season, they were always singing, making up new words for ballads. "If we see a bird, we sing about it, or it might be about a young boy kissing a girl and telling her how beautiful she is."

That reminded me to ask about the courting yard. Did boys and girls still meet there in the evening to sing, dance, and flirt? No. The courting yard still existed, but it was no longer an important part of social life. "Things change," an elder said, meaning, *What can you do?* Most of the teenagers were attending school in Chiang Rai anyway. More Akha were falling in love with and marrying non-tribal members. At least, now that coffee was creating jobs, the young people were moving back home.

Why had so many Akha converted to Christianity? This was a touchy subject. No, it was not because it was too expensive to sacrifice animals in Akha rituals. A lot of conversions occurred because other family members converted. But, Wicha said, the Christians made everything easy. You could go to heaven without making any sacrifices.

Mike Mann and ITDP

THE NEXT DAY, I met Mike Mann, whose father, Dick Mann, had been a coffee pioneer in Thailand. In 1959, when he was two years old, Mike Mann arrived in Thailand with his missionary agronomist parents and grew up there, visiting villages and hiking the mountains with his father. The younger Mann returned to the United States to attend California Polytechnic, where he earned an undergraduate degree in international agronomy and a master's in plant pathology. In 1990, he came back to Chiang Mai, Thailand, to carry on his father's work with hill tribes through what was eventually named the Integrated Tribal Development Program (ITDP). The best of the ITDP coffee beans went to Starbucks, but others were sold as the Lanna Coffee brand. (Lanna is the name of a former kingdom in northern Thailand.)

When Mike Mann arrived in Doi Chang that day, with his coffee manager, Boonchu Kloedu, a Karen tribal member, I feared he would be defensive about the success of Doi Chaang, since Mann had helped form an Akha farmer's cooperative in Doi Chang in 2002, about the time Wicha was beginning to help Adel. Then

Mann had sponsored a Lisu Doi Chang cooperative three years later. Mann had also arranged for coffee from Doi Chang to be part of the Thai Starbucks blend, Muan Jai, introduced in 2004.

But as Doi Chaang Coffee became a huge success, and prices for freshly picked cherries and processed village beans rose, the farmers abandoned ITDP. Many started roasting their own coffee. "Our last major purchase from Doi Chang was in 2010, when we bought over 50 tons, but it tapered off in 2011," Mann explained. "People sold to the Doi Chaang co-op or started their own businesses. They learned about the importance of coffee quality from us and some marketing strategy, but now they could do it on their own. So we put our resources in other places. We are not about taking over, but promoting and building awareness." Mike Mann and Wicha had met at a coffee conference in 2006, he said, but otherwise they appeared to have kept their distance from one another, and there clearly was some tension there. Both claimed credit for improving coffee quality, for instance.

Then we headed for the village, meeting on a terrace at the home of an Akha named Akaw, who had moved to Doi Chang eighteen years ago and had been one of the original ITDP co-op members. We were joined by Teenoi, a Chinese coffee farmer, and Bancha, a Lisu and one of long-time village chief Beno's sons. They had invited Mike Mann back to Doi Chang to discuss the possibility of restarting the co-op, since coffee prices were declining. They apologized that more farmers weren't there, but most had gone to a funeral in Maemon that morning.

It was an ideal opportunity to ask the farmers about their holdings and operations, with Mike Mann translating. Akaw owned 20 rai at a high altitude near Ban Mai, so his harvest had not yet begun. Teenoi owned a total of 30 rai in various parcels, and Bancha had similar holdings. During the harvest season, they hired pickers from other villages, paying them either a daily wage of 200 baht (about $7) or 4 baht per kilo. In the early harvest season, when there were fewer ripe cherries, the pickers wanted to be paid by the day, but at the height of the season, when a skilled, hardworking harvester could pick 100 kilos, they wanted to be paid by the kilo. The farmers complained that they had to pay for gas to pick up their workers every day. "They make more than we do," groused Akaw, but that was clearly far from true.

Akaw and Teenoi sold their cherries to Doi Chaang, but they were not satisfied with the 18 baht per kilo they were getting, and they complained that they had to wait for a month or more to get paid. I made a mental note to ask Adel and Wicha about this allegation. Bancha processed and roasted his own coffee, which he sold as Lisu Doi Chang Coffee. But he, too, was interested in exploring other options. Maybe he would rejoin ITDP.

The meeting ended without any resolution, in part because only three farmers were there. After the meeting, Mike Mann commented: "They are hedging their bets. We are the David of the Thai coffee industry against a bunch of Goliaths." By that time, he represented twenty-five villages in Thailand in five provinces, and the Fair Trade certification, which ITDP had pioneered in Thailand, had become a bureaucratic and financial nightmare. "It used to be that ITDP paid a premium fee for the amount of coffee we sold with the Fair Trade label. But they changed that about three years ago so that the farmers themselves had to pay." In addition, in Thailand, cooperatives had to be formed on the provincial level, but Fair Trade insisted that each of the five ITDP cooperatives pay separate fees. So Mann abandoned the Fair Trade certification in favor of Starbucks' C.A.F.E. Practices, a stringent company standard.

My Last Day

ON MY LAST day of this trip, Bancha, a vigorous, nice-looking man of forty-eight with a thick mop of black hair (in contrast to his bald father), invited me back to see the three caged civet cats he had recently acquired. He wasn't sure he'd be able to sell the civet coffee for the big prices he had heard about. So far, his well-cared-for civets hadn't produced much.

We walked up the nearby hill to the Doi Chang Resort, where Bancha showed me the small room where he and his younger sister, Chome, roasted and bagged their beans for the Lisu Doi Chang Coffee brand. There I met Chome, who spoke very good English, having worked for IMPECT before returning to Doi Chang to join the family coffee business and start the resort. She spoke fluently and earnestly about "indigenous people" and "sustainability," and she said she had started a women's group in Doi Chang. She was applying for a grant to go to Missoula, Montana, to study for three months, hoping to become a more savvy businesswoman. She showed me a mockup for Abeno Coffee, a new brand she wanted to launch with her father's face on it, in obvious imitation of Piko's image on the Doi Chaang bags. She suggested that I stay at her resort on my next visit, and she could translate when I interviewed her father.

Back at the Doi Chaang compound, Nuda explained how she made soap. As I was about to leave, she took a solid silver Akha bracelet off her wrist and insisted that I take it to my wife. "Nuda, I can't take this, it's yours," I said. "I really want you to have it, Abopala," she said, pressing it on me. I was touched, and I liked the new nickname I had earned this trip—I was Abopala, which means "honored old white man."

As Adel drove down the mountain, we chatted, and his English was much better than I had realized. I asked him whether the Lisu had looked down on the Akha when he was a child. Yes, and perhaps there remained some vestige of that prejudice "in their hearts," but no one would say it aloud. The younger generation was growing up without such prejudices, he said, and in the future Akha and Lisu might intermarry more frequently.

I told Adel that I had grown up in the American South in the 1950s, when blacks and whites could not use the same water fountains or schools. He was surprised. I told him that had all changed, in my lifetime, and that now whites and blacks could intermarry without huge concern, and that it was amazing how cultures could change so dramatically and quickly. But subtle prejudices remained.

We got to the airport. I thanked Adel again and grabbed my suitcase, already looking forward to my next visit to the village of Doi Chang, when I would arrive in time for the annual Academy of Coffee celebration the following April.

CHAPTER 9

Carry On

O N THE MORNING OF Thursday, January 23, 2014, I turned on my computer as usual in my home office in Vermont, where I was beginning to write this book. Before I went back to my draft chapter, I checked the inbox of my e-mail and saw a message from John Darch Senior with the subject heading: *Wicha Passed Away January 22.* I stared at it dumbly for a moment. What? I opened the e-mail and read:

Dear Mark,

It is with deep sadness that I'm writing to inform you of the sudden passing of our dear friend and founder, Wicha Promyong, who died unexpectedly in Doi Chang Village, on Wednesday, January 22.

As you know, for more than a decade, Khun Wicha dedicated his life to the well being of the Akha hill tribe of Doi Chang Village, and it was his innovation and passion that led to the creation and success of Doi Chaang Coffee.

There simply are no words to express our shock and heartbreak over the loss of such an amazing inspirational person, and our deepest sympathies are with his wife, children and our extended family at Doi Chang Village.

I thought you would like to know before it is announced publicly today.

—John

I couldn't believe it. Wicha had seemed indestructible, almost an elemental life force. A subsequent message from Darch read in part:

Wicha . . . appears to have had a massive heart attack. We are all feeling so much distress by the loss of such an inspirational man and I can't imagine the grief of his wife, children and everyone at Doi Chang and so many throughout Thailand and Asia, and indeed the world. He touched and was loved by so many. I loved him deeply as a brother and will miss him so much, but I have wonderful memories.

A few weeks later, Darch Senior recalled the aftermath of Wicha's death. "My first concern, after the personal shock and loss of a dear friend, was that I was worried everything would be in chaos. He was buried within twenty-four hours of his death in a family plot in Chiang Rai. Sandra has strong inner strength. She went up there and became mother to Wicha's family and to the Akha in Doi Chang."

When Darch Senior arrived in Chiang Rai a few days later, he and Anand Pawa went straight to the Doi Chaang Coffeehouse to offer their condolences to Nuch, Wicha's widow, and their children. Nuch had at first refused to believe that Wicha was dead, sleeping overnight in the room with his body and telling herself that he would wake up the next morning. Now she had come to terms with his passing. "God has called him home—he needed Wicha's help," she told Darch.

Nuch spoke of Wicha and all he had done, and she committed herself to continuing the business and coffeeshop. Among his many other projects, Wicha had been planning to create a restaurant in their old home just over the bridge on the Mekong River, where the children had grown up. He had also designed a home there, where they would live. It was near completion. Nuch showed Darch a photo of Wicha on the roof with a picnic basket.

Over dinner, Nuch complained that Wicha would never go to a doctor, that he pulled his own teeth with pliers rather than go to a dentist. For infections, he would buy over-the-counter antibiotics. Nuch said that he was finally scheduled for a checkup on February 4. He knew something was wrong with him; he didn't have his same old energy. The morning he died, he was talking on his cell phone with Koon, his youngest daughter, when he suddenly said, "Oh, I have to go." She thought he was going to a meeting. He put down his clippers, cigarette, and phone on the table, and apparently just lay down and died.

In the morning, Darch and Anand Pawa drove up to Doi Chang village. "Miga ran and threw herself at me and clung, totally intense, and she cried and cried and cried for four or five minutes. I stroked her hair, saying, It's OK, OK, OK," Darch remembered. Then more Akha women—Nuda, Apeu, Dawan, and others—came for hugs, and finally Adel greeted Darch, saying, "Please don't leave us." Darch assured him, "I will never leave you, you are my brother."

Perhaps in honor of Sandra Bunmusik, a devout Buddhist who had done so much to contribute to Doi Chaang Coffee's success, they then held a Buddhist memorial service for Wicha in the Academy of Coffee, with saffron-clad monks leading chants and blessings. "We spent two days in Doi Chang," Darch recalled. "There was no discussion of business, just friendship and family stories, and expressions of the deep love and devotion they had for Wicha." Then Darch and the other Canadians went back to the Bangkok office to reassure the staff there.

A few days later, they returned to Doi Chang, where they calmly discussed the future of Doi Chaang Coffee. "The message from Adel, Miga, Lipi, and Nuda was that everyone was OK," Darch said, "They were in control of operations. They didn't need us for their business to be successful. They politely said, 'We are not dependent on you, but we don't want you to leave, you are our new father.' It was very touching. It came through to us that they were strong, they would continue, everything would be good."

Adel and Miga said that, now that Wicha was gone, they would focus primarily on coffee. They would continue with the honey, soap, tea, and other ancillary products, as well as the cordyceps, but coffee was the main concern. They planned to be out of debt in three years. The mushrooms and plans for new drinks would be put on hold. "We didn't challenge anything," Darch said. "We just listened very carefully. They had a lot of confidence in themselves. Wicha had done a tremendous job of succession planning."

As word of Wicha's death spread, hundreds of people from around the world called or wrote to express their sorrow and to remember Wicha fondly. One of the most informed messages came from Jacques Op de Laak, the retired Dutch agronomist who lived in Chiang Mai:

I was shattered by the sudden, unexpected and untimely death of Khun Wicha, founding member of Doi Chaang Coffee Company. I never knew he had heart problems, and he certainly didn't look like someone in poor health. Ever so cheerful, kind and amiable.

I first met Khun Wicha at an Agricultural Fair at Chiang Mai University (CMU) in 2005 and instantly we became friends. I found that he was involved with Doi Chang village for some years already, that coffee growing was in full swing, and that farmers were enthusiastic and energetic in expanding the crop and profits from it. Afterwards I visited Doi Chang many times, and what Khun Wicha had told me was entirely confirmed. These villagers had been bitten by the coffee bug.

I was highly surprised and in the end thrilled to see what was happening there. In the 10 years (1983–1992) that I was working at the Coffee Research Centre at Chiang Mai University to promote coffee among the northern Thai highland farmers, I was convinced that Arabica coffee could and should work here. Only I *hadn't seen it till then!* Doi Chang taught me that Arabica coffee could and *did* work.

It is simply incredible what Khun Wicha and his handful of Akha farmers have accomplished in a relatively short time. What has happened and is still happening there is unique. Nowhere in northern Thailand can one find such a vast area under (good-looking) coffee trees, nowhere else does one find the dedication, drive and determination of the Doi Chang coffee farmers to grow a crop which is not the easiest to grow, at least not in a sustainable way.

Nowhere else is there a single village with an entire population dedicated to cultivating this crop. Truly, Doi Chang deserves the title of *Coffee Village.* And all this because of a humble, tiny Thai man who, through vision and compassion, lifted the villagers to great heights. Surely, without an appropriate "breeding" ground, nothing can be achieved. The Doi Chang farmers had the right mentality and insight and feeling for the crop. Khun Wicha just managed to "fertilize" this ground in the right way to get optimal results.

During my visit in November 2013, I had recorded a few songs as Wicha and I sat around the fire. As I listened to the recordings again, I felt deep sorrow, but I was also moved by how beautiful and sensitive his voice had been. I had turned on my recorder partway through "Kumbaya," so I uploaded it to YouTube, along with some photos of Wicha, the Akha, and Doi Chang. You can see and hear it there.

The Festival in Doi Chang

I ARRIVED FOR my third visit in Doi Chang on April 15, 2014, the night before the seventh anniversary celebration of the Academy of Coffee founding—an excuse, as Wicha had told me, to gather Akha from surrounding communities. This year, in the aftermath of Wicha's death, the festivities wouldn't be as ambitious as previous events, nor would tribal members come from so far away. During the day, there were various games and performances on the large drying patio, including *takraw*, a game that Wicha had told me he excelled at as a young man. It's a fierce kind of soccer-volleyball in which players kick a lightweight rattan or plastic ball (similar to a large whiffleball) over the net, spiking it with incredible pinwheels in which players look as if they will land on their heads but somehow come down on their feet. Akha women in traditional dress pounded bamboo pole-drums in rhythm on the ground, and an older Akha woman sang a full-throated traditional song. Others played drums, gongs, and flutes.

I also met a group of Akha women in their twenties, most of whom lived in the village and worked with their family's coffee business. All had gone to school in Chiang Rai and seemed savvy and well educated. Nun told me that she had studied linguistics at Chiang Rai Rajabhat University, and that she and her sister had started a coffeeshop in the city. I told her I was looking for Meeyae, the Akha teacher, to give her an Akha-English-Thai dictionary by Paul Lewis, so she called her cell, and Meeyae soon appeared. I inscribed the book to her and told her I hoped she would use it to teach her students to be literate in Akha. Meeyae seemed grateful for the book, but she said she was two months pregnant, and after she gave birth, she would be taking time off from teaching.

By now, tables had been set up on the drying patio for the evening's entertainment. I joined the Canadians at their table—Darches Senior and Junior, Anand Pawa, Eric Lightheart—which also included Keith Crosby, a Canadian geologist who had worked for John Darch Senior when he chaired Asia Pacific Resources (APR), the Thai potash project in Udon Thani. Crosby had been the only foreigner to remain with APR when Italian-Thai Development bought it in 2006. Now Crosby was working with Darch on several new potash projects that might ride to success on the coattails of the Italian-Thai development, if that company finally got the long-anticipated green light to begin mining operations.

While walking around, I met a very friendly Akha man who introduced himself. "My name is Tee, not coffee!" he said, and laughed. He gave me his card, which said that his name was Kritipong Jupoh (Tee) and that he lived with his Japanese wife, Nobuko, in Mae Suai, at the bottom of the mountain. He taught political science part-time at Chiang Rai Rajabhat University and said that he had been all over the world, had visited California and Ohio, and had returned to his home in Chiang Rai Province in 2003. He had come up the mountain to enjoy himself at the festivities, but also to attend a meeting of Akha World (www.akhaworld.com), a Chiang Rai organization trying to save and maintain the traditional Akha way of life.

The program from the main stage began as dinner was served. Niwet Phori, the young nurse practitioner at the Doi Chang health clinic, served as master of ceremonies. Before the music started, he introduced Adel, Piko, and other village elders. Then Sandra Bunmusik translated as John Darch Senior and Eric Lightheart gave heartfelt tributes to Wicha. Darch later told me that Sandra didn't speak because she would have broken into tears.

Then I spoke. Sandra translated as I explained that I was writing a book about Doi Chang and its coffee. I said that I had brought the 1984 book *Peoples of the Golden Triangle* on a previous trip, and everyone had really enjoyed looking at the pictures, so I brought another copy and was giving it to Adel to keep, but that it was really for the whole village. Then I explained that I had also given the Akha-English-Thai dictionary to Meeyae, and that anyone could ask her to look at it. Finally, I said that I had loved getting to know Wicha and that we shared a love of singing and playing the harmonica, and I would miss his joy in life. I said I had sung "Kumbaya" with him and made a YouTube video of it, and that I wanted to play the song on my harmonica in his honor. And then I did.

The evening entertainment was geared toward a distinctly younger and more raucous audience. A young Akha man and woman sang a duet in their native tongue, but it was clearly modern, influenced by popular Thai music. There were various dances by traditionally clad Akha from Doi Chang, but also from other nearby villages, some with the high conical headdresses of the Ulo Akha, including three women from the neighboring village of Saen Charoen, who took the stage for a rice dance, sweeping round bamboo winnowing containers in rhythm. I had met and spoken to one of them before the dance. She was quite tall for an Akha woman and had a rather sexy, husky voice. She ended up doing a kind of Akha striptease by herself—not really taking off clothing, but suggestively showing her shoulder and swaying her hips —to much catcalling and applause. Finally I realized that she was a he. "Ladyboy," said an audience member, laughing and applauding.

I had hoped that the aging, legendary rock musician Surachai Jantimatorn, whom Wicha's children knew as Uncle Nga, would play this year, as he had in April 2013, but he couldn't come. Instead, Todd Lavelle, a Scranton, Pennsylvania, native now famous as Todd Tongdee in Thailand, his adopted home, brought his traveling world music show, including bands from Yunnan Province in China and an African group from Ghana. He sang only briefly, because he was hoarse from previous performances, but he too gave a heartfelt tribute to Wicha in Thai, Akha, and English. He dubbed his show the Doi Chaang Akha-World Musiq Festival.

The next day, I got a chance to talk to Todd (Lavelle) Tongdee, who had met Wicha twenty years ago. Tongdee had first come to Thailand on a Fulbright Scholarship. He worked in a refugee camp on the Thai-Cambodian border, then earned his living as a singer and wrestler, eventually becoming a celebrity with his own Thai television show. He got involved with the Akha when he heard and disliked a popular Thai song called "Mida," about a young Akha girl who would teach anyone about sex. In other words, it purveyed the old stereotypical myth of Akha promiscuity. In response, Tongdee interviewed Akha elders and wrote a song about the Akha Way, using Akha drums and musicians, for his *Rhythm of the Earth* album.

He ran into Wicha in Chiang Rai and learned that he was helping the Akha with coffee, so he came up to play for the Doi Chaang Coffee festival for the first time in April 2011 and had been back every year since then. I asked how he would characterize Wicha, and he called him a "pisser," which in his native Pennsylvania means someone who is direct, determined, and funny. "It's someone who knows what they are going to do, and they go for it, regardless of what anyone else thinks," he said.

Visiting Doi Lan and Saen Charoen

ON THIS FINAL research trip to Thailand, I also wanted to visit two other coffee towns—Huey Hawm, the first coffee village in Thailand, and Doi Tung, the once impoverished mountain where the aging Princess Mother had established a model coffee-growing resort community. But first, I ventured out of Doi Chang to the nearby villages of Doi Lan and Saen Charoen, with Anand Pawa, who would translate for me.

Lipi drove us down the paved mountain road and turned left to Doi Lan, about 4 miles away. This was the Lisu village where

Dutch anthropologist Otome Hutheesing had lived, but when we stopped in the middle of town at a little store, we found a group of Loimi Akha teenagers, home for the holidays from Chiang Rai and Chiang Mai. One, a girl nicknamed Pal, spoke good English. She introduced us to their parents across the street, who explained that they had fled the violence in Burma, moving to Doi Lan twenty years previously, and with the help of the Lisu village chief, had gotten their Thai ID cards a decade ago. They all grew coffee on the hillsides above and sold it to Doi Chaang. Doi Lan was part of the Geographical Indication (GI) Doi Chaang district, the equivalent of a Bordeaux wine district for coffee.

We drove up through the coffee trees, then further east to where the road dead-ended on a barren hillside. Down the mountain, I could see fields burning, although even agricultural burning was technically illegal now. Bits of ash floated by, and visibility was limited by the smoke. April is the hottest time of the year in Thailand, so even in the mountains, it reached 90°F or more. The rainy season had yet to commence, and the red gashes on the hillsides at lower elevations, where coffee did not grow, were ugly. By June and July, however, they would be lush with corn, tomatoes, and rice.

On the way back through the village, we stopped at a house and spoke to Alema, a middle-aged Lisu woman who had grown up in Doi Lan when it was purely a Lisu village. When I asked if she knew Otome Hutheesing, she said that she was her cousin, though Otome was actually an honorary family member. Alema said that it was difficult to live off her coffee earnings, since she only owned 5 rai, and her husband was in prison, so she had to hire help, and this year, Doi Chaang paid only 18 baht per kilo. But it was still better than growing tomatoes, which is what she used to do. Yes, she remembered when the logging company cut down all the trees along the road to Doi Chang. There were 140 households in the village, still predominantly Lisu.

We then drove a bit farther down the mountain to Saen Charoen, an Ulo Akha village about 6 miles from Doi Chang. The roads were extremely steep, but luckily were paved with concrete. Most of the village is too low in elevation to grow coffee. The houses we passed were modest, except for one imposing, modern home. Lipi said that it belonged to the ladyboy who had performed at the festival. He toured internationally and was quite wealthy. I asked if there were any Akha ladyboys in Doi Chang, and Lipi said that there were, but that they were still closeted.

We drove down until the road dead-ended in a beautiful little compound owned by an Akha couple. The husband had grown up in Saen Charoen and met his future wife, who lived in another village, when they were walking along mountain trails, before there were roads. They had five children, one of whom was married to a Frenchman in Chiang Mai. His oldest son lived with them and worked on their 20-rai farm, further up the mountain. They grew corn but used to grow tomatoes. They didn't use pesticide on the corn or burn their fields. His other children lived in the city because of the lack of job opportunities in this beautiful area.

Moving to the Village

ON SATURDAY AFTERNOON, I moved to the Doi Chang Resort, owned by Chome, the daughter of Beno, the long-time Lisu headman, which would give me a chance to stroll around the village. But Chome wasn't there yet. After some confusion, since no one spoke English, Chome's assistant, an older Thai woman named Pom, opened one of the small A-frames up the hill, and I helped her make up the bed. It was a small room with a fan and a bathroom, adequate but far from elegant—not exactly what North Americans would call a resort.

At 7 p.m. I walked down to the Catholic church, where I found a big crowd of Akha, some of the women in traditional headdresses, all holding small candles and standing around a bamboo pyre that a priest lit in the courtyard. From the pyre, all the candles were eventually set aflame, including the one I was given. Then we all filed into the church for an Easter eve service. Most people sat on the wooden floor, but a man tugged me to a seat on a low bench at the back reserved for elders. During the service, small children ran in and out. I heard "Apoc Miyeh" repeatedly, the name of the supreme Akha God, and I realized that the Catholics had adopted it as the name for the Christian God. Finally we blew out our candles, and the service ended with communion.

I walked back up the hill to the resort, enjoying the warm night air. There were no streetlights, just lights in houses dotting the valley like fireflies. Chome was back from the valley, and we talked for a while. She verified much of what I had read in Otome Hutheesing's book about the Lisu. Yes, the Lisu were status-conscious and valued money, and yes, the women did most of the work. Families still negotiated a bride price before marriage. Chome said that she wanted to make her place an ecotourist resort that stressed organic coffee and the quiet appeal of the village. I noted that I was her only guest, and she said that she needed a better Internet presence and media coverage. A young Thai couple had stopped earlier for dinner and looked at a room, but they didn't stay. I told Chome that the man had told me there didn't seem to be much to do, and he couldn't believe how quiet it was on a Saturday night. *That's the point!* Chome observed.

It certainly wasn't quiet the next morning, when I was awakened at precisely 5 a.m. by a cacophony of amazingly vehement roosters, one of whom seemed to be a few feet from my bed. They inspired various dogs to join in the chorus. That morning, after breakfast, I walked down to a Protestant church for what I thought would be a 9:30 a.m. service, but no one was there. Instead, I heard distant singing and traced it to a valley far below to the right, where I could see people walking along a trail. I made my way down dirt roads and paths and found a small Akha Easter service underway in a clearing in the woods. There were about forty people from all generations gathered around a wooden cross, and a young minister presiding in the middle. An older Akha woman chewing betel nut sat near me. One little girl sat in the crotch of a tree, and a teenaged boy wore a baseball hat that said OBAMA on it.

A man holding a hymnal invited me to sit next to him on a makeshift bamboo-pole bench, and he pointed to the words as he sang. The hymnal must have been the work of Paul Lewis, because I could actually read the Akha words phonetically, so I sang along. Then some teens sang a song with guitars. The minister read John 20 from the Akha Bible, in which Mary Magdalene discovers the empty tomb, then gave a lively commentary on it. The service wasn't nearly as formal as the Catholic mass the previous evening. At the end, everyone got a glass of water or Sprite and a red hardboiled egg, which is another spillover from traditional Akha culture, though it reminded me of Easter egg hunts.

On the way back to the resort, I thought about the impact of religion on the Akha. Their traditional belief system is complex and evolved over centuries to fit their lives in the mountains, explaining life and death, honoring the ancestors, celebrating the seasons and harvests, placating the spirits. Their rituals helped maintain balance and gave meaning to everything they did. Now, in the space of a few decades, that way of life was nearly gone, and in its place were these imposed forms of Christianity and Buddhism. Yet they, too, had their beauty and rituals, and the Akha had made them their own in many ways.

Chome and Beno

BEFORE OUR INTERVIEW back at her resort, Chome showed me her thesis, "Lisu Women's Identity and Self Over Three

Generations: A Case Study of the Life Experience of a Lisu Woman," for her master's degree in Women's Studies at Chiang Mai University, in which she concluded that "these complex constructed identities have resulted in inconsistencies in these women's concepts of self, [which are] fragmented and fluid." She also showed me her handbook from the Economic Empowerment Fellows Program, sponsored by the Maureen and Mike Mansfield Center at the University of Montana in Missoula, where she would be going in October. She had e-mailed me that she also hoped to learn from American coffee roasters.

Chome was born in 1967, the third of five siblings. As a little girl, she helped her mother harvest opium from their small field up the mountain. When she was nine, her father enrolled her in a Christian school in Chiang Rai, and though she never converted, she attended a series of Christian schools until she studied bookkeeping in college. She only visited Doi Chang sporadically, usually for the rice ceremony in August or the Lisu New Year in January or February. When she came home for a visit as a young teen, she discovered that a few Akha families had moved to Doi Chang, and it seemed that with every subsequent visit, more Akha relations had joined them.

Chome never married. "I was too shy, because I didn't grow up in the community," she said. "My mother sewed me a nice dress and my grandmother gave me a lot of silver jewelry." But no husband courted her or was willing to pay for her bride price. After college, she met Dutch anthropologist Leo Alting von Geusau, who hired her in 1991 as a bookkeeper for his Mountain Peoples Cultural Education and Development Foundation, later renamed Inter Mountain Peoples Education and Culture in Thailand Association (IMPECT).

She worked at IMPECT in Chiang Mai until returning to live in Doi Chang in 2009, as the coffee boom was building. Her father gave his oldest son Bancha 25 rai of land, Chome and her brother Charlie 10 rai each, and her younger brother and sister smaller amounts. Before she arrived, they called their brand Ban Doi Chang Coffee, an obvious attempt to ride on the success of the Doi Chaang packages. "It is our community, so it is a name anyone can use." Then they created the Lisu Coffee brand in 2010 and began roasting their own beans the following year. After discovering that some Lisu in other villages used the same name, they registered the Doi Mork brand, "mork" meaning cloudy and overcast, as the mountains often are. Chome then decided to switch yet again to Abeno Coffee, with a picture of her father on the package.

Chome had also founded a Lisu women's group, which had grown to twenty women, including a few Akha and one Chinese, and had taken them to IMPECT meetings in Chiang Mai. Finally, she had begun the Doi Chang Resort and restaurant, and she owned the small grocery store across the main street.

I asked Chome what she thought of Wicha and Doi Chaang Coffee, and she immediately bristled. "Mr. Wicha was too strong in his talk," she said, adding that he had alienated not only the Lisu but some of the Akha. She admitted that "Doi Chaang Coffee has done some amazing things for the community," but she added, "they say it is the people's company, but they run it with just their group." Of Adel and Miga she commented, "They can continue and learn." Despite her interest in learning more about the coffee industry, she had so far not attended the free classes at the Academy of Coffee. Her big challenge was how to attract more people to her resort. From November to January, quite a few Thai tourists stayed there, but customers were scarce the rest of the year. More tourists seemed to be finding their way up the mountain, but they only visited the Doi Chaang Coffee complex, the first inviting place they came to. Chome somehow needed to encourage them to drive further down the mountain, into the village.

Then, at his home nearby, we interviewed Beno, her father, and I met Amima, her mother, though she didn't talk much. Yes, Beno had first brought coffee seedlings to the village in 1977, but many had been killed by coffee leaf rust, and there was no profit in it. Beno remembered the 1985 army raid that destroyed the opium, and the subsequent public ceremony to burn opium paraphernalia. He confirmed that my understanding of the background history of Doi Chang was accurate. Many Lisu had been very angry when the agricultural research station took over so much land up the mountain, where they had grown poppies, but Beno approved of the takeover, saying that it would "promote good things," that they needed to know about macadamia and coffee. Yet neither the Department of Agriculture nor the Thai-Germans had taught them how to market their products.

Chiang Mai Interlude

IN CHIANG MAI, the big city three hours to the south, Nong, the cordyceps lady, kindly offered to be my guide and act as my translator. My first stop in Chiang Mai was the Payap University Archives, a Thai Baptist institution that housed the papers of Paul Lewis, the missionary anthropologist. I found fascinating material he had written about the Akha in the 1970s, leading up to the time when the first Akha moved to Doi Chang. Here are excerpts from Lewis's observations in 1976 and 1977:

> [Thai government agents] sometimes use visits to the tribal village as an excuse to get lots to drink, smoke, and eat—and the smoking includes opium. They are not above extortion in opium-related matters, or outright thieving.

When there are large caravans of opium traders from Burma moving through Akha country, the Akhas are wise enough not to even go near these heavily armed semi-military units. The modern weapons they carry... were provided originally to "fight Communism," but now are used to make a "killing" in opium...

There may be some changes which are overdue, however, such as coming to have respect for women as human beings. The Akha society is highly male-dominated. I recently met two Akha women who had been forced to leave their village during the time of the ancestor offering, since they were divorced and had no "male" through which they could be related to the ancestors. They were really put in an extremely difficult position...

Akhas are at the bottom of the socio-economic ladder, which might be partly related to the fact that they are the newest tribal group to migrate to Thailand. Akhas are finding themselves forced into contact with non-Akhas in Thailand more often and more intimately than ever before. This is due primarily to the related factors of population explosion and a lack of adequate land for cultivation...

Akhas tend to be poor, sick, and culturally innervated. Akha culture is hanging by a thread. There are still many very fine Akhas in every village, however, who are anxious for a better day to come. For various reasons they seem to feel that they themselves will not see that better day, but at least they want it for their children...

Akhas, as a tribe, are suffering the general effects of the pressure to change, which is very strong and broad. The rate and quantity of change which is going on around them is surprising and unsettling to most of them, who tend to want to move back more closely into the womb of their culture and let the rest of the change swirl by them—but they have found the current is too strong and they cannot get back to that particular womb...

If the day comes when the Akha children might have one or two years of preliminary instruction in their own language, I would hope that many of the Akha proverbs and stories could be written down and used in the teaching. But my own feeling regarding this perplexing problem is that the Akhas themselves will have to deal with it in their own time and in their own way...

Thais and foreigners have no idea how intelligent some of the tribal people can be...Since the tribal people do not as yet have any organization which brings them together in meetings, something must be worked out to see that leaders from each tribe can meet together regularly...Just give the tribal people a chance, and over a period of time they will develop the needed skills to come to logical and workable conclusions as they discuss various problems...

Perhaps the most hopeful [opium replacement] crop is coffee. I have been pushing this for some time with Lahus, but feel now that an extra push needs to be given to all tribes, including the Akhas, who always seem to be so far behind the other groups...

Paul Lewis came across as a decent, thoughtful man who had tried his best to help all of the hill tribes, especially the Akha. And the incredible coffee success in Doi Chang made Lewis look prescient, although some of the problems he wrote about nearly forty years ago remained, even as I read about them in the Payap University Archives. Akha culture was still hanging by a thread, and the old folktales were being lost, perhaps along with the language. Still, strong-minded young women like Miga, Nuda, and Chome were evidence that some things had changed for the better, along with better health care, sanitation, and a sustainable income from coffee.

During my stay in Chiang Mai, I was able to interview several people, including Lamar Robert, an American economist who had spent most of his career in Thailand as a consultant, including work for the Thai-German Highland Development Project in Doi Chang in the 1980s. He recalled that when he first went to Doi Chang in 1984, "the main road had beautiful multicolored poppy blossoms on both sides." In Doi Chang he attended a 1986 meeting to introduce coffee cultivation in which "the emphasis was not on how much money could be made from coffee, but rather on what a demanding crop it is to produce and how it requires special attention." He did not recall any effort to help with marketing the coffee for a decent price. Robert's impression was that in Doi Chang, "the Akha were like the poor stepchildren, who had to move to this location, and out of the kindness of their hearts the Lisu let them move there. I didn't see anyone really taken advantage of, but it was obvious who was the guest, who was the owner."

At his home, where he kept beautiful songbirds and cultivated bonsai trees, I also interviewed Bandid Jangnam, the first director of the Wawi Highland Agricultural Research Station in Doi Chang. He showed me a slide show of his early days in Doi Chang in the 1980s—burned-over fields, opium poppies, a truck stuck in a muddy road. He had previously worked at a district office and remembered his colleagues telling him not to take the job in Doi Chang, which was known as a violent drug outpost. When the agricultural station confiscated the land, "the villagers wanted to kill me," but he became friends with Beno, the headman, and took him to the hospital when someone shot him in the hip. At first, when they gave the farmers coffee seedlings, "they didn't want them," he said. "Coffee leaf rust was a big problem." They had more success when rust-resistant Catimor was introduced. The Akha were relative newcomers and had less land, and so they were more willing to work for wages at the agricultural station.

In 1987, Bandid and his wife, Wiangjan, had bought a small roaster and created what was essentially the first Doi Chang coffee brand. Their daughter Pop remembered helping her mother iron the aluminum bags shut. They abandoned the small roasting project because they could sell only a few bags to friends, but Bandid showed no resentment about not having been part of the local coffee boom.

Bandid retired in 1993. Prasong Munsalong, his first assistant, was now the head of the Wawi station. Prasong, whose home is also in Chiang Mai, was there for this interview as well, and I saw him again when I went back to Doi Chang. Perhaps because he is still employed, Prasong was much more circumspect in his few remarks to me, though there was an interesting photo of him in Doi Chang as a much younger man, sitting in a bamboo hut and holding a rifle.

As the interview ended, Nong brought Jacques Op de Laak, who also lived in Chiang Mai, though he had not seen Bandid and Prasong in years. We drove with Jacques up Doi Suthep, the mountain towering over the city, to visit the high, remote Coffee Research Centre of Chiang Mai University. From 1983 until 1992, the Dutch agronomist had worked there when it was called the Highland Coffee Research and Development Centre, and where he developed the rust-resistant Catimor coffee in the experimental fields. As we strolled the fields, Jacques showed us signs of rust on the older Catimor. The rust was apparently adapting to it. "This is why they are working on a new strain."

Back down the mountain, we went to see anthropologist Otome Hutheesing. Now age eighty-four, Otome verified much of what she had written in her book about Doi Lan. Mostly, I talked with Mimi Saeju, thirty-three, a Lisu woman who lived with and cared for Otome and her long-time partner, Michael Vickery, a retired American teacher. Mimi spoke excellent English. She moved from Doi Lan when she was seven to go to school and, though she never returned to live there full-time, she has kept in close touch with her parents and other villagers.

Mimi and Otome both expressed deep concern about the situation in Doi Lan. In the 1980s, a Thai general bought a large piece of land in the village and established a coffee plantation, which infuriated the Lisu, some of whom were paid a pittance to work there. After someone tried to shoot him, the general fled, but he left an anti-coffee legacy among the villagers. Now the success of Doi Chaang Coffee had driven up the price of land in Doi Lan, and few natives could afford to buy it. Consequently, many lived in poverty or had to go to Korea for menial jobs. Mimi's sister, for instance, worked in a Korean leather bag factory for three months. Another big problem, she said, was that Lisu women in their forties, too old to make a living as prostitutes anymore, had returned to Doi Lan in desperate poverty. Some had turned to drug dealing. AIDS was still a big hidden problem.

It was clearly painful for Otome to hear these sad stories about life in Doi Lan, the village whose initial disruption she had documented in the 1980s. I asked what might be done, and she shrugged, helpless. She had no easy answers.

Huey Hawm, a Karen Coffee Village

MY NEXT JOURNEY was a five-hour drive west to Huey Hawm in Mae Hong Son Province. My driver, Richard Mann, then twenty-seven, was the grandson of the Richard "Dick" Mann who pioneered coffee cultivation in Thailand fifty years ago, in Huey Hawm. So I was going to origin, so to speak. ITDP coffee manager Boonchu Kloedu came along.

Huey Hawm was a charming, isolated mountain village. Like Boonchu, the 380 villagers were Karen tribal members, most of whom had been born there. The native name for the village is Chawti, which means "elephant" in Karen, so it, like Doi Chang, was named for the elephants that once roamed those mountains. The farmers gathered eagerly as Boonchu gave out partial payment for this year's coffee harvest. According to Richard, they would use the money to pay for items such as propane, a motorcycle or car, repair work, building materials such as roofing or teak, and food supplements such as salt. Otherwise, they were nearly self-sufficient. Each family processed its own coffee cherries.

Below the houses, in the valley, I could see rice paddies and sheep grazing next to fishponds. As a young man, Dick Mann had introduced sheep to the village, which is now one of the few places in Thailand that makes and sells domestic woolen clothing. Mann also encouraged fish farming, and ITDP set up a revolving fund for interest-free loans to villagers.

On the surrounding forested mountainsides, shade-grown coffee grew on about 500 rai (200 acres). Above the village is a spring with a water filtration system and concrete storage tank, which Starbucks had paid for in 2004, when the giant roaster began buying coffee beans from the village. The Starbucks purchase was a turning point for coffee in the village. Thalu, a wizened ninety-four-year-old, commented, "I remember when your grandfather [Dick Mann] told us not to cut down the coffee trees, when the price was so low. He said the time would come when coffee would sell better, and when Starbucks came, that happened." Thalu praised the Manns for coming back regularly through the years, unlike other charities, which is why the missionary organization is respected and why the villagers are Christians.

Back in Chiang Mai, Richard Mann took me to the ITDP offices, where I saw photos of other impressive village projects, including Ma Oh Jo, another Karen village. Twelve years ago, Richard had to walk there, but now there's a dirt road. ITDP started with a water/latrine project, then agricultural help with growing beans and other subsistence crops, a school, and now coffee, a biogas project, and a fish pond. "I hope the government will pave the road so we can get the coffee out with big trucks," he said. We also visited the Lanna Café, where ITDP sells its beans, which are roasted next door.

Akha Ama Coffee

IT TURNS OUT I missed visiting another important coffeehouse in Chiang Mai called Akha Ama ("Ama" means "mother" in the Akha language), founded by a young man named Lee Ayu Chuepa. In 1998, at the age of thirteen, he left Maejantai, the small Akha village where he grew up, to attend a Buddhist temple school in Lampang. He never converted, but he liked the monks' philosophy and way of life. Lee then went on to study English at Chiang Mai Rajabhat University, becoming the first person from his village of thirty-two households to graduate from college. He interned for the Child's Dream Foundation, a Chiang Mai charity that attempts to empower marginalized children and youth.

Lee went on to work full-time for the charity for over three years, an eye-opening experience. "I used to think I was a very unlucky person because I'm born in a village, and nobody even spoke Thai, much less English, so I had to start from zero to learn how to speak Thai. But with Child's Dream, when I went to the refugee camps, I realized how many people are more unlucky than I am. People who don't even have a leg, because they stepped on a land mine. So many children dying because of malnutrition and malaria and disease."

Still, Lee longed for home. "I missed my roots." On his visits back to Maejantai, a mountain village not too far to the west of Doi Chang in Mae Suai District, he lamented that most children had no money for education beyond the village primary school. They moved to the lowlands to work in gas stations, restaurants, karaoke bars, or construction sites, often becoming addicted to drugs and becoming HIV-positive.

He told his parents that he wanted to help alleviate the poverty in some way. The Akha grew apricots, plums, cherries, peaches, persimmons, vegetables, and a little rice, but none were cash crops. They also grew coffee, but received a pittance for their beans. "I chose coffee as my project," Lee said, "because it is value-added once you roast it, it is well known in the whole world, and I had noticed that it was growing in popularity in Thailand."

After visiting Doi Chang, Doi Tung, and coffeeshops in the lowlands, in March 2010 Lee, then twenty-four, opened the Akha Ama Café in Chiang Mai in order to roast and sell the high-grown beans from his village, beginning with his parents' harvest. The second year, five other families joined, then twenty households—i.e., most of the village.

At the time, he didn't even drink coffee, but he was a fast learner and very ambitious. He gave away free samples to restaurants and cafés in Chiang Mai. He submitted green beans to an international European barista competition, scraping together the 350 Euro submission fee, and was astonished when the Thai coffee was chosen as one to brew for the contest.

In 2013, Lee visited the United States for the first time, making a pilgrimage to Stumptown Coffee in Portland, Oregon, where he became an eager student of this renowned "third-wave" roaster.

"It was one of the best moments in my life to study about coffee at Stumptown. I think I'm the most lucky person in the world. I learned many things from them, especially coffee roasting, cupping, the grading of green coffee beans, wholesale and retail accounts and overall management." He also learned that processing the beans was an all-important step.

Back in Chiang Mai, he opened a second coffeehouse. About 40 percent of the customers who drank Akha Ama coffee at the Chiang Mai cafés were *farangs* seeking a great coffee experience in a foreign land, but the beans were also sold in other coffeehouses, hotels, and restaurants in Bangkok and Phuket and through the company website, www.akhaama.com.

Life in the village of Maejantai improved in a few short years. "My motivation is to support those farmers, those families, to be able to come up with a higher quality of life, and to be able to pay for their children to go to school." He wanted them to be able to "go out into the world and harvest good knowledge and come back."

An Akha Meeting

AFTER CHIANG MAI, I joined Tee Jupoh, the Akha professor I had met at the Doi Chaang festival, and who had agreed to translate for me. We drove north of Chiang Rai to the Meachang District to a meeting of the Association for Akha Education and Culture in Thailand (AFECT). In 1977, Paul Lewis had observed that "the tribal people do not as yet have any organization which brings them together in meetings." Now they did. The official AFECT meeting would take place in the Vocational Training Hall for Highland People, owned by AFECT and financed by the Japanese Embassy. The room was also used for festivals, conferences, training, and sleeping quarters.

I met Athu Pochear, the AFECT director, a dynamic, fit man in his forties, who welcomed me warmly. Over an informal dinner, Asawin Jupoh—known as Win, a young man from Saen Charoen, down the mountain from Doi Chang—and another Akha described their recent visit to an Akha village in Laos, two days' walk from the nearest town, where the villagers still grew opium poppies as their primary cash crop. The villagers were incredibly poor and ate mostly bamboo shoots. "It was like walking back in time fifty years to visit an Akha village in Thailand," Win said.

Win, who was related to Tee, grew wild coffee in Saen Charoen, having moved back home to care for his mother. He didn't know how many rai he had—he just let it grow wild and harvested what he could. He spoke bitterly about Doi Chaang Coffee, saying that Piko's family was getting rich while keeping the villagers poor. He was also unhappy because Doi Chaang wouldn't buy his coffee, which was not in the approved GI district. I observed that without Doi Chaang's success, no one else would be getting good money for their coffee, either. Tee later told me to take Win's complaints as perhaps "half true."

Athu led an animated conversation about how to preserve the Akha way of life. Many Akha villages no longer had people in all of the traditional roles such as the *pima*, *dzoema*, and *nipah*, so he proposed that one of each should be hired to roam among ten villages, and that the fund should also pay for sacrificial water buffalo. Tee didn't take an active part in the conversation, complaining that it was always big talk but no action.

In the morning, we moved our sleeping mats and I helped set up tables and displays for the big AFECT meeting that day. Over a hundred people assembled, as Athu showed old videos of traditional Akha village life and a television talk show in which he and Todd Tongdee hosted older Akha playing bamboo flutes and other instruments. At the formal meeting, Athu suggested that AFECT should sponsor roaming *pimas* and other ritual specialists, but since no one could figure out how to pay for their time or travel expenses, nothing came of it.

Two Days in Doi Tung

I LEFT THE AFECT MEETING to catch a ride further north to Doi Tung, the mountain that the elderly Princess Mother had made her project in 1987, and which is now a major tourist destination. Charly Mehl, an American who had lived in Thailand most of his adult life and had worked for the Mae Fah Luang Foundation for twenty years, arranged for my visit and came up from his Bangkok office to be my host. He did much of the research and planning for the impressive Hall of Opium I had visited the previous year, and he had also worked in Doi Tung, so he was greeted fondly by old acquaintances. During my two days there, we visited the coffee processing mill, roasting facility, and café at the bottom of the mountain. Doi Tung Coffee is sold in many Thai grocery stores as well as the Doi Tung Lifestyle shops on the mountain and in Bangkok. We also toured the nearby weaving, pottery, and paper factories. Atop the mountain, we saw many coffee trees and the macadamia nut processing plant, strolled through the beautiful gardens, and toured the home (now museum) of the late Princess Mother.

We also went through the Hall of Inspiration, which tells the history of the royal Mahidol family, including the story of the slum girl who became a nurse, married King Mahidol (a physician), and became the Princess Mother of current King Bhumibol. She was given the nickname Mae Fah Luang, "Royal Mother from the Sky." Somewhat to my surprise, the hall really was inspiring, including information on royal water projects and interviews with hill tribe members who had been helped by the project.

Charly Mehl arranged for me to interview two veteran Doi Tung coffee farmers, Saeyo Yangpaingku, sixty-five, an Akha, and Chumporn Apirattachai, eighty-nine, a Lahu. I asked them what it had been like before the Princess Mother arrived. They grew rice, corn, beans, and opium poppies, but there wasn't enough land for sufficient subsistence food, the trees were mostly gone, and they were caught between various feuding drug warlords. Then the army came and destroyed their poppy fields, leaving them in desperate shape. They tried to hunt for wild pigs or deer, using the MI6s or AK47s that were all too prevalent, but the game had disappeared along with the forests.

So of course they were willing to plant trees for the Princess Mother   it prevented them from starving. Then they worked on the royal coffee plantation and later rented or owned their own coffee trees. "It was good to be paid for our work," they said, "but much better to be owners."

Villagers were issued official Doi Tung IDs, which made them part of the privileged families who could take advantage of the program. To limit population growth and prevent a rush to the area, the project would not allow anyone else to move there permanently. Saeyo's original Akha village had been right in the middle of the current royal garden, but the village did not have to be moved far. He admitted that he had been an opium addict when the Royal Project started. "I didn't feel like working, and I had to lie and cheat to get money for opium," he recalled. So he was glad to be put on the "1000 Day Program," a strictly enforced opium intervention that lasted nearly three years. Unlike many other such programs, it actually worked much of the time. Chumporn, the Lahu man, never had a drug problem, and at age eighty-nine still harvested some of his own coffee on the steep mountainside. Both men agreed that their lives were better now than before the Royal Project.

The Mae Fah Luang undertaking at Doi Tung was supposed to be a thirty-year project, slated to end in 2017. It will be interesting to see what kind of transition of power (if any) occurs at that point. It is clear, though, that coffee has helped make a difference in the lives of people on this mountain, as it had in Doi Chang and Huey Hawm.

Before going back to Doi Chang, we drove along a narrow ridge to another Akha village called Pha Hee, sitting right on the Burmese border. It was set in a steep valley, so that no one could enter except from the top or bottom. Charly Mehl said that the village used to be a well-known smuggling byway for opium, with a cave at the bottom of the valley for hiding the contraband, and it may still be used for illegal methamphetamines coming in from Myanmar. Regardless, its hillsides are now covered with coffee trees, and the eighty-nine households of Pha Hee don't sell them to Doi Tung but roast their own. I saw their traditional Akha gate, with the carved male and female figures, which had just been replaced.

I met Kertu Bayche (his Thai name is Aran), the young village headman, who showed me his Phahee Coffee bag, featuring a coffee bean with a stem that looks remarkably like a poppy seedpod, in a sly reference to their former crop. Kertu said they sold their coffee to middlemen or other villages. He had visited Doi Chang, which had partly inspired his efforts.

Complications in Doi Chang

I RETURNED TO Doi Chang, where Tee and I visited the health clinic. It had seven employees, including a nurse, nicknamed Puck, and Niwet, the head nurse practitioner. They could stitch people up, but they had to send major cases down the mountain to the hospital in Mae Suai. The clinic offered family planning, pregnancy monitoring, childhood vaccinations, a chronic disease and nutrition clinic, and drug addiction treatment and rehabilitation. The bustling, well-equipped clinic displayed DONATED BY DOI CHAANG COFFEE on many pieces of equipment, and the dental chair in one room was part of a container of medical equipment that the Canadian company sponsored, although no dentist yet came to the clinic, and the dental chair remained uninstalled. Nonetheless, it stood in stark contrast to the empty, desolate clinic building seen in the 2010 Global Television documentary.

Niwet wasn't there that day. Puck said that undernutrition was no longer a big problem in Doi Chang, but that overeating (especially meat) was leading to more chronic diseases, just as in the developed world. She conducted home visits in the village, mostly to the elderly homebound or postpartum mothers. In the past, the elderly were cared for by their children, but now many children lived elsewhere. Doi Chang was a major hub for drug smugglers, which is why there was an army base there, but addicts were treated in strict confidence. Health care was free to anyone with a Thai ID, but there was a small charge to immigrants without identification papers.

Later, Miga, Nuda, Dawan, Lipi, and I had a lively discussion about the Akha way of life. Miga was contemptuous of the written form of the Akha language, which she said was only created so that missionaries could translate the Bible. I protested that the language might be lost otherwise, and that the written version could be used to write down Akha legends, many of which she and Adel had never heard, but which I had read in a book by Paul Lewis. She insisted that Akha was an oral tradition and should not be written. I said that I worried that the old customs might be lost, that the Akha language itself might be lost as Thai culture invaded Doi Chang. She shrugged, implying, *That's just the way things go.* Lipi interjected that he hated missionaries, who tried to force their ideas into your head.

We talked about traditional Akha medicinal herbs, which they all believed could work. Leebang, the man with a limp, was badly hurt in a motorcycle accident, and rubbing herbs on his leg made him much better. They joked that they could cut me and show me how they could cure me. They said that Akong, the master roaster, kept an herb garden outside the Academy of Coffee and was a great healer. There is a place in the village where there is a hole with magic healing earth, which you could roast and consume to cure what ails you. Nuda later took me to see this red clay, dug out just off the main road, but I never got to roast and eat it.

They also said that there were rituals and chants, and then the healer would blow breath on the hurt place. This was not just a *pima* who did this, but any older family member who knew the proper chants and methods. I asked about shamans, and yes, they have them, and yes, they go into a trance to see your tree of life and how it is doing.

They confirmed that in an Akha wedding, they throw rice and dung. The idea of the dung is that a couple will withstand together the worst that life can bring. But when I asked about the courting yard, Miga insisted that it was only a story made up to show how promiscuous Akha girls supposedly were. The Akha village elders, however, confirmed that it had existed, but was now a rarely used ceremonial area. Young people no longer sang, danced, and flirted there. They were too busy in school or watching television.

After that meeting, Tee and I visited Agui Chermui, the chief *pima*, in his village home. His was a traditional Akha home, with an ancestor shrine hanging in a corner of the women's half of the house. Agui was very proud that he is one of only three *pimas* in Thailand who can sacrifice as many as three water buffaloes and one horse at a funeral for an important deceased Akha.

I also spoke with former headman Beno's daughter-in-law, Atum. She was an Ulo Akha from another village. She had three children, all of whom were being raised as Lisu, and she had essentially lost her own Akha identity and culture, since she lived on the upper Lisu side of the road. She knew of nine other Lisu-Akha couples in Doi Chang—all Lisu husbands with Akha wives. Akha women are known as hard workers and good mothers. I asked Atum if she missed the Akha Way, but she just said, "The husband is the head of the family, and a wife must follow."

Then we visited the current village headman, Aja, who was elected in 2010. On call twenty-four hours a day for any village crisis, he earned a salary of 8,000 baht per month ($270). Typically, he would adjudicate border disputes, since there are no official boundaries or even legal ownership. But only one case in four years had gone to the courts. I asked whether some kind of zoning regulations might be necessary, with the explosive growth in the village. Aja said there was already a kind of zoning—there was a community forest, farming fields, and an area for houses. But no one would dare suggest further zoning restrictions.

Aja admitted that addiction and gambling were sometimes problems and that the money from coffee had exacerbated them. Akha men would start with Ya Ba and then go on to heroin addiction. He was concerned that the traditional Akha way of life was eroding, but this was a new generation, and they had a choice. You could not force anything on them. You could not take away computers and television sets.

Aja also owned 40 rai and grew coffee. He processed his own beans and sold them in parchment to roasters in Chiang Mai, Bangkok, and elsewhere. I asked why he didn't sell to Doi Chaang Coffee, and his face clouded. He then told me that he was one of nine Akha who formed a kind of cooperative back when Wicha and Adel were growing the Doi Chaang Coffee business. Each of the nine was responsible for processing coffee cherries from a group of farmers, then delivering the beans to be roasted for sale by Doi Chaang. For this service, the processors had received 2 baht per kilo.

But Wicha and Adel grew unhappy with this arrangement and accused the processing groups of delivering inferior beans. They suspected that people were buying cheaper beans from lower elevations and otherwise cutting corners on proper fermentation, depulping, and drying. In 2010, Doi Chaang Coffee bought a large, expensive processor, enabling them to purchase the ripe coffee cherries directly from the farmers, thus cutting out the middlemen processors. Aja remained extremely bitter about this development. "Together, we worked hard to develop the business, to get the Geographical Indication registration completed. Then they abandoned us." He blamed Wicha for influencing Adel.

The AAA Doi Chang Coffee Farm, just down the road on the opposite side from Doi Chaang Coffee, is owned by Adel's first cousin Apa, who was another of the nine original processors. The AAA managers roast their own coffee and rent out guesthouses. They also host the "Korea Barista School," where Korean baristas can come for a few days to see how the coffee they brew is grown, harvested, and processed.

I had known that the new processing machinery, installed in 2010, allowed Doi Chaang Coffee to buy directly from the farmers, thus guaranteeing that the coffee was authentic and grown locally. But I hadn't realized what bitterness this rift had caused. When I asked, Adel explained that it had been a difficult decision, but he was in no way Wicha's puppet. "Wicha had a big heart. He was always working, always thinking. People spread rumors that Wicha was using the Akha, but the ultimate goal was to help the farmers. If you listen to rumors, you won't do anything, you'll just lie in your bed and worry." He and Wicha were true partners, he said, and they discussed everything together.

Adel said that some of their coffee had been rejected for low quality in 2009. He had tried to talk with the head of each processing group, but each said, "It's not my problem. You have to take responsibility." So he held an emotional meeting in which he announced his plans to eliminate the middlemen processors. "Yes, I had to cut off my own brother Leehu and my friends." In the four years since that decision, Adel had tried to rebuild trust and relationships. "I still give advice and counsel. I will help anyone who is struggling." His brother Leehu, unlike Aja, had fully reconciled.

I asked Adel whether they would be able to carry on without Wicha's charismatic leadership. "Wicha is irreplaceable," Adel said. "No other man in the world could do all that he did. But yes, of course we will carry on." Wicha was the company's public face, but everyone worked to execute his ideas behind the scenes, and Adel and Miga were confident that they could continue effectively. I asked if Adel would be comfortable talking to the media, and he said he would. "It's always easy to tell the truth."

The Quiet Coffee Millionaire

TEE TOLD ME that I really ought to see one more coffee operation that no one had told me about. Beche Coffee lay off the dirt road that ran behind the Doi Chaang coffeehouse. I had driven to the end of that road with Leebang to see his Doi Yama Coffee, but now Tee and I turned left off the road and came to a compound where a brightly colored truck was being loaded with coffee, part of four containers that would be shipped from Bangkok to a broker in Indonesia. Inside the warehouse, full burlap bags of coffee were stacked along a wall behind a long table at which women were sorting through piles of green coffee beans.

Precha Beche, thirty-nine, was busy monitoring the operation. Tall and thin, with close-cropped hair, he didn't look like a typical Akha, nor did he have the friendly, outgoing manner of Adel. Instead, he was low-key, with the matter-of-fact manner of a powerful businessman used to getting his way. On the main road through the village, he owns a gas station, mini-mart, commercial space, fifty apartment units, and a coffeehouse with a small roaster that he said was just there for show. Precha explained that he had begun buying land in Doi Chang in 1992, when he was seventeen years old, starting with 20 rai, and planting coffee, when no one saw any future in it. People thought he was crazy, but he kept buying land. He now owned 700 rai of coffee in Doi Chang, high on the road to Ban Mai, and another 500 rai at a lower elevation near the town of Wawi, where he grew trees imported from Java.

He also buys coffee from many other places, including Mae Suai, Doi Lan, Huey San, Wawi, and as far away as Nan Province, negotiating payment depending on the quality level. Then he grades them all, selling into both the specialty and commodity-grade market, shipping to brokers in Indonesia (two-thirds goes there), Thailand, Japan, Taiwan, and Malaysia. He sells about a million kilograms (a thousand tons) of coffee per year, about half of Doi Chaang Coffee's production. He also keeps a low profile.

Precha converted to Christianity when he was fourteen, but that did not prevent him from marrying three women—one Akha, one Lisu, and one Thai—though he now has only two wives and eleven children. He flew to Brazil in 2012 to look at huge automatic coffee harvesting machines that shake cherries loose, and he planned to return there to purchase the first such harvester to be used in Thailand. He would use it to harvest robusta coffee trees that he would plant in the lowland near Chiang Rai, where he already owned 1,000 acres.

He was skeptical about how much credit should be given to Wicha for his (Precha's) success. "Wicha was a trend-maker, who made the name Doi Chaang famous for world-class coffee, but the name is meaningless to me. I only care for customer satisfaction." He buys coffee beans from anywhere to resell, not just from the Geographical Indication area around Doi Chang. Yet I couldn't help thinking that his location in Doi Chang must have contributed to his success.

Good-bye to Doi Chang

MY LAST NIGHT in Doi Chang, I had dinner alone with Miga in the small covered area next to the kitchen on the far side of the Academy of Coffee. She told me that this was where she found Wicha the morning of his heart attack. Usually she was hesitant to speak English with me, but now she forgot to be anxious. "I miss Khun Wicha too much," she said, lighting another cigarette. Three weeks before, as I sat next to the wall by the fire, I had said, "This was Wicha's place," and Miga had blurted out, "Everywhere around here is Wicha's place."

Now she told me that every night she and Wicha would talk seriously for an hour or so. He didn't joke with her, as he did with others. He reviewed the day, telling her what she did right or wrong. He taught her that she must learn to control herself, or she would be controlled by someone else. She cried as she told me this and said that she rarely cried in front of anyone. Yes, she had cried when Khun John first came after Wicha's death. "He is a good man, and so is John Leck [Darch Junior] and Anand." I got up and hugged her. She apologized. I told her it was good to cry.

She remembered how Wicha would teach her things. "Miga, see that red flower? That means that the rainy season is about to begin." Or "Miga, see that yellow plant? That means that there will be a good harvest." Things like that. She said she did not like to dream about Wicha, because then she woke up to the reality. "He was like a father to me." And she stamped out her last cigarette of the night.

The next day, I said my good-byes to Miga, Adel, Nuda, and everyone who had called me Abopala. Good-bye, Doi Chang, unique, alive, beautiful, complex, growing, changing, compelling coffee village.

What Next?

WHAT DOES the future hold for the two interrelated ventures on either side of the globe, both relatively recent, both very much works in progress? The Canadian Doi Chaang Coffee enterprise was small but growing, with gross sales breaking $3 million in 2014. With the help of food broker Danny Tam, the company began to expand further in Ontario through deals with Sobeys East Stores, which provided a wedge to get onto Sobeys West shelves back in British Columbia. In ninety Loblaw stores, Doi Chaang Aroma cups were being tested in bins in the coffee aisle, where customers could grab a capsule or two as an impulse buy. "We see more customers demanding organic Fair Trade products in the Toronto area," Darch Senior said, "so we are arriving at a good time." Meanwhile Canterbury's John McGowan, based in Oakville, Ontario, was finding smaller diners, restaurants, and university accounts.

The company's European expansion also seemed encouraging. DRWakefield, the UK green coffee bean importer, bought three Doi Chaang containers in 2014, then resold them to various roasters to whom the Akha Beyond Fair Trade story was appealing. Ben Roberts, owner of Beanpress Coffee Company in Dorset, was one of those roasters who bought a few bags of Doi Chaang beans. He loved both the coffee and the story. Then, when he discovered that

Terry Darch, the younger brother of the founder, lived only 20 miles away, he got in touch, which led to a meeting in 2014 with John Darch Senior and Junior. Roberts hoped to establish himself as an agent for Doi Chaang in the UK, becoming a master roaster and distributor. "The United Kingdom sends a million tourists a year to Thailand," he said. "We love Thai cuisine and culture, but people don't know about great Thai coffee, despite the coffee boom."

That same year, Oro Caffè, based in Udine in northeastern Italy, bought its first container of Doi Chaang beans and began to promote them heavily on its Italian website and in its advertising. Elisa Toppano, the founder's daughter and heir apparent, planned to purchase two containers the following year. Oro Caffè used Doi Chaang beans in its premium blend as well as selling it as a single-origin choice, with sales in Italy, Germany, Austria, and Saudi Arabia. Younger sister Ketty Toppano moved to Toronto to start a Canadian branch of the Italian company, so the cobranded Doi Chaang-Oro Caffè beans, roasted in Italy, were now being sold in Ontario, just as beans from the Vancouver company were becoming more popular there as well.

The Darches had yet to figure out how to crack the huge, enticing market to their south in the United States, at least in any meaningful way. Yet Doi Chaang certainly had devotees there, such as Henry Kalebjian, owner of Henry's House of Coffee in San Francisco. An Armenian immigrant who had been roasting at the same location since 1981, Kalebjian adored Doi Chaang's taste. "There is no acidic aftertaste, it's smooth with a brown sugar sweetness, rich and nutty," he said. "There is a magic inside. You can drink cup after cup without tiring of it." He gave away roasted samples, even to people he waylaid in the supermarket coffee aisle. "And every single person comes back to my shop to buy it."

Meanwhile, in Vancouver there were a number of staff changes. Near the end of 2014, Anand Pawa, who had served as such a vital link between the Canadian and Thai businesses, announced that he was moving back to Bangkok, where his aging father wanted him to take over the family business, selling medical equipment. Anand Pawa hoped to remain involved with Doi Chaang, continuing to serve as an advisor for those in Thailand as well as Canada.

Around the same time, public relations manager Katharine Sawchuk resigned in order to return to school. "My two years at Doi Chaang have been special and fulfilling," she said. "I'm proud of what we've accomplished together as a team, and what I have done with the company's communications (both online and offline) from the ground up. It's exciting to hear more people gush about how much they love the coffee in person and on social media. It makes me happy I was able to put Doi Chaang's reputation as a sustainable, ethical and high quality coffee out there in front of the coffee-loving public. I'm leaving a group of intelligent, unique and caring individuals. They will be greatly missed."

To replace Katharine Sawchuk and Anand Pawa, the Darches hired Brittany Brown, a young woman with a diploma in public relations with experience in social media, brand awareness, promotions, and strategic planning. She had also spent three years managing Esquires Coffee House in South Surrey, near Vancouver. She described herself as "creative and passionate" and said that she thrived in quick-paced environments.

That same fall, sales manager Sanja Grcic married and moved to Croatia. To give fuller attention to existing accounts, and seek new ones, George Goldsmith, a veteran food products salesman in his forties, came aboard in late August 2014 as the first full-time sales rep for Doi Chaang Coffee in Canada. He spent every day on the road visiting retail outlets, making sure stores were fully stocked, setting up sampling demonstrations, and meeting with store managers. In his first three months, he was able to add ten new accounts, such as Gourmet Warehouse and Budget Foods. "I think we're just scratching the surface with this company," he said. "There is definitely opportunity out there." Although he only showed up at the office for Tuesday morning sales meetings, he was impressed with the energetic, idealistic, goal-oriented team there. Ironically, Goldsmith didn't drink coffee himself, but he believed in the Beyond Fair Trade concept and felt that the story behind the coffee was important.

Tanya Jacoboni took over some of Grcic's role in dealing with accounts with head office purchasers, with whom she organized promotions, advertising spending, and any other matters best dealt with at the main office. She supervised Goldsmith and any other sales people who might be added, as well as dealing with all brokers and distributors.

In the village of Doi Chang, the Akha were continuing to grow and thrive, with plans to expand their coffeehouses into other countries, launch the cordyceps business, and encourage the growth of coffee trees on up to 10,000 acres within the Geographic Indication region near the mountaintop. To handle all of the beans, the company installed a new processing plant down the mountain in Mae Suai, next to a second large drying patio.

Phitsanuchai Kaewphichai, the Thai entrepreneur who served as Wicha's unpaid background advisor for many years, began to take a more active role following his friend's death and now became Khun Ar Phitsanu—Uncle Phitsanu—to the Akha. He began the process of standardizing Doi Chaang coffeehouses throughout Thailand, for the first time applying stringent quality codes to any establishment that displayed the Doi Chaang logo. By the end of 2015, he planned to have one hundred official Thai franchises, in addition to 200 independent coffeehouses that used the village's beans. Malaysia would have eighteen Doi Chaang coffeehouses, China would have five, Korea hosted three, and one opened in Singapore, with ongoing negotiations for franchises in India, Japan, Cambodia, and Australia. Anand Pawa, now back in Thailand, traveled to India to set up a Doi Chaang Coffee franchise system there, with plans to open the first coffeehouse in Mumbai early in 2016.

Phitsanu also owned several Doi Chaang coffeehouse locations in Asian airports and met frequently with Adel and Miga in Doi Chang and in Bangkok with Paolo Fantaguzzi, who was finalizing the design of his brewer, grinder, and roaster, and who imported all other coffee machinery and set up other services for coffeeshops.

Adel and Miga planned to have long-term infrastructure in place and paid for within three to five years, so that they could begin to take profits rather than plowing them back into capital improvements. They hoped no longer to have to borrow money to pay for coffee cherries every harvest season. They would then begin to pump 30 percent of their profits into the Doi Chaang Coffee Foundation, which would fund a new day care, school, and hospital for the village and surrounding area.

All of these plans received a big boost in November 2014, when, after six months of negotiation, Adel, Miga, and others at Doi Chaang Coffee Original announced a new joint venture with Vara Food & Drink Company, a non-alcoholic subsidiary of Singha Corporation, a wealthy organization that makes the most popular Thai beer. This new entity, unpoetically named DVS 2014 Company (D for Doi Chaang, V for Vara Food, and S for Singha), would be the sole distributor for both raw and roasted beans and other Doi Chaang products, aside from existing clients, such as the Vancouver roasting company, which already dealt directly with Doi Chaang Coffee Original, the parent Thai company. But in the future, as current agreements expired, or clients agreed, the new joint venture would handle that distribution as well. John Darch Senior and Junior planned to continue to deal directly with

Miga and Adel in Doi Chang village, as they always had. "DVS 2014 will mainly handle our retail market such as capsule coffee," said Phitsanu, "and will sell our roasted coffee beans in modern trade outlets."

The immediate impact of the Singha investment was the ability to purchase half of the 2014–2015 season's coffee cherries without having to borrow money. The harvest came from approximately 6,000 acres of producing coffee trees, which yielded 10,000 tons of coffee cherries. Once processed, that produced 2,000 tons of parchment coffee. Half would be financed and sold to DVS, while the other half would go to Doi Chaang in Canada and elsewhere.

Now it appeared that plans to fund the Doi Chaang Coffee Foundation and its projects could go forward much more quickly. Not only would 30 percent of Doi Chaang Coffee Original's profits go into the Foundation, but so would 15 percent of the DVS profits. In addition, Khun Santi Bhirombhakdi, Singha's chairman, pledged to contribute supplementary funds from his personal foundation. Plans for a new day care center in Doi Chang village, to accommodate the growing number of children in the boomtown, were a first priority.

As the Advisory Chairman of Doi Chaang Coffee Original, "Uncle Phitsanu" would monitor the new joint venture, along with the Doi Chaang coffeeshop franchises and another joint venture with Ital-Thai Services Company, Paolo Fantaguzzi's coffee brewers and roasters, imported machines, and service.

Lessons from Two Continents

A s WITH MOST ongoing stories, we are left with more questions than answers. Can Doi Chaang Coffee of Vancouver provide a model for a new form of capitalism, as John Darch Senior hoped? Or is this nothing more than a quixotic, well-intended venture by a wealthy investor who wanted to leave his mark on the world by doing something meaningful for the Akha? How much did the Akha side depend on Wicha Promyong's energy and enthusiasm to succeed and to maintain its success? Can the village handle its sudden wealth gracefully? Will the joint venture with Singha mean that the Akha become just another part of the corporate world? Will other villages—in Thailand or other countries—be able to replicate this success? How have the two cultures, Canadian and Thai/Akha, meshed or clashed? What lessons can the Doi Chaang Coffee experience teach the world of the future in social, cultural, ethical, and business terms?

I think there are some tentative answers, based on the research and interviews I have conducted for this book. The particular model provided by Doi Chaang Coffee, in which half of the

Canadian company was essentially gifted to a consortium of Akha farmers, is not necessarily a model for others to follow, but it does provide an example for those who want to break free of the traditional, prevailing capitalistic model, in which cheap commodities have been extracted from poor developing countries, then processed and sold in developed nations—where most of the profits remain.

As the anthropologist Eric Wolf observed in his classic 1982 work, *Europe and the People Without History*, "The world of humankind constitutes... a totality of interconnected processes." The story of opium and coffee in Doi Chang and elsewhere provides one fascinating thread, stitching together the disciplines of history, anthropology, sociology, psychology, medicine, and business, and offering a way to follow the interactions that have formed a global economy. While this book has concentrated on coffee and opium, similar stories could be told for other products. The European countries extracted furs, silver, gold, diamonds, slaves, spices, sugar, tea, coffee, cocoa, tobacco, opium, rubber, palm oil, and petroleum from Asia, Africa, and the Americas. As North America, taken over by white Europeans, developed industrially, it too joined the conquest.

As the world has become more of a global village, a place in which a coffee harvester high on a remote mountainside can stop to talk to someone hundreds or thousands of miles away on his or her cell phone, the inequities built into the world's economy have become more glaring. Fortunately, this has been accompanied by a heightened awareness about how products make their way to Western marketplaces. Increasingly, people are showing concern about and interest in not only the quality of the products they purchase, but who made them and under what conditions, and how they were paid. That is the basis of certifications such as Fair Trade. Yet Fair Trade establishes only a kind of minimum wage, arguably not a particularly fair one—it's better than the coffee C-market, but still inadequate. The "Beyond Fair Trade" model established by Doi Chaang Coffee really does make a substantial difference, and I hope that in the coming decades, true partnerships between producers at origin and retailers in developed countries will become commonplace.

The other model that Wicha's vision helped establish was roasting at origin, so that more of the profits remain with the villagers. As John Darch Junior emphasized, coffee becomes a substantially value-added product after it is roasted. Traditionally, green coffee beans have been exported, with a few exceptions, such as Café Britt, which roasts Costa Rican beans in Costa Rica, Peruvian beans in Peru, and Colombian beans in Colombia. Now, with coffee consumption increasing in origin countries such as Brazil, more roasters should be able to keep more of the profits in-country.

After coffee is roasted, it stales quickly when exposed to oxygen, and for many years, that meant pre-staling packaged coffee, since freshly roasted beans produce carbon dioxide, and the "de-gassing" process would burst airtight containers. But one-way valve bags can now keep roasted beans fresher for months, which makes it possible to roast at origin and ship throughout the country and even across borders, as Café Britt has demonstrated.

In the coming years, we are likely to see a slow shift in the inequity built into our capitalist system, as "developing" countries attain greater wealth and the global playing field becomes "flatter," as economist Thomas Friedman puts it. Thailand has, in fact, come far along that path, as have China and India, for example. There are still glaring contrasts between extreme wealth and poverty in those countries (as in North America, for that matter), but I hope that the model of compassionate capitalism that John Darch Senior and Wicha Promyong attempted to model will inspire people in other countries around the world. Coffee is a perfect product for that model, but as Darch told me, "I am not a coffee person. We focus on the highest quality, but it could have been any commodity that I tried to help sell. I am passionate about people, especially underdogs who, through no fault of their own other than the accident of birth, seem to have the world against them. This just happened to be in Thailand, and it happened to be coffee."

In my conversations with him, Darch emphasized that he was not acting out of guilt when he created the new coffee company. He had no regrets in having promoted his various mining ventures, though over the years he had become more concerned about the environmental impact of such extractive industries, and he was haunted by the deaths in the Rovic diamond mine collapse. "My move to coffee wasn't waking up and thinking I *hate mining and want to pay for my sins*. Our society is built on the use of natural resources. We need mines, unless we want to go back to living in caves. Coffee is renewable and sustainable, but it must be processed and transported, all of which requires oil, gas, electricity, and trucks. The metal for those trucks had to be mined." Darch noted that everything we use has been "either grown, mined, or pumped out of the ground."

I pointed out the irony that Darch made a good deal of money from selling his Thai potash concession and is still promoting other potash ventures, and that he used part of that money to establish an organic coffee company. Potash is one of the three primary ingredients in chemical fertilizer. Wasn't that a contradiction? Darch demurred. "Potash is essential to improve the strength of plants, to make them grow better, resist diseases, and feed more people. If we didn't mine that potassium, billions of people would be worse off." It was great that the Akha could recycle their pulp as organic fertilizer, but Darch insisted that "in certain areas of the world," organic was not an option.

In one of my interviews with Wicha, I asked him whether he was uncomfortable with Darch's profits from potash. "No," he said, "John is a good man." Wicha disliked all chemical fertilizers and thought that the "green revolution" had done more harm than good, and if Darch ever wanted to use potash in Doi Chang, he would refuse. But he had no problem with accepting Darch's help. "We are family," he insisted.

Darch acknowledged that, in the past, the mining industry had often been irresponsible, focusing on profits more than people and the environment. "We need watchdogs but not fanatics. There is a fine balance. Some activists just want to stop anything."

I asked whether he expected to recoup his substantial investment in Doi Chaang Coffee. He hoped he would. He was irritated when people regarded it as "a charity under the guise of a business," and he repeatedly compared the venture to a junior mining company in the developmental stage, where early investments were not expected to yield a profit, but in the long term they might succeed. Yet he admitted, "Most of my former mining friends were skeptical, asking, Why? Where is the profit?" Darch's old mentor, David Giddings, is one of the cynics. "John really cares about the people up there in the village," Giddings said. "This is probably the first time in his life he's done something so generous and misguided. I don't think he'll ever get his money back. It's not impossible, but I don't think it will grow sufficiently big to float, even on the Vancouver stock exchange."

Darch has no plans to take the small Canadian coffee company public, but he is looking for a "strategic partner" to take the company to the next level. He cited the success of Kicking Horse, the British Columbia coffee company started in a garage that sold for millions. Indeed, he might try to entice Kicking Horse CEO Elana Rosenfeld into becoming a partner in Doi Chaang.

I would not be surprised if Darch Senior did indeed get his money back. He is a powerfully persuasive salesman. "I have always had confidence in my ability to find a way, and that way would become apparent as everything unfolded," Darch observed, looking back on his career. "I never began a project because I had dreams about how much money I could make, but because I believed in the projects and what they could be. I could visualize them up and running."

It's become clear to me, as I have researched topics as varied as coffee, Coca-Cola, public health, psychology, astronomy, mirrors, or renewable energy, that *unusual individuals have made all the difference.* There have always been driven, visionary leaders who have made change happen. True, they came along at a particular time in history and they happened to take an interest in a particular topic or venture. But without their ideas to drive others to action, little would have been accomplished.

It occurred to me that John Darch Senior and Wicha Promyong, who grew up in such different circumstances, were surprisingly similar personalities. Both men refused to accept limitations. Both had enormous energy, required little sleep, and enjoyed multiple challenges. They were excited about new projects and possibilities but weren't the best of managers. Each needed pragmatic people to keep them somewhat grounded in reality. While both men claimed not to care about money as their ultimate goal, they enjoyed establishing wealth-creating businesses. Ultimately, despite their rather large egos, both men acted selflessly to help others.

"I see myself as a catalyst," Darch said. "I enjoy telling the story of the Akha and seeing it evolve." He acknowledged that he had a hard time "going in a straight line" and always had to have several enterprises going on simultaneously, just as Wicha did. "The sadness of his passing is hard to express," he added. "He truly touched my heart. Wicha literally gave his life to others. But nothing would ever have been enough for him. He would always be looking for something new."

The same could certainly be said of Darch. "John has always been a very busy man," observed Rupi Khanuja, Darch's long-time financial officer. "I enjoyed working with him because I got

260, BEYOND FAIR TRADE

to be challenged and learned a lot. I enjoyed the road shows, seeing how he presented a project. It takes a certain charisma to sell a hole in the ground, telling people what you are going to do. But he was always well-prepared and scrupulously honest." Working with John Darch also had its challenges. "He doesn't seem to sleep. I was working eighteen hours a day, and the worst thing I ever did was to give him a laptop and teach him to e-mail. I created a monster."

But once leaders such as Darch and Wicha establish companies (or other leaders I have written about who championed scientific advances, products, or programs), their legacy often lives on when they are gone. That certainly seems to be the case in the village of Doi Chang, where the Akha are carrying on with hardly a bump following Wicha's untimely demise. "And if I pegged out tomorrow," Darch said, "the wheels are turning enough so that Johnny (Darch Junior) and everyone else could carry on."

It would be a mistake to promote the myth of superior leaders who did everything alone, however. It is impossible to list everyone who made this joint international venture a success, but clearly Adel, Miga, Nuda, Lipi, and other Akha were essential in the village, while John Darch Junior, Anand Pawa, Tanya Jacoboni, and other staff in the Vancouver office and at Canterbury Coffee rose to the challenge in Canada. John Darch Senior points out that one key person is often overlooked—Kornkranok "Sandra" Bunmusik. "Sandra really was the catalyst, in her own soft way, in persuading Wicha and I to deal with one another smoothly. Many times, as we tried to move forward, she was the voice of reason." She was always with Wicha when he traveled to represent the company, keeping him focused.

As for possible cultural clashes within a business co-owned by Akha farmers and Canadian businessmen—yes, there have been some miscommunications, though the arrival of Anand Pawa, who grew up in Thailand and was educated in British Columbia, helped considerably. Goodwill, frequent visits, and respect for one another resolved most issues. Wicha never did understand why he couldn't send Akha to Vancouver to set up roasting and distribution, though.

I have already noted that the ripples from the establishment of Doi Chaang Coffee, in both Canada and Thailand, have been substantial and perhaps impossible to measure. One of the primary goals for both Wicha and Darch was, as Darch wrote, "to eliminate the coffee grower's cycle of poverty by promoting education and health care, encouraging cultural identity and pride, and returning the majority of the revenues to the growers." In large measure, those goals have been achieved, though the intervillage school that Wicha envisioned has yet to be built.

Still, success has brought its own set of unanticipated problems. While the Akha may take pride in their cultural heritage, that heritage is being eroded with increased contact with other cultures. All village farmers, Akha as well as Lisu, do not share equally in the profits, and some original association members remain bitter over the 2010 split that occurred when Wicha and Adel decided to do their own processing and buy just-harvested coffee cherries directly from the farmers.

Darch couldn't forget the comment of a veteran business acquaintance, who cautioned him as he was beginning his roasting venture that new wealth in a poor community or family often leads to unpredictable results. "The people you are helping now are fully committed, but be careful of the second and third generation. Growing up with more money, education, and opportunities, they may not have the same level of dedication to the business. You may encounter levels of resentment because everything doesn't come as easily as they expect." In other words, human beings are likely to take for granted what they already have.

It was clear to me from my time in Doi Chang village that along with the extraordinary success of the coffee venture came unanticipated problems, such as unplanned congestion and the cultural influences of television and computers. And a few succumbed to the temptations of drug abuse and gambling. But what were the alternatives? Would it be better to leave the hill tribes in poverty, marginalized in a society that stereotyped them as lazy, stupid, and inferior? It was clear that they could never go back to their traditional way of life, living freely and independently, hunting and growing subsistence crops on rotating fields. Nor could they go back to a reliance on opium poppies as their primary cash crop. The Akha and Lisu had to join the national and global economy. "We aren't of a mind to say, 'You continue in your grass huts as you were,'" said Darch. "Education, health, respect, and independence are key."

Without the help of the Canadian company, it is unlikely that the Thai operation would have grown the way it has. "If we had not come along, Doi Chaang would probably still be a small operation in northern Thailand. I don't think they would have been so successful without the kick-start from Canada and the attendant international media exposure," Darch says. "Thais love such attention from the foreign press, which gives status and credibility to domestic businesses." Darch acknowledged, however, that the Thai business is already a success, whereas "our Canadian enterprise has a long way to go."

No one knows what the future will bring, either in politics or business. It seems likely that Doi Chaang Coffee will continue to thrive in Thailand. The brand is recognized as top-quality coffee produced and roasted domestically, and the franchise system is expanding into Korea and other Asian countries. There may be some new competition when the ASEAN free trade agreement commences at the end of 2015, allowing coffee grown in neighboring Asian countries to be imported without the current 90 percent tariff. Since the Doi Chaang name and brand image are already well established, however, it should continue to do well.

Let the last word go to John Darch Senior. "It is our belief," he wrote to me at one point, "that when the growers are able to significantly benefit from the sustainability and prosperity of their goods, they gain financial independence, security, dignity, and control of their own well-being. With basic survival no longer their priority, farmers are motivated to sustain production and quality control, and a strong, respectful partnership is formed."

ACKNOWLEDGMENTS

ROB SANDERS of Greystone Books was immediately enthusiastic about the Akha, their coffee, and the Vancouver firm that roasts the Thai beans. My thanks to him for taking on this project, and particularly to Lesley Cameron, the freelance editor engaged by Greystone to help whip my manuscript into shape.

Many people in Thailand, Canada, and elsewhere made this book not only possible, but a pleasure to research and write. That includes all of those included in the list of interviews below. I owe a large debt to Paul Lewis, retired missionary and anthropologist, for his ethnography and books on the Akha and for sharing his personal insights, and to retired missionary and agronomist Dick Mann for letting me read his unpublished memoirs. Both Lewis and Mann live at Pilgrim Place in Claremont, California. I am also grateful to Matthew McDaniel, founder of Akha Heritage Foundation, for letting me read his unpublished writings, even though I do not agree with some of his criticisms of missionaries (especially his unfair attack on Paul Lewis's family planning activities). John

McKinnon and Duangta Sriwuthiwong were generous in sharing their unpublished primary source documents about the village of Doi Chang in the 1980s. Ronald Renard wrote a great book about opium reduction in Thailand and provided me with invaluable contacts and suggestions.

Anthropologists Deborah Tooker, Otome Hutheesing, and Cornelia Kammerer wrote extremely helpful books and articles as well as sharing further insights, and Otome welcomed me to her home in Chiang Rai, along with Mimi Saeju and Michael Vickery. Nong (Chayanin Sritisarn) was a great driver and translator during my research trip to Chiang Rai, during which I interviewed Bandid Jangnam and Lamar Robert, who graciously invited me to their homes, while Jacques Op de Laak took me up the mountain to revisit his coffee research station. Jitra Samsa welcomed me to the Payap University Archives, where her staff was helpful and accommodating.

Richard Mann and his father, Mike Mann, of the Integrated Tribal Development Program (ITDP), were generous with their time and knowledge, and I enjoyed my lengthy road trip with Richard and Boonchu Kloedu to see the village of Huey Hawn and the ITDP headquarters. Kritipong "Tee" Jupoh was a terrific, thoughtful translator and companion during our forays in the village of Doi Chang and elsewhere. Charly Mehl came all the way from Bangkok to take me around Doi Tung and answered all of my subsequent questions with patience. He also read and commented on parts of my manuscript, as did Phitsanuchai "Chai" Kaewphichai, who has been an advisor to Doi Chaang Coffee since its earliest days.

Mostly, I have to thank the main subjects of my story, starting with John M. Darch, whose contributions to this book were generous and undemanding, and his son John A. Darch, who also proved to be an enjoyable and amusing companion. Anand Pawa not only translated for me in Thailand but showed me around Vancouver. Danika Speight and Sanja Grcic both shared their first trips to Doi Chang with me as well as welcoming me to Canada. The rest of the Vancouver Doi Chaang Coffee gang, including Tanya Jacoboni, Katharine Sawchuk, Jackie Kingston, Senni Dempster, and Katharine Regan, were all friendly and helpful. At Canterbury Coffee near Vancouver, I wish particularly to thank Eric Lightheart, whom I met again in Thailand, for his time and enthusiasm.

While in Thailand, Sandra Bunmusik was an integral part of my experience in both Bangkok and the village of Doi Chang, where she provided quiet support as well as translating lively conversations and speeches at the Academy of Coffee annual festival.

In the village of Doi Chang, my deepest thanks go to Miga Saedoo and Adel Saedoo for sharing their time and expertise, and to siblings Lipi, Jay, and Dawan Wuiyue for their friendship, and particularly to Jay for leading me up the muddy coffee slopes to find wild civet coffee. I was touched when Bujoh "Nuda" Piaocheku, who makes soap and cordyceps, gave me a traditional silver Akha bracelet to take home to my wife.

Thanks to Chome Leeja for hosting me at her resort in the village and translating for me when I interviewed her father. Another Lisu, Poomjit (Toon), was a thoughtful host at his charming resort, Baan Suan Doi Chaang, on the road up to the agricultural research station. In fact, everyone I encountered in the village was helpful and friendly, whether during a casual drop-in or an Easter service, or whether they were agricultural research personnel or soldiers encountered on the road.

Finally, I want to express my thanks to Wicha Promyong's family for their kindness to me on my last visit to Thailand, following Wicha's tragic and untimely death. In our brief but intense time together, I had become friends with Wicha, who was a truly remarkable man. I can only imagine the loss they feel.

TO CONSERVE SPACE, I am including this note, highlighting books and interviews that were helpful in my research. For the full bibliography, see my website: www.markpendergrast.com.

ABOUT THE AKHA AND OTHER HILL TRIBES

Anderson, Edward F. *Plants and People of the Golden Triangle: Ethnobotany of the Hill Tribes of Northern Thailand* (1993).

Goodman, Jim. *The Akha: Guardians of the Forest* (1997).

Goodman, Jim. *Meet the Akhas* (1996).

Grunfeld, Frederic V. *Wayfarers of the Thai Forest: The Akha* (1982).

Kammerer, Cornelia Ann. *Gateway to the Akha World: Kinship, Ritual, and Community Among Highlanders of Thailand*, dissertation (1986).

Kunstadter, Peter, ed. *Southeast Asian Tribes, Minorities, and Nations.* Vol. 1 and 2 (1967).

Lewis, Paul W. *Akha Oral Literature* (2002).

Lewis, Paul W. *Ethnographic Notes on the Akhas of Burma* (1969).

Lewis, Paul and Elaine. *Peoples of the Golden Triangle* (1984).

McCaskill, Don, and Ken Kampe, eds. *Development or Domestication? Indigenous Peoples of Southeast Asia* (1997).

McKinnon, John, and Wanat Bhruksasri, eds. *Highlanders of Thailand* (1983).

McKinnon, John, and Bernard Vienne, eds. *Hill Tribes Today: Problems in Change* (1989).

McKinnon, Katharine. *Development Professionals in Northern Thailand: Hope, Politics and Practice* (2011).

Morse, Eugene. *Exodus to a Hidden Valley* (1974).

Tooker, Deborah E. *Space and the Production of Cultural Difference Among the Akha Prior to Globalization* (2012).

COFFEE

Op de Laak, Jacques. *Arabica Coffee Cultivation and Extension Manual for the Highlands of Northern Thailand* (1992).

Pendergrast, Mark. *Uncommon Grounds: The History of Coffee and How It Transformed Our World.* 2nd edition (2010).

KING BHUMIBOL

Dejkunjorn, Vasit. *In His Majesty's Footsteps: A Personal Memoir* (2001, 2006).

Grossman, Nicholas, and Dominic Faulder. *King Bhumibol Adulyaduj: A Life's Work* (2012).

LISU

Berlinski, Mischa. *Fieldwork: A Novel* (2007).

Hutheesing, Otome Klein. *Emerging Sexual Inequality Among the Lisu of Northern Thailand: The Waning of Dog and Elephant Repute* (1990).

OPIUM

Booth, Martin. *Opium: A History* (1996).

Chouvy, Pierre-Arnaud. *Opium: Uncovering the Politics of the Poppy* (2010).

McCoy, Alfred W. *The Politics of Heroin: CIA Complicity in the Global Drug Trade* (2003).

Renard, Ronald D. *Opium Reduction in Thailand 1970–2000: A Thirty-Year Journey* (2001).

THAILAND

Phongpaichit, Pasuk, and Sungsidh Piriyarangsan. *Corruption and Democracy in Thailand* (1994).

UNPUBLISHED SOURCES

Richard Mann autobiography, Matthew MacDaniel autobiography, John McKinnon papers, and Duangta Sriwuthiwong report.

USEFUL WEBSITES

www.akha.org
www.doichaangcoffee.com
www.hackwriters.com/saveMathewMcDaniel.htm
www.hilltribe.org/akha

INTERVIEWS CONDUCTED IN PERSON, BY PHONE, OR BY E-MAIL, 2012–2014

Names listed as in the text: Adel Saedoo; Aje Yaebyangu; Dr. Anant Suwanapal, Linda Aylesworth; Bancha Leeja; Bandid Jangnam; Scott Bearss; Beno Leeja; Leo Brandenberg; George Brazier; Philip Calvert; Chome Leeja; Scott Coats; Sharon Cramen; Keith Crosby; John A. Darch; John M. Darch; Louise Darch; Terence "Terry" Darch; Kenneth Davids; Dawan Wuiyue; Ksenia "Senni" Dempster; Robert Denning; Hagen Dirksen; Duangta Sriwuthiwong; Mark Duffield; Murray Dunlop; Paolo Fantaguzzi; David Giddings; Sanja Grcic; Michael Howard; Otome Hutheesing; Tanya Jacoboni; Jay Wuiyue; Henry Kalebjian; Cornelia Kammerer; Rupi Khanuja; Jacquelyn Kingston; Kornkranok "Sandra" Bunmusik; Nootcha "Kwan" Promyong; Todd "Tongdee" Lavelle; Paul Lewis; Eric Lightheart; Lipi Wuiyue; Norman Lock; David Long; Shawn MacDonald; Sergio Magro; Mike Mann; Richard Mann (grandfather and grandson); Matthew McDaniel; John McGowan; John McKinnon; Charly Mehl; Miga Saedoo; Mimi Seaju; Misaw;

Robert Napoli; Greg Noga; Bujoh "Nuda" Piaocheku; Jane O'Connor; Jacques Op de Laak; Sherman Pao; Patchanee Suwanwisolkit; Anand Pawa; Phitsanuchai Kaewphichai; Piko Saedoo; Lacio Pontes; Prasong Munsalong; Katharine Regan; Ronald Renard; Lamar Robert; Ben Roberts; Paul Royce; Brian Saul; Katharine Sawchuk; Robert Schwab; Danika Speight; Danny Tam; Kritipong "Tee" Jupoh; Deborah Tooker; Poomjit (Toon); Simon Wakefield; Jeff Weaver; Wicha Promyong; and David Williamson.